Organization Development in Health Care

High Impact Practices for a Complex and Changing Environment

A volume in
Contemporary Trends in Organization Development and Change
Therese F. Yaeger and Peter F. Sorensen, *Series Editors*

CONTEMPORARY TRENDS
IN ORGANIZATION DEVELOPMENT AND CHANGE
Therese F. Yaeger and Peter F. Sorensen, *Series Editors*

Organization Development in Health Care

**High Impact Practices for a Complex
and Changing Environment**

Edited by

Jason A. Wolf
The Beryl Institute

Heather Hanson
Kaiser Permanente

Mark J. Moir
Sanford Health

INFORMATION AGE PUBLISHING, INC.
Charlotte, NC • www.infoagepub.com

Library of Congress Cataloging-in-Publication Data

Organization development in health care : high impact practices for a
complex and changing environment / edited by Jason A. Wolf, Heather Hanson,
Mark J. Moir.
    p. cm.
Includes bibliographical references.
ISBN 978-1-61735-351-2 (pbk.) – ISBN 978-1-61735-352-9 (hardcover) –
ISBN 978-1-61735-353-6 (e-book)
1. Health services administration. 2. Organizational change. I. Wolf,
Jason A. II. Hanson, Heather. III. Moir, Mark J.
RA971.O678 2011
362.1068–dc22

                                                    2010052693

Printed in the United States of America

CONTENTS

Foreword ix

Therese Yaeger and Peter Sorensen

Introduction xi

Jason A. Wolf, Heather Hanson, and Mark J. Moir

PART I
CHANGE

1 Understanding the Multifaceted Nature of Change in the Healthcare System 3

Dawn E. Bowden and Stanley J. Smits

2 Developing a Change-Ready Organization: Building Internal Capacity for Change 25

Stacy B. Cupisz, Joanne Schlosser, Beth B. Stiner

3 Guiding Health System Change: Leadership Strategies for Organization Development 43

Josephine M. Kershaw and William E. Ruse

PART II

LEADERSHIP

PART III

ENGAGEMENT

PART IV

NEW VIEWS

FOREWORD

Therese Yaeger and Peter Sorensen

This series on Contemporary Issues in Organization Development (OD) is dedicated to and concerned with the most important issues in the field. The first book on Global OD followed by the volume on Strategic OD, clearly dealt with two of the major issues in the field, issues which define the new OD. A third book, *Optimizing Talent* (2010), by Linda Sharkey and Paul Eccher addressed the critical issue of the workforce talent and its impact on Organization Development.

This fourth volume follows this theme with probably one of, if not *the* most important, issues not only for OD but for our society in general—the current state and future of healthcare. Here we are dealing with literally life and death, with a situation of unequalled magnitude of change, and an environment of uncertainty and increasing turbulence. What is and what will be the role of OD in this critical area?

As editors of this series we are proud to present the fourth volume—a volume which addresses in a comprehensive manner, the practice, potential, and promise that OD has to make to one of the truly challenging change situations of our time—the promise of effective health care delivery for all.

Organization Development in Health Care, page ix
Copyright © 2011 by Information Age Publishing

INTRODUCTION

Jason A. Wolf, Heather Hanson, and Mark J. Moir

This handbook focuses on the critical nature of Organization Development (OD) in health care and how it applies in this unique environment, examining its broad use from hospital settings to corporate offices, from small systems to multinational corporations. It tells the stories of how OD is applied in these settings, providing research-based practical processes and methods, while sharing compelling cases of how the compassion and care associated with health care is wound tightly with the OD work it encompasses. The handbook also presents a comprehensive look at how OD can play a role in the critical transformation facing health care today. It concludes with an open discussion on the future applications of OD in health care. Within each section is a collection of case studies and research on new methodologies that demonstrate that OD is an invaluable asset for change in health care.

PART I: CHANGE

Part I includes three chapters that open a broad conversation on how change has and will impact healthcare organizations at the systems as well as at the individual levels. The first chapter in Part I, "Understanding the Multifaceted Nature of Change in the Healthcare System," by Dawn Bowden and Stanley Smits, describes five major classifications of change

Organization Development in Health Care, pages xi–xvi

ongoing in the healthcare system: *scientific, professional, economic, political,* and *cultural.* They argue that each genre of change has its own rules and modus operandi, interaction effects on other types of change, and its own degree of "manageability." They conclude with the challenge of getting all the stakeholders and change agents at the table to coordinate and implement effective, system-wide improvements.

The second chapter, "Developing a Change-ready Organization: Building Internal Capacity for Change," by Stacy Cupisz, Joanne Schlosser, and Beth Stiner, suggests that while an abundance of literature has been written on change management models, theories, failure rates, and techniques, less has been written about what it takes to develop skilled change agents to successfully implement change. The authors complement what currently exists in the literature with additional methods on how organizations can increase their core competence in managing change. These methods involve developing engaged, confident, capable leaders who are able to effectively address the people side of change, which is a critical lever in the success of any change effort.

The final chapter in Part I, "Guiding Health System Change: Leadership Strategies for Organization Development," by Josephine M. Kershaw and William E. Ruse, suggests that it is necessary for healthcare leaders to be visionary experts in strategic management and organization development. Leaders must determine the most important priorities to address in their organizations, formulate a change-management plan, and steer the organization through the necessary steps to achieve objectives. The chapter presents four leadership strategies that promote organizational growth and survival through the turbulence of the present healthcare environment.

PART II: LEADERSHIP

Part II takes a deeper dive into the impact that leadership has in the healthcare environment. It offers an intricate look at leadership development and proposes models on how leadership and leadership teams can positively influence healthcare organizations. The first chapter in the section, "The Strategic Role of Organization Development in Talent Management and Transforming Leadership: CEO and OD Executive Perspectives," by Rosa M. Colon-Kolacko, suggests that successful healthcare organizations are those that are led by great leaders and that develop teams of leaders to drive business results. The chapter explores cases that describe leadership strategies and tools to diagnose leadership needs and impactful interventions. The author proposes an integrated framework for developing healthcare leaders that accelerates clinical transformation and develops a great place to work. The key drivers of this framework include talent management, succession planning, coaching, and leadership development.

In the second chapter, "The Multidisciplinary Healthcare Leadership Model," by Charlotte Lofton and Howard Straker, the authors propose that leadership is a result of the interaction of the team of healthcare practitioners from various disciplines. This cross-discipline collaboration brings forth inherent complexity to the system described through the lens of complex adaptive systems. The model presents a dynamic, multidisciplinary, multilevel perspective of leadership that emerges from within the team. This framework provides the OD practitioner with a tool for diagnosis and intervention for leadership emergence in healthcare teams.

The third chapter, "Collaboration in Health Care: A Complex Proposition for One Leadership Team," by Daniel Dangler and Susan Burns-Tisdale, suggests that the collaboration and leadership needed to foster multidisciplinary teams is not a common condition within health care. The inherent complexity within the system rejects teamwork and the coordination needed to transform the results. In order for successful teaming and collaboration to occur in health care, a very different set of assumptions must first be applied, requiring people to stretch beyond their own belief system and assumptions about processes, themselves, and others. The authors explore a case on how to apply a research-based methodology for collaboration, and how the leader—and subsequently, the team—gained insights and learning to achieve impressive results.

PART III: ENGAGEMENT

Part III includes two chapters that add to the expanding conversation around engaging employees. They offer a case of how partnerships can lead to successful engagement and suggest new ideas on how we can look at engaging employees in health care. The first chapter, "Promoting Employee Engagement in Health Care," by Tabitha Moore, provides a case study of a large private teaching hospital eager to improve employee satisfaction and to reduce employee turnover within their support services departments. It discusses an effective partnership process that helped support this objective and has led to both quick improvement and lasting engagement in these units.

The second chapter, "Intrinsic: The Missing Link to Creating a Culture of Well-being and Employee Engagement," by Rosie Ward, discusses employee engagement as an emotional attachment between an employee and his or her workplace, linking it to several measures of organizational effectiveness, including higher levels of productivity, more innovation, greater customer satisfaction, and higher profitability. The chapter suggests that organizational well-being and performance are too often addressed ineffectively with traditional behavior change approaches. A new perspective on organizational well-being and effectiveness is offered with practical tools for how leaders can put these concepts into practice in any healthcare organization.

PART IV: NEW VIEWS

The last section of the handbook includes five compelling chapters that take a bold step into new and innovative approaches to change, leadership, and engagement within health care. In the opening chapter in this section, "Leading Important Conversations: The Schwartz Center Rounds®," by Kathryn Kaplan, Schwartz Center Rounds® is introduced as an integrated and robust program for courageous conversations and strategies to facilitate dialogue across and entire healthcare system. The author presents a case study outlining seven challenges to the rounds process and strategies to overcome barriers and increase overall engagement. Findings suggest that the synergy of the Schwartz Center Rounds® with OD in health care creates a potent process for developing healthcare professionals and influencing culture change.

The second chapter in this section, "The Value of Appreciative Intelligence in Senior Living," by Diane Doumas, identifies what appreciative intelligence is and how leaders in senior living can apply the strategy in day-to-day operations. While the case examines senior living, the chapter provides an important insight into the application of appreciative processes across healthcare settings. By tapping into the inherent caring capacity of healthcare workers, this method nurtures the sharing of unique perspectives, valuing of contributions, and creating environments that are founded on principles of openness, care, and appreciation.

The following chapter, "Span of Control: Designing Organizations for Effectiveness," by Kelly Topp and Jon Desjardins, discusses a critical consideration in healthcare operations: the number of direct reports a leader can effectively manage, or *span of control* (SOC). The authors suggest that there have been challenges in addressing appropriate SOC due to the significant number of factors that need to be taken into consideration when determining the optimal number of direct reports for a manager. The chapter explores whether it is appropriate, given the complexity of health care, to have SOCs that are more than double what they are in less complex industries, and what can be done to optimize the number of direct reports a manager might have. It concludes by offering a systematic approach for exploring, analyzing, and optimizing an organization's SOC, while highlighting the role of the OD practitioner in this process.

The fourth chapter in this section, "Innovation and Engagement: What Works When Good Intentions Aren't Enough?," by Lisa Kimball and Carlos Acre, introduces the concept of *Positive Deviance* in healthcare settings. Positive Deviance (PD) is based on the belief that in every community there are certain individuals or groups whose special practices or strategies enable them to find more successful approaches to behavior change problems than their colleagues who have access to exactly the same resources. The authors suggest that the PD process is a great example of an engagement process-driven OD intervention, one different from some of the analytic quality problem solving approaches more familiar in hospitals. They conclude by identifying special challenges and opportunities when introducing and facilitating a process-driven intervention like PD in hospital settings.

The final chapter in this section, "Organization Development in the New Age of Healthcare Reform," by Diane Dixon, shares three case examples of successful healthcare reform efforts and describes how organization development processes played a valuable role in facilitating transformational change. The cases reveal that to achieve any aspect of healthcare reform requires collective transformational leadership that makes effective use of organization development processes to facilitate complex system change. Leadership collaboration and teamwork across multiple stakeholder boundaries are fostered by strategic change facilitation, strategy development, team development, and organizational learning. It provides this handbook with a valuable discussion of the role of OD in the transformation of health care today.

SPECIAL PERSPECTIVES

At the completion of the topic sections, we offer a challenge to OD practitioners and healthcare leaders alike. In "Learning to Resist 'Resistance to Change' in Academic Medicine," Marv Weisbord reminds us of the challenge of change in healthcare settings and uses academic medicine as his setting for exploration. It provides the important perspective that, as OD practitioners and healthcare leaders, we need to be willing to engage in our environments in the appropriate way. In fact, the author's experience facilitated an internal shift in some long standing beliefs in OD and even stimulated him to drop the term *resistance to change* from his vocabulary. It calls us to think how our experiences and environment will influence OD in health care for the future as well.

CONCLUSION

We close the book with the chapter "Organization Development in Health Care: The Dialogue Continues," from the editors, Jason A. Wolf, Heather

Hanson, and Mark Moir. The chapter reflects on the challenges offered and opportunities conveyed in this handbook. It recognizes the challenge of change we face in the healthcare environment and offers thoughts on next steps.

In reflecting on this work, we see it in some ways as history and in other ways as predictions surrounding very practical and applicable uses of OD in health care. Through the sharing of practices and processes, revealing outcomes, and connecting each concept to a living case of how OD has impacted the healthcare field, we hope this handbook provides a unique resource for OD and HR professionals, healthcare executives, MHA students, and the academic community. We also hope that it serves as just the beginning of an important and extensive dialogue.

Jason A. Wolf
Heather Hanson
Mark Moir
August, 2010

PART I

CHANGE

CHAPTER 1

UNDERSTANDING THE MULTIFACETED NATURE OF CHANGE IN THE HEALTHCARE SYSTEM

Dawn E. Bowden and Stanley J. Smits

ABSTRACT

Opinions abound about how to change the healthcare system. Yet few of those offering solutions appreciate the variety and complexity of change ongoing in the system. Using the *Seven Natural Rings of Reality* model (Boulding, 1964; Haines, Aller-Stead, & McKinlay, 2005) as a point of departure, we describe five major classifications of change ongoing in the health care system: *scientific, professional, economic, political,* and *cultural.* We then argue that each genre of change has its own rules and modus operandi, interaction effects on other types of change, and its own degree of "manageability." We conclude with the challenge of getting all the stakeholders and change agents at the table to coordinate and implement effective, system-wide improvements.

Countless stakeholders are advocating for changes to the healthcare system (HCS) in the U.S. Few, we argue here, understand and appreciate the complexity of the system, the nature and extent of the changes continuously

Organization Development in Health Care, pages 3–23

occurring in it, and the structural interdependencies resulting in unantici-
pated impacts in various parts of the system caused by changes in other
parts. Further, we contend, from an organizational development/change
management perspective, that bringing increased rationality, integration,
and stability to the HCS may be as challenging as introducing the next array
of transformations.

The calls for changing health care found in political debate (Alonso-
Zaldivar, 2009), the popular press (*The Economist*, 2009b), reports from
panels of experts (Institute of Medicine, 2001), presentations by industry
leaders (Edington, 2007), and academic publications (Spear, 2005) tend
to focus on three primary issues: improved access to care for the millions
of Americans who are not currently connected to the HCS via insurance;
cost reduction and containment so that comprehensive health care can be
provided without bankrupting families, government, or the economy in
general; and substantial improvements in the quality of care to avoid sense-
less injuries and deaths resulting from treatment errors (the "Do no harm"
ethical mandate) and a general desire on the part of multiple stakeholders
and change advocates to improve the overall health status of the citizenry.
No one can deny the worthiness, importance, or urgency of these national
goals; but it is important to acknowledge that they are not new; rather, they
are still unresolved after decades of serious attempts at change (Nembhard,
Alexander, Hoff, & Ramanujam, 2009).

Here, we attempt to convey the dynamic complexity of the HCS in order
to provide context for the efforts underway to increase access, control costs,
and improve quality. We start with an overview of the total system including the dynamic, interdependent nature of its components, describe five
major types of change ongoing within the system, and we conclude with
suggestions for system improvements. We advocate more sophisticated use
of information technology to improve system-wide communication, understanding, and monitoring; describe how persons acting in the role of *system
spanners* could improve coordination and integration across and among
system components; and we promote the use of *relational coordination* by
change agents and managers.

PERSPECTIVES ON HEALTH CARE AS A TOTAL SYSTEM

To help put the HCS in perspective, we turn to a multi-level model originally developed by Kenneth Boulding in *The Meaning of the 20th Century* (1964)
to represent the hierarchy and integral networking of living systems. His
model was updated by Haines et al. (2005) to further the science of systems
thinking relative to enterprise-wide change initiatives (Figure 1.1).

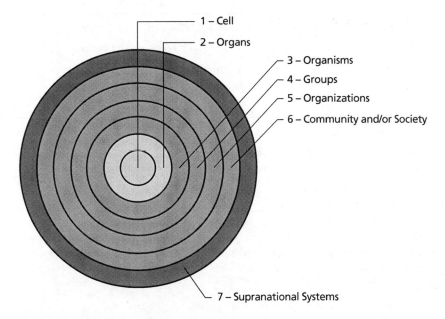

1 – Cell
2 – Organs
3 – Organisms
4 – Groups
5 – Organizations
6 – Community and/or Society
7 – Supranational Systems

Figure 1.1   The seven natural rings of reality.

The further one moves outward through the seven rings of the model, the more complex the system becomes, the greater the difficulty with execution, and the greater the need for integration. The relationships between and among the levels are as important as the individual levels themselves. All of the inner levels are automatically included in—and impacted by changes in—the outer levels. Thus, solutions to a system-level problem are typically found at, and must be affected by, the next higher level of the system or at the interaction of the system levels (Haines et al., 2005; Midgley, 2008).

The 7-ring model can promote systems thinking while providing a direct linkage to many traditional OD interventions. Specifically, OD interventions can facilitate change at the various ring levels and at the intersections between the levels (Haines et al., 2005). This is exemplified in the correlation between each ring, the intersections (3A, 4A, 5A, and 6A), and the traditional OD goals and interventions as shown in Table 1.1.

APPLICATION TO HEALTH CARE IN THE U.S.

We begin the application of the model to the HCS by briefly discussing each ring and its contribution to the total system. We revisit these concepts in later sections when we discuss the dynamic complexity of the system, the five major arenas of change, and the implications for theory, research and practice.

TABLE 1.1   Relationship Between OD Goals and the Rings

Ring	OD Goals	Examples of OD and Change Intervention Topics
Ring #3: Organisms/ Individual	Improve personal competency and effectiveness (Trustworthiness issues within oneself)	Leadership Development Core Competencies Core Values Management Development
Intersection #3A: One-to-One Interpersonal Relationships	Improve interpersonal and working relationships with others (Trust issues between individuals)	Performance Management Incentive Compensation Programs Conflict Management
Ring #4: Work Teams/ Groups	Improve the effectiveness of the work team (Empowerment and role/ relationship issues)	Problem Solving Decision Making Group Development Group/Team-Based Compensation
Intersection #4A: Inter-Group/Cross-Functional Groups	Improve the working relationships and business processes between departments (Horizontal collaboration/ integration issues)	Total Quality Management Productivity Improvement Process Improvement Appreciative Inquiry
Ring #5: Total Organization	Improve the organization's structures and processes to achieve business results (Alignment and attunement issues)	Cultural Change/Transformation Systems Dynamics Complex Adaptive Systems Operational Planning
Intersection #5A: Organization Environment	Improve the organization's sense of direction, response to its customers, and proactive management of its environment (Adaptation to environmental issues)	Strategic Planning Strategic Thinking Systems Thinking Value-Chain Management Needs/Stakeholder Analysis
Ring #6: Environment (Community/ Society)	Societal/community improvement	Societal Change Initiatives Community Activism Political Involvement Special-Interest Groups Community Development

Source: Adapted from Haines et al., 2005.

- 1 – Cell and 2 – Organs: The building blocks of the human body, major targets for treatment, and the focus of much of the basic laboratory research and clinical trials activity in the HCS.
- 3 – Organisms: Individual patients interacting one-on-one with professional caregivers; the principal leaders and change agents shaping the HCS.

- 4 – Groups: Families, teams, providers, and functional departments, to name a few of the many entities included in the HCS.
- 5 – Organizations: The diverse array of private, public, and not-for-profit organizations participating in the HCS: hospitals, clinics, health plans and payers, health services organizations, professional associations, and trade and industry associations, just to list a few.
- 6 – Community and/or Society: State and local planning bodies; regulatory agencies; committees; boards; activist organizations; and federal programs such as Medicare, Medicaid, and the Veterans' Health Administration.
- 7 – Supranational Systems: Oversight bodies for the world's health, such as the World Health Organization (WHO) and the Centers for Disease Control and Prevention (CDC).

All parts of the HCS are impacted by transformational changes to any one component of the system and, to lesser extents, to transactional improvements. For example, the 1940s and 1950s saw tremendous advances in our ability to combat infectious diseases and prevent life-threatening post-surgery infections. The long-term consequence of scientific breakthroughs in immunology and antibiotics, technical advances in radiology and laboratory diagnostic procedures, emergency medical services, and countless other advances and improvements is increased longevity. Increased longevity, in turn, has slowly changed the nature of the healthcare services model from one of acute care to one primarily focused on care for chronic conditions (Institute of Medicine, 2001).

With advancements in knowledge and technology come increased service options and increased demand. The family physicians who made house calls in the early 1900s to deliver babies, care for children suffering from chicken pox, and attend to terminally ill grandparents have been replaced by a vast array of specialists. According to the Accreditation Council for Graduate Medical Education, today "physicians specialize in one of 120 disciplines including internal medicine, cardiology, adult cardiothoracic anesthesiology, hand surgery, pediatric endocrinology, and abdominal radiology" (Nembhard et al., 2009, p. 29).

The HCS is unlike any other industry in the U.S. It has evolved to meet the incentives offered, particularly for the reimbursement of care providers. Consumers do not set or drive prices, despite the fact that the money to pay for services is provided by them through taxes for government programs, payroll deductions for employer-provided benefits, and out-of-pocket expenses such as co-payments and payment for non-covered benefits. Further, the American public rejected a capitated health model because of concerns that value would be reduced and choices limited. Thus, it is no surprise that the current healthcare model in the U.S. is structured as a non-market-based payment system that incents volume versus performance or outcomes. While certain care processes and payment policies may improve the care and outcome for the patient, they may actually decrease revenues for providers creating a misalignment of provider incentives (Chua, 2006; Institute of Medicine, 2001).

> **Example:** Nurse practitioners with training in simple infectious diseases can provide comparable quality for the lower-tier disorders (Cooper, Henderson, & Dietrich, 1998). Despite the training and qualifications that provide full capability to perform these tasks, many states have regulations preventing nurse practitioners from diagnosing diseases or prescribing treatment (Christensen, Boehmer, & Kenagy, 2000).

In summary, the HCS responds to multiple changes at multiple levels in both predictable and unexpected ways. Changing the HCS is not the biggest challenge. Stabilizing it for efficiency will be more difficult because it changes naturally in known and unknown ways that are difficult to anticipate, understand, manage, and control. Change initiatives undertaken to resolve present problems may impact other parts of the system years later with no clear cause-and-effect relationship between past actions and long-term future impacts. As Senge warned us, "Today's problems come from yesterday's 'solutions'" (1990, p. 57).

> **Example:** After decades of major investments to improve the diagnostic testing, clinical interventions, and the efficacy of drugs available to patients in the U.S., these major advancements now contribute to soaring health care costs. The overuse of diagnostic procedures and subsequent treatments is dictated by several factors: First, a desire to be thorough and provide patients the best possible care; second, protection against liability in the event the patient sues the physician for not doing her or his best to treat them; and third, because physicians are reinforced with monetary rewards for the overuse: "[M]ost doctors in America work on a fee-for-service basis; the more pills they prescribe, or tests they order, or procedures they perform, the more money they get—even though there is abundant clinical evidence that more spending does not reliably lead to better outcomes." (*The Economist*, 2009a, p. 13)

DYNAMIC COMPLEXITY IN THE HCS

Taken as a whole, the HCS is highly complex, multidimensional, interactive, interdependent, and dynamic. This means that at any given time parts of the system are in chaotic states in which processes are largely not manageable in the usual sense, and selected consequences are time-delayed and therefore unpredictable. At the same time, other parts of the system may be static and in need of change. Chaos theorists describe this dual condition as the result of the "simultaneous influence of counteracting forces":

> Organizations also have counteracting forces at play. Some forces push the system toward stability and order; these include the forces of planning, structuring, and controlling. Some other forces push the system toward instability and disorder: the forces of innovation, initiative, and experimentation. The coupling of these forces can lead to a highly complex situation: a chaotic organization. (Thietart & Forgues, 1995, p. 23)

These counteracting forces are operative in each organization within each of the seven rings of the model described above. The result is what Senge (1990) labeled *dynamic complexity*.

Senge described *dynamic complexity* as "situations where cause and effect are subtle, and where the effects over time of interventions are not obvious" (1990, p. 71). He gave us three major symptoms indicative of this condition: There is *dynamic complexity* when:

- the same action has dramatically different effects in the short run and the long,
- an action has one set of consequences locally and a very different set of consequences in another part of the system, and when,
- obvious interventions produce non-obvious consequences. (Senge, 1990, p. 71)

To deal with *dynamic complexity*, Senge advises managers and change agents to learn to see interrelationships rather than linear cause-and-effect chains, and to observe the processes of change rather than snapshots. In other words, he advises us to observe the patterns of change and underlying structures "that recur again and again" (1990, p. 73).

Two types of change are ongoing in the HCS, *transformational* and *transactional*. Cawsey and Deszca (2007) present a useful description of these two types of change, which we attempt to paraphrase and summarize here. *Transformational* change typically occurs in response to the external environment and involves some combination of factors associated with environment, leadership, mission and strategy, and organizational culture. Because it challenges the core assumptions and values of the organization, transformational change is difficult to manage. Anderson and Anderson (2001), in fact, argue that transformational change cannot be managed because it involves moving from a known present state to an unknown future state. "Unpredictable, uncontrollable, and often messy," they say, "the change process must be crafted, shaped and adapted *as it unfolds*" (Anderson & Anderson, 2001, p. 4, emphasis original). When completed, the outcome is a radically changed organization that then needs to revamp its internal systems to restore stability and improve efficiency and quality, which are often disrupted by the radical change processes.

Transactional change is aimed at refinements to the day-to-day activities of the organization. As such, transactional change is manageable and typically does not trigger transformational change. *Transactional* change is seen in "ongoing quality improvement initiatives, management development programs, work realignment, and other incremental interventions aimed at refining and improving internal practices... to improve performance" (Cawsey & Deszca, 2007, p. 62). This is the type of change often reported in the healthcare literature as the HCS attempts to improve the quality of care (Gittell et al., 2000; Shortell et al., 1995).

Transactional and transformational changes are happening simultaneously in various parts of the HCS, thereby adding to stability (transactional) and disrupting stability (transformational). Current efforts to eliminate waste and cut costs are primarily transactional changes, while some considerations, like a public health insurance program to compete with private insurers, would result in transformational change. Transformational change is sometimes described as "punctuated equilibrium: an alternation between long periods when stable infrastructures permit only incremental adaptations, and brief periods of revolutionary upheaval" (Gersick, 1991, p. 10). Most recently, efforts by the Joint Commission, the Institute for Healthcare Improvement, and the Agency for Healthcare Research and Quality (AHRQ) have been promoting and driving numerous transformational changes.

Organizational transformation as punctuated equilibrium has been found to occur under two major conditions: major changes in the environment and chief executive officer succession (Romanelli & Tushman, 1994). Lengthy periods of equilibrium are attributed to what Gersick (1991) calls "deep structures," ingrained patterns of activity developed over time to maintain the organization's existence. Schein (1985, 1992) described similar patterns of behavior as strong organizational cultures designed to resist changes to its underlying basic assumptions. And de Caluwé and Vermaak (2003) refer to such long periods of counterproductive stability as "dysfunctional static equilibrium," often caused by oscillation. They attribute oscillation to structural conflict, that is, pursuing conflicting and competing goals. The example of oscillation they give describes attempts to cut costs interrupted by attempts to increase quality, interrupted by attempts to cut costs.

In brief, the HCS, like all complex systems, is susceptible to dynamic complexity and the difficulties engendered by unintended and delayed consequences. Similarly competing goals within and among major components of the HCS can keep parts of it in a state of dysfunctional static equilibrium while transformational changes in one or more major parts of the system can push it toward chaos and make the HCS appear to be unmanageable.

TYPES AND DRIVERS OF CHANGE IN THE HCS

The present HCS is the result of decades of change driven by advances in science, technology, social policy, professionalism, and the natural forces working within a market system. Here, we briefly describe five distinct arenas of change operative in the HCS. While the different forms of change may be found in any ring of the *Seven Natural Rings of Reality* model presented earlier, each type tends to be more typical in some rings than in others. And from our perspective, each type of change is driven, managed, and controlled by relatively unique sets of factors. While different, each of these types of change influences other parts of the system where its impacts often must be accommodated, assimilated, and integrated.

Scientific Change

The basic science of the HCS dominates Levels 1 and 2 of the model (Cells and Organs). Extensive research has been done and progress has been made within these levels, including the development of new cures and treatments, DNA modeling, clinical and laboratory technologies to assist in identification and treatment of specific maladies, and achievement of a significantly improved understanding of how the body works. Scientific change follows careful rules, often in the form of established protocols, as new drugs are tested and readied for approval and new clinical trials evolve into standard treatments. Outcomes from the scientific method are published in scholarly journals controlled by editorial boards made up of expert scientists. The published results drive change in several ways, including new research to extend and apply the findings; new treatments; and, in time, new consumer demand. The problem today seems to be translating the volume of research into practice: The estimated "number of published randomized control trials, the gold standard for evidence of clinical and organizational effectiveness in medicine, surpassed 1 million 10 years ago and continues to increase at a rate of 10,000 annually" (Nembhard et al., 2009; p. 27). Not surprisingly, this volume of scientific output overwhelms implementation practices: The results of clinical trials take an average of seventeen years to become standard clinical practice (Institute of Medicine, 2001). This phenomenal volume of change stimuli is the result of huge investments by society and companies: The budget for the National Institutes of Health was reported to $15.6 billion in 1999, the same year pharmaceutical firms invested $24 billion in research and development (Institute of Medicine, 2001).

Example: Since the first bariatric surgical procedure was conducted in 1954, there have been numerous scientific studies leading to impressive improvements in the surgical tools and procedures, and increased usage to combat severe clinical obesity. Unfortunately, obesity rates continue to rise.

Professional Change

As indicated earlier, advances in knowledge helped differentiate physicians into 120 specialties. These specialists work in concert with dozens of other professional caregivers, such as physical therapists, nutritionists, and pharmacists. The nursing profession alone has more than 50 specialties (Nursing Degree Guide, 2009). Members of each of these professional entities are educated in programs in which the content is controlled by accreditation bodies and faculty curriculum committees and is updated frequently to incorporate the relevant innovations from clinical trials. Upon graduation, many healthcare professionals join professional associations, read professional journals, and participate in the continuing education and social action promoted by their associations. With specialization come multidisciplinary and interdisciplinary approaches to the delivery of care and the challenges of coordination and integration. In brief, these multiple professional groups selectively process the innovations generated by science and influence each other's innovative practices as they sort out the scope of their professional responsibilities, standards of practice, and interprofessional relationships.

> **Example:** Strasser and his associates developed a conceptual model of interdisciplinary teamwork; published it in a special issue of a professional journal devoted to stroke rehabilitation (Strasser & Falconer, 1997); responded to Kizer's (1998) initiative to transform the Veteran's Health Administration (VHA) with a proposal to experiment with ways to improve interdisciplinary teamwork in 50 VA Hospitals; demonstrated that the quality of teamwork could be improved, especially through more effective physician leadership of the team (Smits, Falconer, Herrin, Bowen, & Strasser, 2003); demonstrated via a clinical trial that improved interdisciplinary teamwork resulted in improvements in stroke patient outcomes (Strasser, Falconer et al., 2008); and further applied the findings by advocating for improved teamwork in the VHA and Department of Defense (DOD) polytrauma teams treating wounded soldiers returning from Afghanistan and Iraq. (Strasser, Uomoto, & Smits, 2008)

Economic Change

Funding is needed at all levels of the HCS to produce innovations in treatment and technology; professional education; service delivery; community, national, and international infrastructure; adequate staffing throughout the system; and all the other components involved in healthcare services. In difficult economic times, parts of the system lose some degree of effectiveness, thereby affecting other parts of the system. The monies that drive the system are largely market-based, with other funding coming from public and charitable sources. The operation of the total system is expensive and is getting more expensive each year: According to the Congressional Budget Office, Americans spent 16% of gross domestic product (GDP) in 2007—approximately 2.3 trillion dollars—on health care (Eckles, 2008), and this amount is predicted to go to 25% of GDP by 2025 unless ways are found to control costs. At a personal and family level, most people rely on health insurance to meet treatment costs, and most health insurance coverage is provided, in large part, by employers as a benefit. In the U.S., there are both public and private insurers, but the dominance of the private insurers distinguishes this system from the rest of the world. In 2006, 62.2 percent of the civilian population under the age of 65—161.7 million people—were covered by employment-based health insurance, while 70.9 percent of the workers age 18–64 had employment-based coverage (Employee Benefits Research Institute, 2008). Currently, nearly 50 million Americans have no health care insurance coverage, and public policy makers are struggling to find ways to provide coverage, and therefore system access, for all.

> **Example:** Today's employee benefit healthcare coverage can be traced to several programs in colonial times, but the first group and prepaid plans can be traced to Baylor University Hospitals in Dallas, TX, in 1929, eventually leading to the development of the Blue Cross/Blue Shield plans. In the early 1930s, Kaiser Permanente, a group practice-based health maintenance organization (HMO), was started to serve workers building an aqueduct to bring fresh water from the Colorado River to the city of Los Angeles. Immediately after WWII, Kaiser opened its plan to the public. During WWII, there was fierce competition for attracting workers. Fringe benefits became the recruitment strategy of choice. Group health plans were further encouraged through an IRS ruling in 1943 allowing employer-provided health benefits to be tax exempt for employees and tax deductible for employers. The major insurance carriers introduced major medical and comprehensive medical plans in the 1950s and 1960s, leading to substantial increases in group health coverage. During this same period, costs also began to increase dramatically. (Pierce, 2005; Porter & Teisburg, 2006)

Political Change

Here, we combine social policy development as it impacts health care, government-sponsored programs and initiatives, and government oversight and regulation in the single term *political change*. We are referring to all the collective inputs to the HCS that come from social action by power coalitions and elected representatives engaged in democratic processes and the art of compromise. The federal government, often in conjunction with the states, operates huge programs like Medicare, Medicaid, S-CHIP, and the VHA. The states are heavily involved in regulating and managing the delivery of health care, starting with the licensing of healthcare professionals, establishing oversight and regulatory boards for hospitals and other care-rendering facilities, and monitoring the health of its citizens through state boards of health.

> **Example:** In 1998, Dr. Kenneth W. Kizer, Undersecretary of Health, undertook the transformation of the VHA: "[T]he VA, as it is commonly known, is far and away the nation's largest integrated health care system. It has an annual budget of over $17 billion, two hundred thousand employees, 173 hospitals, and over 1,000 sites of care delivery. It is also the major provider of graduate medical and other health care professional training and one of the largest research organizations in the United States." (Kizer, 1998; p. 1)

Further, the ongoing discussion of whether to offer a public or private option to healthcare access, or a combination thereof, is arguably a social and economic issue. However, it has more often presented itself as a political debate. This bipartisan debate questions citizen rights to health care and is predicated on insurance reform efforts, as opposed to reform of the delivery system. Thus, the focus of reform on payment and coverage/insurance has ignored a systems perspective and the organization of care delivery. Healthcare reform focused on coverage is required, though the debate assumes the current care delivery system as a starting point instead of determining how the system can be organized in a more optimal way to support delivery of care for patients. Bohmer (2009) recognizes this misdirected focus on payment and ensuring coverage for all Americans as a management problem. Policymakers cannot solve the systemic issues, but managers in practice can design the way their organizations work to create more effective models of care delivery that work toward systemic change (Bohmer, 2009).

Cultural Change

Cultural change is less discernable than any of the four arenas of change described above. It evolves over decades and is only partially observable until it reaches a tipping point and there is general awareness that a paradigmatic shift has occurred. Americans have been slowly moving toward maintaining wellness rather than treating injury or disease as a primary goal of the HCS. This is exhibited in efforts to maintain healthy lifestyles through increased attention to diet, exercise, product safety, and the avoidance of environmental stressors and pollutants. In parallel, there has been a move toward alternative forms of health care, an increased concern about quality, and a determination to maximize value rather than passively accept care as defined by caregivers and insurance companies. The challenge is that many business models are focused on delivering "sick care" versus general health and well-being. This is further perpetuated by the need for continued profits from these existing business models, which are organized by individual products, business units, and organizations, as opposed to coordinated care across the system. In 1973, the HMO Act by Congress was designed to reward a new way of payment, from sickness-based to prevention-based. The subsequent conversion to for-profit models and insurance consolidations that was encouraged by the government disrupted the supranational system. The result was business models that benefit from quarterly profit versus investment in infrastructure for community and individual health. However, business models that are designed to profit from patient wellness and consider the patient experience across the system do exist within the current HCS.

> **Example:** Kaiser Permanente and Geisinger Health System are providers that own hospitals and clinics. They also operate insurance companies and employ their own doctors to effectively offer an integrated delivery system. Success for these organizations is realized through the retention of the members within the system and maintaining the long-term health of those members. Integrated delivery organizations are incented to save costs through the delivery of preventative and self-management services instead of restricting access to care (Christensen, Grossman, & Hwang, 2009). Keeping the members healthy and satisfied increases the profits from wellness-based compensation which is determined by the health outcome achieved instead of from a sickness-based and fee-for-service compensation model characterized by billing for services rendered.

IMPLICATIONS AND CHALLENGES

We hope that the brief descriptions and examples in the above section suffice to communicate the nature of change occurring in the five defined arenas of change (*scientific, professional, economic, political,* and *cultural*) so that we can make two observations here relevant to change management:

- First, managers and change agents from one arena of change have less influence and little control over the changes occurring in other arenas. Similarly, the types of change (transactional vs. transformational) initiated, managed, and controlled differ across arenas along with the techniques employed and the stakeholders served. Therefore, the art and science of organization development and change management will vary greatly *within* each of the five major arenas of change, *between* highly interdependent change arenas within the HCS where there are strongly shared interests, and *among* the five major change arenas. Clusters of current OD and change management strategies are likely to work best as applied within a given arena and less well when generalized across the HCS.

- Using today's theories, tools, and techniques (Hughes, 2007), the degree to which change is manageable (planned, efficiently implemented, and evaluated for impact) varies from one change arena to another. Clearly, managers within each arena promote, manage, and control change somewhat differently when compared to other arenas of change. We have presented the arenas in the above section in the order of manageability, with change in the *scientific* and *professional* arenas being the most manageable, and change in the *political* and *cultural* arenas being the least manageable.

Substantive system-wide improvements in health care will require new forms of communication, cooperation, and coordination among the stakeholders, change agents, and change managers from all five arenas of change. Here, we present broad suggestions for meeting these system improvement requirements.

OD Challenges

Greatly Expanded Use of IT

The HCS response to dramatic improvements in knowledge and technology has been specialization. This is true within the seven rings of the model presented earlier and within the five arenas of change. Specialized parts of the HCS are often internally efficient, effective, and managed well in terms of change. The system-wide problems arise between and among the highly specialized components due to a lack of understanding, coordination, and cooperation. This lack of "fit among the parts," often in the form of contradictory objectives and duplicated efforts, is a major cause of the system inefficiencies leading to waste and increased costs.

Historically and culturally, the HCS developed a manner that relied on case notes, hand-written patient records, and concerns about privacy and confidentiality that resist current advances in the application of information technologies (IT). We suggest using greatly expanded and more fully implemented IT to provide the accurate information needed for system-wide understanding, monitoring, efficiency, and effectiveness. Resources are available from the American Recovery and Reinvestment Act in the amount of $30 billion to improve healthcare information (Halamka, 2009). But it will take far more than fiscal resources to achieve the many system integration objectives made possible by transformative applications of IT. First of all, it will require buy-in from the leadership of the major components of the HCS; stakeholder relaxation of cultural and social taboos that resist such information exchanges; and new models and competencies by OD, IT, and HCS experts working collaboratively for change. Some of the scholarly literature dealing with innovation networks (Dhanaraj & Parkhe, 2006) and organizational responses to innovation (Guo, 2004; Hargrave & Van de Ven, 2006) provide starting points for this effort. However, it will also take a radical rethinking and redesign of IT to model the complexity of the HCS and communicate its dynamic properties in the form of feedback loops and simultaneous adjustments.

System Spanners

Attention has been paid to the role of boundary spanners in helping improve patient care involving multidisciplinary caregivers: "Boundary spanners, also known as cross-functional liaisons, are individuals whose primary task is to integrate the work of other people" (Gittell, 2002, p.1409). The impact of boundary spanners on improving services to patients has been demonstrated by Gittell et al. (2000) and Shortell et al. (1995). Here, we are suggesting a similar role for persons attempting to bring about communication, coordination, and collaboration among various components in the HCS. We suggest the development and employment of *system spanners* to help bring about better fit and collaboration among selected components of the HCS. Each HCS component, as described by the *Seven Natural Rings of Reality* model (Haines et al., 2005), has high priority interdependencies with selected rings below and above it in the system. For example, graduate medical education entities (ring 5) have high-priority interdependent relationships with scientists conducting relevant clinical trials in their specialty areas (rings 1 and 2), their graduates and professional peers involved in direct patient care (ring 3), and with accrediting bodies and professional associations (ring 6). Such educational institutions would be wise to develop and deploy system spanners with the expertise needed to monitor and understand developments in these related rings and to help translate relevant innovations into practice within their educational institutions.

Relational Coordination

Assuming a more sophisticated, more comprehensive deployment of IT can produce the information and communication needed for increased understanding of the total HCS, and that system spanners will be able to keep related parts of the system in close contact, the next OD question becomes one of how to get the diverse HCS stakeholders to develop some common perspective on the issues facing the system and agreed-upon strategies for resolving them. The goal is to get shared perspectives among key stakeholders about mutual self-interest and to develop greater awareness of the integrated effort required for sustainable HCS improvements. Here, we briefly make two points: First, health care is delivered locally, regulated locally, and often innovated locally. OD models and experts should target helping with the creation and operation of local healthcare innovation networks in a manner similar to the hub firm orchestrated networks described by Dhanaraj and Parkhe (2006). They suggest that the first task of orchestration for the innovation network is "ensuring *knowledge mobility*," which they define as "the ease with which knowledge is shared, acquired, and deployed within the network" (p. 660). They contend that ideas from one group can help solve problems in another group, "but only if the distributed resources of the network are mobilized to be efficiently deployed across organizational boundaries" (p. 662). Secondly, we suggest greatly expanded use of *relational coordination* at the local level among system spanners, boundary spanners, and stakeholders as a coordinating mechanism within, between, and among HCS components. This form of coordination is described by Gittell as "communication- and relationship-intensive" (2002, p. 1408). As such, relational coordination appears to fit well with the suggestions for bringing stakeholders together for innovative change suggested by Hattori and Lapidus (2004).

Implications for Managers

Change agents and managers need to focus on selected aspects of the total HCS, starting with their "within-ring" priorities, where they have the capacity to make improvements. While they have little capacity to change parts of the system outside their ring, they do need to maintain awareness of the relevant interdependencies with other parts (rings) of the total HCS. As Tushman and Nadler (1986) told us decades ago, this is *job one* for managers:

> There is perhaps no more pressing managerial problem than the sustained management of innovation. There is nothing mysterious about innovation ... it is the calculated outcome of strategic management and visionary leadership that provide the people, structures, values, and learning opportunities to make it an organizational way of life. (p. 92)

That said, how does one lead and manage change within a system as complex and dynamic as today's HCS? We recommend a four-step process described briefly here:

1. First, it is important to clearly define the key innovation objectives within one's organization and arena of change. With so much change in process everywhere in the HCS, it is easy to get caught up in fads engaging almost exclusively in *mimetic isomorphism,* "conscious and unconscious modeling as less successful entities copy those perceived as more successful" (Smits, 2004), to keep up with others in one's segment of the industry. Imitating others may be one way to change, but setting well informed, thought-out, and defined innovation priorities in keeping with your organization's strategic imperatives is a better way to approach innovation management.
2. While one should plan and prioritize innovation efforts based on strategic objectives, one should not innovate in a vacuum. Rather, it is important to understand and monitor the key relationships between your initiatives and other relevant components of the HCS. Similarly, a continuous effort should be made to anticipate the impact that changes in other parts of the HCS will have on your overall strategy, operations, and planned innovations. If you do this well, you will be engaging in the *system spanning* role we advocated earlier.
3. Practice *rational coordination* as a key part of your change management activities. Many people involved in the HCS have a strong desire to improve the lives of others; they are people-oriented. And as such, they respond more fully and enthusiastically to cooperative approaches to problem solving and innovation, the key attributes of *relational coordination.*
4. The congruence between values and decision-making will affect the ultimate success of achieving a given goal. Christensen and Overdorf (2000) define values as the "standards by which employees set priorities" (p. 69). All participants within the system must make decisions. The decisions made at a practitioner and manager level must be consistent with the strategic direction of the future HCS.

CONCLUDING COMMENT

We conclude with a summary of the challenges faced by persons seeking to improve theory and practice throughout the HCS. We presented the HCS in the context of a multidimensional, interactive, interdependent system (*7 Rings Model*), discussed five major types/arenas of change (*scientific, professional, economic, political,* and *cultural*), and described the interplay between two major categories of change (*transformational* and *transactional*) within the rings and arenas. This level of dynamic complexity can be overwhelming for stakeholders wanting to contribute to system improvements.

To address this, we offer with some practical advice for OD theorists and change managers.

Transformational change, by definition, is disruptive to the status quo. It moves one or more major elements of the system in a new direction, such as when a new breakthrough technology displaces a traditional one. Such change, while welcome, often causes inefficiencies while equipment is being replaced; caregivers are retrained; and new protocols and standards of practice are developed, refined, and implemented. *Transactional change* helps resolve the disruption caused by transformational change by restoring order and capturing the benefits of restored efficiency. Stagnant elements of the HCS need transformational change, while chaotic elements need increased stability. This two-act drama (stagnation acting as a stimulus for change and disruptive change acting as a stimulus for stability) is replayed over and over in all parts of the system.

OD theorists have an opportunity to move the HCS forward in a positive manner by creating more comprehensive models that help us better understand the interactive, interdependent nature of the multiple components of this complex and dynamic system. As implied earlier, we think collaborative efforts between OD and IT professionals could result in more sensitive models capable of forecasting and measuring how change impacts both the targeted element of the HCS and related elements. Sophisticated IT-enabled model development could help us better anticipate the triggers for transformational change and increase the efficiency and effectiveness of the transactional changes needed to produce meaningful benefits. Until we have the tools to better understand the totality of the HCS, our ability to lead and manage it responsibly will be problematic.

Similarly, we think managers throughout the HCS need a comprehensive training and development intervention to give them the knowledge, skills, and abilities to manage transactional change efficiently and effectively. Our models and tools for managing this type of change have been in existence for decades, but too few managers are adequately trained to use them. Additionally, many of these change management tools are inadequately researched, thereby making it difficult to refocus and refine them to meet the needs of an HCS constantly increasing in its dynamic complexity.

In brief, the HCS is complex; the shared responsibility for leading and managing its continuous improvement is daunting, and the opportunity for the organization development community is challenging. As Cawsey and Deszca (2007) observed, "Change management is about keeping the plane flying while you repair it" (p. 310). This observation is especially true for the HCS and the patients who rely upon it for continued good health and survival. The challenge of change must be met successfully.

REFERENCES

Alonso-Zaldivar, R. (2009). Hard choice on 4 big issues stymie health push. *The Washington Examiner*, nation. Retrived from http://washingtonexaminer. com/nation/2009/006/hard-choices-4-big-issues-stymie-health-push

Anderson, L. A., & Anderson, D. (2001). *The change leader's roadmap: How to navigate your organization's transformation.* San Francisco: Jossey-Bass/Pfeiffer.

Bohmer, R. M. J. (2009). *Designing care: Aligning the nature and management of health care.* Boston: Harvard Business School Publishing.

Boulding, K. E. (1964). *The meaning of the twentieth century.* New York: Harper & Row, Publishers.

Cawsey, T., & Deszca, G. (2007). *Toolkit for organizational change.* Los Angeles: SAGE Publications.

Christensen, C. M., Bohmer, R., & Kenagy, J. (2000, September/October). Will disruptive innovations cure health care? *Harvard Business Review, 78*(5), 102–112.

Christensen, C. M., Grossman, J. H., and Hwang, J. (2009). *The innovator's prescription.* New York: The McGraw-Hill Companies.

Christensen, C.M., & Overdorf, M. (2000). Meeting the challenge of disruptive change. *Harvard Business Review, 78*(2), 66–76.

Chua, K. P. (2006). *Overview of the U.S. health care system.* Unpublished manuscript, American Medical Student Association. Retrieved from http://www.amsa. org/uhc/HealthCareSystemOverview.pdf

Cooper, R. A., Henderson, T., & Dietrich, C. L. (1998, September 2). Roles of non-physician clinicians as autonomous providers of patient care. *JAMA, 280*(9), 795–802.

de Caluwé, L., & Vermaak, H. (2003). *Learning to change: A guide for organization change agents.* Thousand Oaks, CA: Sage.

Dhanaraj, C., & Parkhe, A. (2006). Orchestrating innovation networks. *Academy of Management Review, 31*(3), 659–669.

Employee Benefits Research Institute (EBRI). (2008, June). *EBRI Datebook on Employee Benefits.* Retrieved from http://www.ebri.org

Eckles, W. (2008). A call for American leadership. *American Journal of Business, 23*(1), 9–12.

Economist, The. (2009a, June 27). This is going to hurt. *The Economist, 392*(8637), 13.

Economist, The. (2009b, June 27). Heading for the emergency room. *The Economist, 392*(8637), 78–91.

Edington, D. (2008, November). *Moving the paradigm from the cost of health care to total value of health care.* Presentation at the 53rd Annual Employee Benefits Conference, International Foundation of Employee Benefit Plans. San Antonio, TX.

Gersick, C. J. G. (1991). Revolutionary change theories: A multilevel exploration of the punctuated equilibrium paradigm. *Academy of Management Review, 16*(1), 10–36.

Gittell, J. H. (2002). Coordinating mechanisms in care provider groups: Relational coordination as a mediator and input uncertainty as a moderator of performance effects. *Management Science, 48*(11), 1408–1426.

Gittell, J. H., Fairfield, K. M., Bierbaum, B., Head, W., Jackson, R., Kelly, M., . . . & Lipson, S. (2000). Impact of relational coordination on quality of care, postoperative pain and functioning, and length of stay: A nine-hospital study of surgical patients. *Medical Care, 38*(8), 807–819.

Guo, K. L. (2004). Leadership processes for re-engineering changes to the health care industry. *Journal of Health Education and Management, 18*(6), 435–446.

Haines, S., Aller-stead, G., & McKinlay, J. (2005). *Enterprise-Wide Change: Superior Results through Systems Thinking.* San Francisco: Pfeiffer.

Halmaka, J. D. (2009, July–August). Your medical information in the digital age. *Harvard Business Review, 87*(7/8), 22–24.

Hargrave, T. J., & Van De Ven, A. H. (2006). A collective action model of institutional innovation. *Academy of Management Review, 31*(4), 864–888.

Hattori, R. A., & Lapidus, T. (2004). Collaboration, trust and innovative change. *Journal of Change Management, 4*(2), 97–104.

Hughes, M. (2007). The tools and techniques of change management. *Journal of Change Management, 7*(1), 37–49.

Institute of Medicine. (2001). *Crossing the Quality Chasm* (Committee on Quality of Health Care In America, Trans.). United States: The National Academies of Sciences.

Kizer, K. W. (1998). *Health care, not hospitals: Transforming the Veterans' Health Administration.* Washington, D.C.: U.S. Department of Veterans Affairs.

Midgley, G. (2008). Systems thinking, complexity and the philosophy of science. *Emergence: Complexity and Organization, 10*(4), 55–73.

Nembhard, I. M., Alexander, J. A., Hoff, T. J., & Ramanujam, R. (2009). Why does the quality of health care continue to lag? Insights from management research. *Academy of Management Perspectives, 23*(1), 24–42.

Nursing Degree Guide. (2009). *Specialties.* Retrieved from http://www.nursingdegreeguide.org/articles/specialties/

Pierce, P. D. (2005). Understanding managed care health plans: The managed care spectrum. In J. S. Rosenbloom (Ed.), *The handbook of employee benefits* (6th ed., pp. 107–153). New York: The McGraw-Hill Companies.

Porter, M., & Teisberg, E. (2006). *Redefining health care: Creating value-based competition on results.* Boston: Harvard Business School Press.

Romanelli, E., & Tushman, M. L. (1994). Organizational transformation as punctuated equilibrium: An empirical test. *Academy of Management Journal, 37*(5), 1141–1166.

Schein, E. H. (1985/1992). *Organizational Culture and Leadership.* (1st/2nd editions). San Francisco: Jossey-Bass.

Senge, P. M. (1990). *The fifth discipline: The art & practice of the learning organization.* New York: Doubleday/Currency.

Shortell, S., O'Brien, J. L., Carman, J. M., Foster, R. W., Hughes, E. F. X., Boerstler, H., & O'Conner, E. J. (1995). Assessing the impact of continuous quality improvement/total quality management: Concept versus implementation. *Health Services Research, 30*(2), 377–401.

Smits, S. J. (2004). Disability and employment in the USA: the quest for best practices. *Disability and Society, 19*(6), 647–662.

Smits, S. J., Falconer, J. A., Herrin, J., Bowen, S. E., & Strasser, D. C. (2003). Patient-focused rehabilitation team cohesiveness in Veterans Administration Hospitals. *Archives of Physical Medicine and Rehabilitation, 84*, 1332–1338.

Spear, S. J. (2005, September). Fixing health care from the inside, today. *Harvard Business Review, 83*(9), 78–91.

Strasser, D. C., Uomoto, J. M., & Smits, S. J. (2008). The interdisciplinary team and polytrauma rehabilitation: Prescription for partnership. *Archives of Physical Medicine and Rehabilitation, 89*, 179–181.

Strasser, D. C., Falconer, J. A., Stevens, A. B., Uomoto, J. M., Herrin, J., Bowen, S. E., & Burridge, A. B. (2008). Team training and stroke rehabilitation outcomes: A cluster randomized trial. *Archives of Physical Medicine and Rehabilitation, 89*(1), 10–15.

Strasser, D. C., & Falconer, J. A. Issue Editors. (1997). Team care in stroke rehabilitation. *Topics in Stroke Rehabilitation, 4*(2), i–98.

Thietart, R. A., & Forgues, B. (1995). Chaos theory and organization. *Organization Science, 6*(1), 19–31.

Tushman, M., & Nadler, D. (1986). Organizing for innovation. *California Management Review, 28*(3), 74–93.

CHAPTER 2

DEVELOPING A CHANGE-READY ORGANIZATION

Building Internal Capacity for Change

Stacy B. Cupisz, Joanne Schlosser, Beth B. Stiner

ABSTRACT

A recent study conducted by IBM (2008) entitled "Making Change Work" confirmed much of what has been written about the topic of change management. Some of the findings in the study can be summarized with the following statements:

- *Change is constant.* The expected level of change is continuing to rise, and many organizations are struggling to keep up.
- *Don't underestimate the power of people.* Efforts that address the "people" side (or "soft" side) of change experience a higher percentage of success than those that do not.
- *The soft stuff is the hard stuff.* Addressing the people side of change is a critical success factor as well as one of the most critical challenges in implementing change efforts.
- *Mind the gap.* There is a growing gap between the amount of change organizations are experiencing and their ability to effectively manage the change.

Organization Development in Health Care, pages 25–42
Copyright © 2011 by Information Age Publishing

In addition, the study found that utilizing experienced and skilled change managers can increase a project's likelihood of success. The article notes projects with a seasoned change master as more likely to be successful than projects where a novice change agent is supporting the effort, illustrating the importance of individuals having experience in leading change.

While an abundance of literature has been written on change management models, theories, failure rates, and techniques, less has been written about what it takes to develop skilled change agents. This chapter aims to complement what currently exists in the literature with additional thinking around how organizations can increase their core competence in regard to managing change through developing engaged, confident, capable leaders able to effectively address the people side of change, a critical lever in the success of any change effort.

CHANGE ACCELERATION

Across industries, organizations are inundated with change (IBM, 2008). In the healthcare industry, leaders are faced with multi-faceted, complex issues and a landscape that is ever changing. In the book *Leading the Revolution in Health Care: Advancing Systems, Igniting Performance,* by Cathleen Krueger Wilson and Timothy Porter-O'Grady (1995), the authors claim that "change is occurring at a rate that makes it impossible to keep up with" (p. xi). Whether the issue is healthcare reform, implementation of a new technology, or the opening of a new addition, successful organizations will require the capacity to not only respond to change, but to lead it effectively.

Banner Health, based in Phoenix, Arizona, is one of the largest nonprofit healthcare systems in the country, employing more than 35,000 employees in seven states. Peter Fine, President and CEO, frequently reminds leaders that effective healthcare leadership requires "a passion for complexity and a high tolerance for ambiguity," given the fast pace and constant change within the organization and the healthcare industry (Fine, 2010). Fine has emphasized the importance of leading change to his leaders as the organization moves toward its vision of industry leadership by the year 2020. Recent actions indicate the rapid pace of change, with highlights from the past three years including

- Investment of over $1.7B in new facility space resulting in a total increase of 798 beds
- Acquisition of a two-hospital system (800+ beds) in addition to two physician groups
- Announcement of a joint venture with a world-renowned cancer partner, M.D. Anderson

In addition to these changes, Banner is also making substantial investments in system-wide initiatives to improve patient care. One such investment is the initiative to implement the Electronic Medical Record (EMR), which involves installing new clinical computer systems and transforming the way care is provided at the bedside. Implementing these systems requires significant amounts of change, from redesigned process workflows to training staff and physicians and improving the hospital infrastructure to support the hardware and software.

Initiatives like these run a high risk of failure. Recent articles highlight other healthcare systems that have attempted and failed with similar efforts. Most notably was the infamous Cedars-Sinai case, where an 870-bed institution mandated physician use of the technology without the support of physicians. This approach resulted in a revolt of physicians and ultimately the removal of the system in 2003, costing the organization $34 million (The Advisory Board Company, 2009).

As Banner prepared for the multi-year initiative in 2005, leaders realized that regardless of how great the technology solution was, it was imperative that the end users support the change in order for the implementation to be successful. Wanting to ensure success in their endeavor, Banner sought to adopt a common change management model that could be applied to the EMR initiative as well as numerous other efforts requiring acceptance of change. The selection process and implementation strategy for this work was owned by the Organizational Development (OD) department, whose function was to support the organization in achieving its strategic objectives through increasing organizational capacity. The authors Stacy Cupisz and Joanne Schlosser are directors in the organizational development department and Beth Stiner is the senior director of the OD department.

The search resulted in the selection of General Electric's Change Acceleration Process (CAP). The model was introduced into the organization in late 2005 as part of a strategy to increase change management expertise internally by training leaders to become change agents. Since 2005, over 500 leaders have become trained in the CAP methodology and deemed "change agents." Since then, Banner has learned many lessons about what it takes to develop confident, capable change agents.

THE CHALLENGE OF LEADING CHANGE

Even though most leaders know that being able to manage change is crucial to their success, there are far fewer that know how to lead change successfully. "Leading change is not easy particularly if it is cultural change you are trying to introduce" (Morton, Newall, & Sparkes, 2001, p. 78). In a 2008 survey, only 38% of CEOs felt that transformational change efforts in their organization were successful, and they agreed that change management was not a core competency within their organization (Isern & Pung, 2007). The days of implementing change through command and control leadership are over. Today's leaders need to know how to empower teams to create solutions as well as engage others in dialogue to ensure a shared vision of the future.

Leading change can be thought of as a three-legged stool, with the legs representing people, process, and content. Our experience and review of the literature supports that the people leg often receives much less attention than the process and content legs. "Project success does not hinge primarily on technology—instead success depends largely on people" (IBM, 2008, p. 2). In reality, well-intentioned leaders and teams often come together to create or improve new processes and end up investing most of their energy into the development of the solution and very little into ensuring that others share the same vision of success.

The change equation developed by General Electric (2003) supports this premise. The equation indicates that there are two elements to ensuring that a change is effective: the technical solution (Q) and people side (A). Both are equally essential for a change to be effective (E).

The Effectiveness (**E**) of the result is equal to the Quality (**Q**) of the solution times the Acceptance (**A**) of the idea.

$$Q \times A = E$$

Figure 2.1 Change effectiveness equation. Reprinted from *Change acceleration process (CAP) change agents workshop*, by General Electric Company, 2003, p. 41. Reprinted with permission.

Consider the following scenario. The Emergency Department (ED) formed a team to create a new patent flow process and invested considerable effort into its development. On a scale of 1–10, with 10 being the highest number possible, the team created a solution (Q) that was 8 out of 10. Outside of some basic training and general communication, not much additional effort was invested in creating a shared need or vision with the staff members not involved on the team. This resulted in 2 out of 10 on the acceptance scale (A). Table 2.1 demonstrates these results.

TABLE 2.1 ED Change Effort: Scenario 1

	Q	×	A	= E
First Attempt	8	×	2	16

With a result of 16 out of a possible 100, how likely is this change to be successful? We would suggest, not very. So the team reconvenes and comes up with a plan. Typically, their focus will remain on reworking the process or providing a technical solution (Q) resulting in an incremental change. Table 2.2 demonstrates these results.

TABLE 2.2 ED Change Effort: Scenario 2

	Q	×	A	= E
First attempt	8	×	2	16
Second attempt (focus on Q)	9	×	2	18

Has much changed? Not much. This scenario is very common. To increase the probability of success, the ED team needs to put equal energy into the "A" or acceptance part of the equation as they have the "Q." Let's look at what would happen if the team invested their energy into increasing acceptance of the solution (A) after the initial attempt as opposed to reworking the process (Q). Table 2.3 demonstrates the results when efforts are placed on increasing the "A" or acceptance part of the solution.

TABLE 2.3 ED Change Effort: Scenario 3

	Q	×	A	= E
First attempt	8	×	2	16
Second attempt (focus on A)	8	×	8	64

Increasing the "A" improves the effectiveness of the change. This example illustrates General Electric's (2003) research finding that 62% of change efforts fail from lack of attention to the people side of change, or simply put, failure to address the "A."

Banner Health decided to adopt and embrace the GE CAP model, depicted in Figure 2.2, precisely because of its ability to help us focus on the "A."

The Change Acceleration Process (CAP) is a set of principles designed to increase the success and accelerate the implementation of organizational change efforts. It addresses how to create a shared need for the change, understand and deal with resistance from key stakeholders, and build an effective influence strategy and communication plan for the change. Benefits include driving fast, yet sustainable organizational change, promoting a positive environment for driving change in human behaviors, eliminating resistance and engaging those affected by the change, and comple-

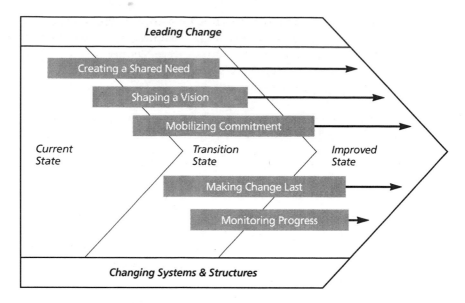

Figure 2.2 The change acceleration process. Reprinted from *Change acceleration process (CAP) change agents workshop*, by General Electric Company, 2003, p. 32. Reprinted with permission.

menting the technical strategy with the human strategy. The model has seven elements, each described in brief below:

1. *Leading Change*: A champion who will lead the effort, ensuring both the "Q" and "A" are addressed.
2. *Creating a Shared Need*: The team identifies the reasons for change, makes certain the reasons are widely understood, and increases the shared need among those impacted by the change.
3. *Shaping a Vision*: The team establishes the desired outcome of change and conveys the vision to key stakeholders.
4. *Mobilizing Commitment*: Key stakeholders are identified, reasons for resistance are ascertained, and actions are developed to gain support and commitment.
5. *Making Change Last*: The team leverages success and lessons learned to stabilize and sustain the change.
6. *Monitoring Progress*: Measures of success are established and monitored so action can be taken to correct when needed.
7. *Changing Systems and Structures*: Reinforcing mechanisms such as reward and recognition structures are evaluated to ensure they incent behaviors that support the change.

758 = Step 8 → monitor performance & create short-term wins

Just like change, the seven elements are dynamic and overlap, and they do not occur in a linear fashion. Individuals trained in CAP leave the session with dozens of tools they can apply to increase acceptance around change.

At Banner, approximately 300 leaders have attended the CAP training. After completing the formal training, there was no formal or structured means of supporting the continued development of the change agents or ensuring that newly learned skills were applied. By 2008, there was a growing concern around the engagement and competence of existing change agents. A survey was administered to assess the current level of engagement of change agents as well as their future level of commitment toward change initiatives. The results were astonishing and validated the concern around change agent capability.

What was most disappointing was discovering that 67% of those trained in CAP were not utilizing the tools. However, what was encouraging was that 97% of the change agents who responded were interested in staying engaged with CAP activities and willing to commit 4–8 hours a quarter to supporting change initiatives. When asked what change agents needed in order to be fully committed and confident in applying their skills, a majority cited a refresher course as well as more experience in applying the tools.

CREATING A SHARED NEED AND SHAPING A VISION

While there was an extensive investment in developing internal change agents, it was evident that Banner had significant room for improvement. Despite having over 300 individuals trained as change agents, the organization was hard pressed to identify a specific number of individuals who could apply their skills with confidence. From this point forward, the OD team committed themselves to a single goal: to create a cadre of engaged, confident, capable leaders able to effectively address the people side of change.

To reignite the engagement of our change agents, a strategy was developed to align them with the organization's top strategic objectives, known as Banner's Strategic Initiatives (SIs). These organization-wide initiatives often require implementation of new processes or technology (Q) at all of our facilities, requiring a tremendous amount of acceptance (A) in order to be successful. While the organization has been successful in achieving the initiatives in the past, a strong theme appeared each year around the lack of "acceptance" of the imposed changes. This made the SIs a prime opportunity for alignment of the change agent role.

At the organizational level, each initiative is assigned a system leader (System SI Leader) to lead the change. While the individual is responsible for the success of the initiative, they do not have direct authority over the people who make the work happen at the facilities. In addition, these leaders are selected because of their expertise around the subject matter (Q) of the initiative and may or may not be equipped with the change skills needed to lead the acceptance of the change (A). Each initiative typically also has a lead at the facility or hospital level to lead the effort locally (Facility SI Leader).

Figure 2.3   Strategic initiative structure.

Every change agent interested in supporting this work self-identified one SI to support at their home facility. Their role was to work with the Facility SI Leader to assist with the acceptance of change. To support the change agents, each member of the OD team was aligned to an SI at the organizational level.

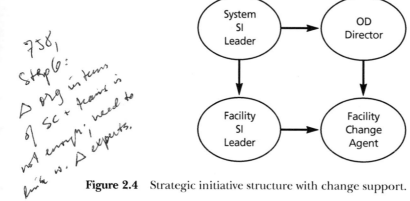

Figure 2.4   Strategic initiative structure with change support.

Each OD Director ultimately serves as the system-level change agent for one or more of the SIs. Her or his role is to support the System SI Leader to increase the acceptance of the change as well as to support, guide, develop, and direct the facility change agents aligned to the same initiative.

To set up the change agents for success, the OD team held an SI orientation session. Attendees received a mini-toolkit outlining one tool for each CAP stage and a partnership agreement to use for ensuring clarity on roles and expectations between themselves and the Facility SI Leader. After the initial orientation, ongoing support was provided through monthly conference calls, hosted by the OD Director and change agents assigned to the same initiative. The calls were used to educate the change agent about the work, share successes and struggles with one another, bubble up themes and challenges, and to provide peer support as needed.

In turn, the facility change agent's role is advising, coaching, and supporting the Facility SI Leader in an effort to increase acceptance of the change and ensure initiative success. Change agents work with the Facility SI Leader in the development of implementation plans as well as facilitating discussions with the team as they need assistance from a change management perspective. Finally, change agents work with each Facility SI Leader prior to each meeting to ensure that she or he has developed an agenda that will achieve the desired outcome and integrated activities around change where appropriate.

Table 2.4 is a summary of materials developed to support the success of the change agents.

MOBILIZING COMMITMENT TO MAKE CHANGE LAST

There was a small window of opportunity to implement this structure and strategy. As a result, a "grassroots" approach was utilized, leaving the change agents with the responsibility for communicating their value to the Facility SI Leaders. Assumptions were made that SI Leaders at the organizational and facility levels understood the "A" side of change and wanted or needed a change agent and had access to resources to be successful. It was also assumed that change agents would have the confidence, skill, and experience to effectively advise, coach, and support facility leaders.

TABLE 2.4   Summary of Materials

Initial briefing	Created a *Guidebook for Supporting the Facility through Change.* The intent of the guide was to further clarify the change agent role and expectations, provide structure and alignment for each strategic project, and provide the change agent with "talking points" to start dialogue with their Facility SI Leader. It includes a toolkit that is organized in alignment with the GE CAP model and a partnership agreement that defines value, deliverables, and scope of work for the change agent.
Monthly call	System change agents host a monthly call with their respective facility change agents with the purpose of sharing system and facility information specific to the project. Other activities include designing work plans, sharing successes and lessons learned, and asking questions related to tools and/or approach.

Although the strategy was simple in theory, implementation quickly became challenging. Early in the process, it was apparent that assumptions around how the initiatives were structured and communicated at each facility greatly varied. In general, the rollout of the SIs varied as a result of facility size, leadership style, and whether or not the facility was meeting the metrics on the specific initiative. Team-based structures varied as well, with some facilities forming teams around every initiative and others deciding to "activate" only some teams while leaving others "dormant." Because of the variation, change agents were faced with a myriad of situations we did not anticipate.

Despite the challenges, early successes also took root. For example, two change agents teamed up on one initiative and formed a successful partnership. Another initiative team developed a work plan for the change agents to provide consistent direction and scope in activities. The work plan included inviting the System SI Leader to the monthly calls, inviting facility change agents to system meetings, and assigning change agents to round in designated areas to observe how a process was working.

As the change agents made their way through the ambiguity, they were hungry to build their confidence and their skills. As a result, a new program, "Applying CAP—The Roadmap Series," was created. The series delivered three interactive sessions to refresh and strengthen change agent skills and confidence using change tools. Within days of launching the series, nearly 80% of the SI change agents registered to attend. The sessions were enthusiastically received by the change agents, with 87% saying that the sessions were beneficial and 97% saying that they would be interested in future change classes.

Toward the end of the first quarter, it was apparent there was still work to be done to implement the strategy. There was still a lack of understanding by System and Facility SI Leaders, leaving the change agents frustrated and discouraged. One individual stated, "As a change agent there has been a distinct lack of support from the facility leads. How many times do you knock on the door to offer support and demo tools before you are seen as a pest?" On the other side of the coin, one Facility SI Leader wrote, "I love my change agent. We have had three wonderful sessions with her and staff has been very engaged in the exercises. We are working on Making Change Last. I would like to be a change agent next year after I learn my new role better. Thank you!"

There were obvious communication gaps at all levels, and the OD team needed to close those gaps for the strategy to be successful. Our biggest challenge was buy-in and support for the strategy from system leads, facility senior leadership, and Facility SI Leaders. The OD team responded with a plan to increase the "A" around the change agent strategy.

Within a couple of weeks, the OD team met with the facility senior leaders and other key stakeholders to provide background of Banner Health's change methodology, the definition and benefits of CAP, and to formally introduce the Strategic Initiative Change Agent Strategy. Results from the meeting included increased support for the strategy, purposeful dialogue between facility senior leaders and facility SI leaders regarding change agent support, and the opportunity for the facilities to shuffle change agent assignments to make the work more meaningful and increase the account-ability for results. Listening to key stakeholders, opening up lines of com-munication, and creating an opportunity for change agents to enhance their skills provided an opportunity to course correct mid-year, with hopes of the strategy taking root and achieving success by year end.

MONITORING PROGRESS

To monitor progress toward our goal of creating a cadre of engaged change agents, we established formal and informal measures. The formal measures included tactics to support the overall goal, as well as leading and lagging measures. Below are some of the measures used on the scorecard.

TABLE 2.5   Organizational Scorecard Example

Goal: **Increase organizational capacity for change through creating a cadre of engaged change agents**

Tactic:	Leading Indicator:	Lagging Indicator:
Increase the number of change agents who apply new skills immediately after training	100% CAP participants identify a project prior to attending training	90% change agents trained apply skills to their project within 6 months of training
Engage change agents through aligning them to a strategic initiative	80% of change agents aligned to an initiative attend monthly change agent calls	75% of SI change agents indicate high engagement and continued commitment to continuing to support the organization with their skills as measured by year-end survey
Develop change agents who can confidently lead change	80% of change agents attend "Applying CAP" series	90% of "Applying CAP" attendees Agree or Strongly Agree that the sessions increased their confidence
Improve resources and knowledge management around change	Design a Web site with tools for change agents and place to track projects	80% change agents agree that the Web site is: • Easy to use • A reliable source of information and • Helpful in growing change agent skills as measured by the year-end survey

The informal measures came from mid-year interviews with both the change agents and the SI owners. The findings allowed us to make course corrections in order to improve our strategy (Q) as well as its acceptance (A) by leaders in the organization. Highlights from this data collection are outlined below.

Change Agent Survey Highlights

- 84% are moderately engaged or completely engaged in their change work:
    "I love helping people walk through issues, mobilize the desire to change, and sustain improvements."
- 27% felt their role was not understood at their facility:
    "One of my major frustrations is to be so willing, able, and ready to help from a skilled change agent perspective and to have little understanding within the organization as to how to use the change agents."
    "I am frustrated with the use of tools on our campus. I believe they are very valuable and being underutilized"
- 87% felt the "Applying CAP" series increased their knowledge around change management:
    "The recent education was very beneficial. Having homework was a great exercise and refresher for me."
- 92% were committed to serving as a change agent for an SI next year:
    "This has been an extraordinary process. . . . I have enjoyed it great-ly and wish I could do it full time! I am attempting to use these tools in my daily role. Thank you for a fantastic opportunity!"

A mid-year check-in with System SI leaders captured feedback on how well OD and the change agents were supporting change management efforts for SIs. As we spoke with the system SI leaders, themes included:

- Where change agents were being utilized, traction and progress around the initiative could be seen
- Appreciation for the information the change agents were sharing with the SI owners and with other change agents across facilities
- Continued uncertainty as to how a change agent could assist on the project when they were not an expert on the subject matter and hesitation to fully engage the change agent in the work

In general, the OD team was able to identify additional opportunities for improvement. Clearly, the biggest problem remained the lack of un-

derstanding around the role, skill, and value of a change agent. Until this
is addressed, the change agents face high barriers of entry to the work and
their role will continue to be sub-optimized.

CHANGING SYSTEMS AND STRUCTURES

The last phase in the CAP model is systems and structures. The purpose
of this phase is to evaluate the systems and structures that are in place in
order to ensure that they support the change that has been implemented.
By addressing systems and structures, Banner can enable acceptance and
commitment to the *new ways* and prevent reverting to the *old ways*.

Through this evaluation, Banner identified changes we will make in our
systems and structures. A few examples of the resulting changes include:

- *Pre-qualification for training:* Individuals who want to attend CAP
  must now identify a project and secure their leader's approval prior
  to being accepted into class. This increases the likelihood that skills
  will be applied immediately after training.
- *Change agent assignments:* Instead of assigning one change agent to
  each initiative at the facility level, we will look at alternate structures,
  such as dedicating 2–3 people to an initiative at a larger organizational level (e.g., regional level) so that one change agent can support several facilities.
- *Select appropriate SIs:* This year, we attempted to support all of the
  SIs. In hindsight, we learned that some are more appropriate than
  others, due to a variety of reasons. In the future, we will apply criteria before committing to support the SI.
- *Utilization of existing forums for communication:* In the future, we will
  be more proactive to request time at large leadership forums to
  ensure that all senior leaders have a better understanding of the
  change agent support strategy for the SIs.
- *Talent management:* We will ensure that active change agents are
  identified in our Talent Management database to ensure accuracy of
  our records and tracking of active change agents.
- *Introduction to the strategy and structure:* We will host an orientation
  to bring together the SI leaders with the change agents in order to
  provide an overview of the alignment strategy and offer a forum to
  discuss expectations around the partnership. Initially, leaders were
  not clear on the value the change agents could bring, so they were
  not fully utilized. By starting off with a meeting to identify the work,
  we hope to create a stronger, more valued relationship.

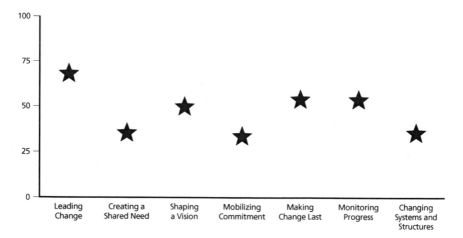

Figure 2.5 CAP self-assessment.

Almost a year into this strategy, a great deal has been learned around what it takes to develop a cadre of engaged change agents committed to increasing organizational capability to change. Using the CAP profile below (Figure 2.5), we assessed our work against each phase of the CAP model. Generally, we can assume the higher the rating, the better we performed on this phase; however, General Electric specifies that in order for the change to be sustainable, the following must be true:

- Mobilizing Commitment, as a standalone phase, must be above 50%
- Leading Change, Creating a Shared Need, and Shaping a Vision must have 2 of the 3 phases above 50% and
- Making Change Last, Monitoring Progress, and Systems and Structures must also have 2 of the 3 phases above 50%

This evaluation validated the need for our efforts to focus on Mobilizing Commitment as we prepare for the year to come.

CRITICAL SUCCESS FACTORS

In returning to the initial questions we set out to address, we will now outline some critical success factors for organizations contemplating a similar effort.

1. What does it take to develop a skilled change agent?
   a. *Purposeful selection*: Do not allow everyone to come to training; more trained leaders is not necessarily better. For the past

few years, the doors were open to anyone who wanted to be a change agent. We believe that a critical success factor is selecting change agents who are meeting performance expectations, are endorsed by leadership, and are supporting an identified project prior to attending training. In addition, targeting high-potential leaders can turn your change agent cadre over faster than you want. We recommend targeting talented leaders who intend to serve in their current role for 2+ years.

  b. *Experiential development*: Development needs to be an intentional blend of the 70–20–10 learning methodology (70% hands-on application, 20% development through coaching and feedback, and 10% classroom or virtual learning).

  c. *Ongoing support*: The infrastructure must be developed to provide change agents with the structure they need to be successful. Lean on the side of more structure, rather than less. Provide the change agents with work plans, monthly calls, sample documents, et cetera. Partner new change agents on a project—either with each other or, ideally, with a more experienced change agent—to build skill and confidence. The support really pays off in engagement and positive outcomes.

2. How do you set the stage for a change agent to be successful?

  a. *Eliminate the dual role*: It is extremely challenging to be effective at being the change agent for a project you are also leading. In looking at our own experience, we would have been wise to take our own medicine and have a non-OD change agent assist us as we developed the strategy. In hindsight, the blind spots are glaringly obvious, but in the moment they went unseen. If you find yourself in the situation of being both the change agent and project lead, find a partner to take on one of the roles so that you can focus on the other.

  b. *Educate others on the "A"*: Change agents do not need to be content experts on the projects they are supporting. Their expertise is around the acceptance of change. Help project leaders understand this before you partner a change agent on the project. Create a brief course for all leaders, starting at the most senior level to help them understand the $Q \times A = E$ equation and the role of a change agent.

3. What should an organization do if they are interested in implementing a similar strategy to improve acceptance around change?

  a. *Allow enough time to create a shared need around the strategy*: We created an idea and quickly moved to implementation with a framework of a plan and improved it during the journey. We saw a "limited time opportunity" to start the year off with the structure and grabbed it. Had we used our first year as a year to build a solid foundation, we might have kicked off the program in the following year with greater buy-in and perhaps different results.

b. *Leverage your allies and advocates:* If you have internal allies, invite them to brainstorm how change agents could most effectively be deployed. They understand the change agent role and have the perspective of what other organizational leaders need.

c. *Conduct readiness assessments:* This would have helped to increase our knowledge about how the rollout and responsibilities for achieving the initiatives were structured. It would have helped to identify key areas of resistance so that we could have managed resources more effectively.

d. *Start communication at the top:* Ensure that senior leaders receive an overview of the approach and an explanation of the "A" side of the $Q \times A = E$ equation. They need to be able to articulate the value of the change agent in order to support their role and alignment to the organization's most important priorities.

e. *Change is not a stand-alone; it has to be integrated into the work:* Leaders often want to create a "change" as a stand-alone team. We have found it more effective to integrate the change agents on the working teams so that they are able to identify opportunities to increase acceptance of change as decisions are made.

A CRITIQUE OF THE CAP MODEL

In this section, we revisit the CAP Model and its relationship to the relative context of realizing successful change. The CAP model provides a framework to increase the success and accelerate the implementation of organizational change efforts. Each of the tools is simple and easy to use. The CAP Business profile, for example, is a tool used to assess a current change effort. It takes approximately 15 minutes for a group or individual to complete. The real benefit is not the tool itself, but the dialogue that results from the discussion that accelerates change.

Change agents often comment that CAP training provides them with tools they can apply immediately. That said, there tend to be two key challenges for change agents in applying the model after training. The first is their ability to string together multiple tools to achieve an outcome, which takes practice and experience. Novice change agents find it difficult to determine when to apply the tools. The second is that to apply the model as a change agent, it helps to have some general consulting skills in order to step into a situation, assess the progress of a project, and identify the right tool or tools to apply. The tools also require explanation to a group, and this can be intimidating to the novice change agent. These appear to be the two biggest entry barriers for novice change agents in applying the model.

Another downside of the model is that the tools that support each of the seven elements vary in their appropriateness and value. As you progress through the seven elements, the material and tools are weaker. For example the material and tools in "Monitoring Progress" element are limited, with the suggestion of creating a scorecard. While the approach is sensible, there are few tools to support the development of an appropriate monitoring process.

Overall, the CAP model provides a solid framework for an organization to think about change. Its focus on the "A" (or acceptance) component in addition to the technical change strongly resonates with people, and therefore increases buy-in to the model up front. Organizations considering the use of the model will find many benefits, but at the same time should plan to address its shortfalls before widespread implementation.

THE WORLD BEYOND

We conclude this chapter by sharing future plans to develop and implement a change agent certification program, and we outline our vision for establishing a Strategic Change Management Office to further provide change capability within our organization.

We are currently in the process of creating a change agent certification program as part of our strategy to develop and maintain a cadre of engaged change agents within the organization. The program will have three levels of change agents, each with skills and commitment building from the previous level. Individuals trained as change agents prior to 2010 will be asked to apply for certification if they wish to continue as a change agent in the organization.

Level 1 change agents will have the skills to confidently use CAP tools and will maintain a sharp skill set through documenting the use of the tools at least two times a year. These change agents will serve as a resource pool for the local facility to utilize.

The Level 2 program will require recommendation by the facility senior leaders and be tied to current performance and future promotional potential. These leaders will be part of a one-year cohort-based program and will be required to take on a system or regional project as part of their certification. Afterwards, they will need to maintain their Level 2 certification through supporting a minimum number of facility and/or regional projects.

Certification for Level 3 will be a longer-term effort that will most likely only be available to a handful of leaders committed to serving the organization as master change agents.

In the longer term, we envision the development of a Strategic Change Management Office that would organize and prioritize all major changes that evolve from our strategies. This would ensure that the high-potential projects are well resourced and supported, and that other less urgent or less important projects are staged to limit the chaos that ensues when the organization is beyond capacity to absorb more change. We are confident that the lessons learned from our experiences will greatly benefit us as we continue on this journey.

Qualitative research contributions: Lisa A. Robinson and Ali Swandal.

REFERENCES

The Advisory Board Company. (2009). *An infamous case: Cedars Sinai CPOE adoption process.* Los Angeles, CA: The Advisory Board Company.

Fine, P. S. (2010, June). *Transitioning from growth to innovation.* 2010 Strategic Initiatives Summit, Mesa, AZ.

General Electric Company. (2003). *Change acceleration process (CAP) change agents workshop.* [PowerPoint slides].

IBM. (2008). *Making change work.* Sommers, NY: IBM Global Management.

Isern, J., & Pung, C. (2007, November). Driving radical change. *The McKinsey Quarterly, 2007*(4). Retrieved from http://www.mckinseyquarterly.com/Organization/Change_Management/Driving_radical_change_2046

Morton, C., Newall, A., & Sparkes, J. (2001). *Leading HR: Delivering competitive advantage.* London: CIPD House

Porter-O'Grady, T. & Krueger Wilson, C. (1995). *The leadership revolution in health care: Altering systems, changing behaviors.* Gaithersburg, Maryland: Aspen Publishers.

CHAPTER 3

GUIDING HEALTH SYSTEM CHANGE

Leadership Strategies for Organization Development

Josephine M. Kershaw and William E. Ruse

ABSTRACT

Given the ever-shifting landscape of healthcare reform, it is necessary for healthcare leaders to be visionary experts in strategic management and OD. Health executives must determine the most important priorities to address in their organizations, formulate a change-management plan, and steer the organization through the necessary steps to achieve objectives. In this chapter, the authors use an organization development perspective with a conceptual framework based on leadership strategies described by Darling and Heller (2009). These leadership strategies consist of (a) attention through vision, (b) meaning through communication, (c) trust through positioning, and (d) confidence through respect. Darling and Heller's (2009) strategies promote organizational growth and survival through the turbulence of the present healthcare environment. To illustrate the practical application of the four leadership strategies, the authors including the former CEO of the Blanchard Valley Health Association, discuss the Blanchard Valley healthcare organiza-

Organization Development in Health Care, pages 43–60

tion's transformational change from its inception as a home for "Friendless Women and Children" to a diversified, integrated delivery system with multisite, regional impact.[1]

LEADERSHIP AND ORGANIZATION DEVELOPMENT

In the dynamic healthcare environment, OD requires a commitment to organizational excellence, as well as the leadership strategies and values that prioritize achievement of that excellence. Important organizational components of this quest for excellence include member commitment, customer focus, constant innovation, and management leadership. To this end, Darling and Heller (2009) suggest four leadership strategies that contribute to organizational excellence: attention through vision, meaning through communication, trust through positioning, and confidence through respect.

Leadership Strategy 1: Attention Through Vision

To perform well within the healthcare environment, where change is paradoxically a constant, most successful individuals in directive roles are capable of assuming both managerial and leadership responsibilities in the interplay of operational conditions and environmental perspectives. These individuals balance a focus on people and initiatives within the organization with a concurrent concern for customers and external environmental influences. The reality of the shifting environment of health care requires this dual functionality of management and leadership roles with the appropriate skills and abilities to accomplish desired results. According to Hughes, Ginnett, and Curphy (2009), dual functionality of "adaptive management leadership" requires managerial leaders to better understand and meet the needs of associates in order to foster engagement and ownership of organizational efforts and results associated with planned systemic change.

Making a positive difference in the development of the organization, the managerial leader's professional fulfillment for success is oriented in service to others. Even initially negative events can be viewed strategically to evoke a positive response, by looking for commensurate strengths, prospective advantages, and hidden opportunities. Consequently, effective managerial leaders have a positive vision that propels their organizations beyond the limitations of the present horizon.

Visionary foresight provides the overall guiding sense for the organization as it navigates through the constantly changing healthcare environment. If an organization were like a human body, visionary foresight, like the five senses, would monitor the external environment, and the organization's mission, like the brain, would be the vital organ that sustained longevity and purpose. The case vignettes that follow trace the life of the Blanchard Valley Health System over several decades. Starting with lessons learned early in the professional life of a young manager, the reader travels through the organization development phases in response to the internal and external environments that propelled an organization from a single hospital to an integrated rural health delivery system. Physician recruitment, mastering the regulatory process, budgeting tied to strategic plans, risk taking, and vision forged a healthy body built to withstand the complexities of the aging process.

Health System Case Study: The Blanchard Valley Health Association

From 1960 until the mid-1970s, Blanchard Valley Hospital (BVH) was a typical mid-size community hospital. Founded in 1891 as the Findlay Home for Friendless Women and Children, the hospital's basic services were obstetrics, pediatrics, general medicine, and general surgery. There were few specialists. General practitioners delivered babies, conducted general surgery, and often served as anesthesiologists. More complicated and tertiary care cases requiring intensive, specialty care were transferred elsewhere. Although completely re-making an organization can be a long and arduous task, it was clear by the latter part of the 1970s that the time had come to diversify into more specialized medical care.

Strategic planning identified several medical and surgical specialists that were needed, but the timeframe for recruitment was measured in years rather than months using traditional recruitment techniques, including national search firms and marketing and advertising in medical journals. Rejecting the piecemeal attempts of one-at-a-time recruiting, BVH decided to recruit directly at residency training sites, including the Ohio State University in Columbus, Ohio.

This strategy proved successful, as ten physicians, who were all classmates at Ohio State, were looking for an opportunity to practice together at any location in the U.S. BVH successfully recruited this group and, over the next three years, the practice of medicine in Findlay and the growth of the hospital changed dramatically. Specialists in the group included orthopedic surgery, obstetrics and gynecology, endocrinology, cardiology, hematology, oncology, rheumatology, and pulmonary medicine. The physicians, who became known as the "Columbus Ten," were committed to excellence and demanded that the hospital meet quality expectations in all of its diagnostic service areas including laboratories, imaging, nuclear medicine, and the emergency department.

Realizing the need to diversify and add new services as the emphasis on health care moved away from the hospital, BVH reorganized in 1983 into a health system where the hospital became a subsidiary of the parent system. The reorganization was timely, as hospital operations were becoming more complex and the healthcare environment was in flux. Moreover, a major healthcare payer, Medicare, dramatically changed its inpatient reimbursement philosophy. Consequently, hospitals were struggling to find new ways to treat patients in their homes or on an outpatient basis. In addition, managed care had entered the national picture. Furthermore, physicians were gaining an entrepreneurial spirit and opening competing business enterprises.

To respond to this changing environment, hospital board members were asked to consider developing a new organizational structure wherein the hospital would become a subsidiary of a parent. Those wishing to focus their energies at the hospital level would remain members of the hospital's governing board. Strategy development and nonhospital-based services would be guided by a new system board whose members would be those former hospital board members who preferred long-range organization development. Thus was born the Blanchard Valley Health Association (BVHA). To solidify the organizational structure, the Association executed a Management Agreement whereby the hospital retained BVHA to provide executive and administrative services to the hospital (BVHA, 1983).

Leadership Strategy 2. Meaning Through Communication

Like BVHA, today's organizations must evolve constantly to keep up with the rapid changes taking place in the environment around them and among the people who work within them. With change comes risk and uncertainty, which can hinder development, particularly if the change process is haphazard and not managed appropriately. Consequently, OD manages this challenge, bringing the organization forward through planned change. Keys to successful OD are a visionary leader who does not fear change and embraces opportunities, attention to process, and focus on goals and organizational values. By recognizing that organizations are social systems, the OD approach eases transitions through planned change that shapes organizational culture, which in turn influences the way people work. In response to the changing conditions of the healthcare industry, an organization must adapt with a continuously learning workforce, innovative use of technologies, and aligned business processes (Graf, 2009).

To adapt, innovate, and align business processes, communication is essential in its role of creating common meaning of values and shared goals that elevate the organization above the change and unrest of the healthcare environment. Thus, meaning through communication enables an organization to maneuver obstacles of change and reach its goals. In OD, change is the ultimate outcome, while development to improve potential effectiveness and increase capacity is the purpose. OD leads to planned systemic changes that enable organizations to achieve their desired goals. Characterized by Beckhard (1969) as "an effort, planned, organization-wide, and managed from the top, to increase organization effectiveness and health through planned interventions in the organization's processes, using behavioral science knowledge" (p. 9), organization development is essentially planning for system-wide change. Planned change incorporates shared interpretations of reality that facilitate coordinated action by work teams.

Increasing organizational complexity and operational connectivity have intensified the need for communication and coordinated efforts among all levels of today's healthcare organization. Such coordinated efforts highlight how teamwork has become a core competence in work environments where collaboration is essential (Laszlo, Laszlo, & Johnsen, 2009). Hackman (1983) identified three factors that contribute to team effectiveness: (1) the group's output meets or exceeds expectations, (2) the group's work processes lead to improvements in ability to collaborate in the future, and (3) the group's collaborative effort contributes to the growth and wellbeing of its members. In the ideal healthcare team, members with complementary skills exhibit commitment and share mutual accountability for a common purpose or set of performance goals.

Case Study: A Young Manager Learns the Value of Meaning Through Communication

Often arising from experience, the wisdom of skillfully communicating meaning that meshes with an organization's culture is lacking in young managers who are anxious to move an organization forward. Within a year of joining the staff of a hospital pharmacy department in Lima, Ohio, a young pharmacist was promoted to chief pharmacist. The 300-bed hospital was growing, had a rapidly expanding medical staff, and served as an internship site for medical school graduates pursuing future practice in family medicine. Unfortunately, the pharmacy department was not of sufficient size to meet the growing demands for pharmaceutical services. Plans to expand the pharmacy department were rejected by the CEO after having been approved by a vice-president. The young chief pharmacist at the time was devastated. Why, he thought, would a CEO reject plans to expand a department into space that was being used less than nine hours per week by volunteers?

A few years later, the young pharmacist, having obtained an MBA in health care, was appointed acting administrator at another facility, Blanchard Valley Hospital in Findlay, Ohio. On day one of his new job, he approved expansion of the pharmacy department into space currently being used by volunteers—and incurred the animosity of 800 auxiliary members. It was on that day that the wisdom of the Lima Memorial Hospital CEO became apparent. The event cemented in the mind of the young acting leader that leadership requires communication and understanding of the impact of unilateral actions on the morale of organizations.

The application of meaning through communication was learned through recognizing that, as nonprofit organizations develop, they rely heavily on volunteers. Leadership, in this instance of dealing with hospital auxiliary members, required a different skill set and a sensitivity to lead by motivation unfettered by the traditional principles of business profit. Moreover, compensation for volunteers is replaced by recognition, and space to call one's own is certainly a form of recognition in the world of volunteerism. Thus, applying meaning through communication involves a vision of the future, coupled with the empathy required to lead people whose lives are dedicated to helping others.

Leadership Strategy 3: Trust Through Positioning

Providing leadership, expertise, and experience in change management, change agents—either internal or external to the organization—usually facilitate OD by initiating and managing change interventions. Many OD interventions are modeled on action research, a

> process of systematically collecting research data about an ongoing system relative to some objective, goal, or need of that system; feeding these data back into the system; taking actions by altering selected variables within the system based both on the data and on hypotheses; and evaluating the results of actions by collecting more data. (French & Bell, 1990)

A value-added customer focus enhances the probability of success by matching the services and products the business is providing to the customers' needs (Vandermerwe, 2000).

Adding value and meeting customer needs requires flexible organizations that may be viewed as open systems, influencing and influenced by both central (e.g., operations) and peripheral (e.g., regulatory) environments (Farris, Senner, & Butterfield, 1973). Through evaluation studies of OD activities and their effects, it has been found that the outcomes of OD activities are not due to any single factor, but collectively result from various human and non-human elements (Koivisto, Vataja, & Seppanen-Jarvela, 2008). In OD, opportunities that arise during times of socioeconomic turmoil must be recognized and seized with appropriate actions taken to assure operational adaptation. Compelling reasons to conduct OD include the changing nature of the workplace, global markets, and the accelerated rate of change (Rouda & Kusy, 1995).

In a global world, it is impossible to manage without mastering the external regulatory environment. A hospital's patients can easily be lost to an aggressive competitor who offers better pricing, better service, or better quality. Moreover, competitors with newer technology can easily gain market share. There is an area of the environment, however, where regional and even national competitors stand on equal footing. It is the regulatory environment that applies to all organizations within its jurisdictional reach. Organizations cannot develop a meaningful strategic plan without mastering, participating in, and using the regulatory environment as a tool for OD.

It has often been observed that health care is one of the more heavily regulated industries in the U.S. Most would argue that the regulatory environment is an impediment to progress, and that may well be the case. Energy companies operating nuclear reactors may argue this point, and justifiably so. Be that as it may, no one can deny that hospitals, nursing homes, medical and paramedical personnel, drug companies, medical equipment manufacturers, and others similarly situated live in a world of extensive rules and regulations. In the healthcare sector, regulations govern access, quality, and cost of care.

Case Study: Positioning in the Healthcare Regulatory Environment

By the mid-1960s, the days of laissez-faire between government and hospitals were coming to an end. In the early and mid 1950s, government had helped expand access by providing grants and loans to hospitals to promote building and expansion. The Hill-Burton program would provide 1/3 of the capital cost of building. With the advent of the Medicare program in 1965 and the companion Medicaid program in mid-1965, the purpose of government turned from promoting access to controlling access. Government had become a purchaser of care for elderly, blind, disabled, and low-income Americans.

The substantial financial interest involved in these major social programs heralded the advent of increased regulation. Consequently, strategic planning required healthcare executives to concentrate on a major source of regulatory information, the Federal Register. Laws passed by Congress were interpreted by administrative agencies and interpretation of congressional intent was often in the mind of the beholder. Forward-thinking executives had to understand the regulations and they had to develop a strategy that included visits to congressional offices in Washington, D.C.

It was in this vortex of change that Blanchard Valley Hospital and its leadership team determined that the future of health care in Findlay, Ohio was as much dependent on its interactions with state and federal congressional offices as it was on advances in science, technology, and medicine.

Two legislative interventions in the 1980s were responsible for BVH's evolution from a single hospital to a comprehensive rural healthcare delivery system. As the hospital formulated its strategic plan, it was necessary to focus on regulations promulgated by the Ohio Department of Health at the state level. Simultaneously, at the national level, it was necessary to monitor Medicare's newly developed prospective payment system, which did away with cost-based reimbursements and set in place a fixed cost-per-stay reimbursement scheme based on a patient's diagnosis—more commonly known as diagnosis-related groups (DRGs).

At the state level, Ohio embraced a strong certificate of need (CON) program in the 1980s. Included in the list of regulated healthcare services was radiation therapy, which affected BVHA because the expansion of specialists on the hospital's medical staff had allowed a significant increase in the number of oncology patients who could be treated locally. A complete oncology program required a combination of surgical, chemotherapy, and radiation therapy interventions. The recently reorganized BVHA had applied for a CON to develop a radiation therapy center; however, the request for a CON was denied by the Ohio State Department of Health, which reasoned that radiation therapy centers should be located in larger metropolitan areas. Since radiation therapy required multiple visits each week for a period of several weeks, the burden of travel aggravated an already stressful situation when local treatment was not available.

The BVHA system appealed the Department of Health's ruling and a hearing officer subsequently ruled in BVHA's favor; but the State of Ohio did not adopt the hearing officer's findings. As a result, the BVHA system was faced with two final alternatives. One was to turn to the courts, which would be a lengthy and costly process. The other alternative was to use the legislative process to change the law to allow more flexibility in locating radiation therapy centers in smaller communities. BVHA worked with its local representative in the Ohio House of Representatives and with the Governor's Office. In the end, BVHA was successful in having the law changed so that a radiation therapy center could be built and operated in Findlay, Ohio. Today, the Radiation Center plays an integral role in providing cancer services to residents of Northwestern Ohio.

On the federal level, the introduction of Medicare's prospective payment system provided a challenge to both BVH and the BVHA system. DRG reimbursement under the prospective payment system varied, depending on a hospital's location, its patient mix, its teaching capacity, and other factors. Hospitals that were located in Standard Metropolitan Statistical Areas (SMSAs) received higher reimbursement rates than hospitals outside an SMSA, or rural hospitals. Although BVH provided a wide range of sophisticated services, it received lower reimbursement rates than hospitals in larger population centers to its north or to its south. During the mid-1980s, the city of

Findlay had a population of less than 35,000 people, which did not qualify for SMSA designation. To qualify as an SMSA hospital, BVH would need to be located in a city with a population of at least 50,000 people.

Regulations implementing the prospective payment system did provide for a category of hospitals called rural referral centers (RRCs). At that time, an RRC was defined as a hospital located a significant distance from an SMSA and providing a wide range of sophisticated services. BVH met all the requirements for RRC designation, except for the distance requirement. In other words, the hospital was too close to a city with a population of 50,000 or more.

When it was determined that reimbursement from the Medicare program could be increased by approximately one million dollars if RRC designation were achieved, the hospital's management team developed a two-pronged approach in their goal to achieve RRC status. The first step was to join with a coalition of hospitals that were seeking similar status. Meetings with these hospitals were held in Washington, D.C. A common strategy was developed that, among other things, mitigated the distance requirement. The next step was to meet with members of Congress, both in the House of Representatives and Senate. Each hospital in the coalition group met with individual members of their congressional delegation. Moreover, members of key congressional committees were invited to meet with the group, and many did so. In a relatively short period of time, amendments were made to legislation and signed by the President providing for more flexible RRC designation. These changes allowed BVH to become an RRC.

Leadership Strategy 4: Confidence Through Respect

Achieving designation as an RRC involved leadership actions in multiple arenas with various stakeholders, health organizations, and public agencies. As a discipline, OD combines research and practical experience in the process of understanding people, business organizations, and their interactions during the system change process. Leadership initiative and organizational values that make possible creative thinking, opportunity awareness, and strategic responses serve to make successful OD possible (Darling, Gabrielsson, & Serist, 2007). Visionary leaders must possess organizational wisdom, defined by Bierly, Kessler, and Christensen (2000) as "judgment and decision making, which requires an understanding of the complexity of a situation, but also requires the ability to make sense and simplify so that action can be taken" (p. 595). To be effective, OD interventions require support from top management, with buy-in from stakeholders throughout the organization.

According to Gabrielsson, Serist, and Darling (2009), managing and leading differ in that

> managers control resources, master procedures and routines, and accomplish goals and objectives, while effective leaders creatively secure and allocate resources, and communicate and coordinate among associates in guiding the organization's operations. (p. 9)

Similarly, Drucker (1999) distinguished between managing (to accomplish, to have responsibility for, to conduct) and leading (to guide in direction, course, action, or opinion). Within the healthcare organization, both managers and leaders are necessary for success. Some people are naturally good managers, while others seem to have innate leadership qualities.

In a world of change, a high degree of positional purpose, goal-directedness, and value-based consistency must be established by managerial leaders in order to withstand the ups and downs of daily activities and maintain continuity (Heath & Heath, 2007). Organizational decision issues such as managing, leading, investing, borrowing, buying, owning, working and innovating permeate the healthcare environment today in ways they never have before (Coy, 2008). As it gained the confidence and respect of surrounding hospitals, BVH continued its external growth, organization development, and horizontal integration progress. Simultaneously, leaders must skillfully navigate in both the organization's internal dimension (including associates and employees) as well as the external dimension of which customers and competitors constitute a major part.

Case Study: Winning the Confidence of Governing Boards and Community Partners

The external dimension of competitors for BVH encompassed smaller facilities in adjoining towns and counties. A notable example was Bluffton Community Hospital (BCH), a small hospital located between Findlay and Lima, Ohio that was searching for a merger partner. BCH hired a consultant who interviewed representatives of two hospitals in Lima and BVH in Findlay. During the discussions, members of BVH's medical staff met with board members and medical staff members of BCH. It was the Blanchard medical staff's commitment to work closely with Bluffton that proved to be the decision maker. The consultant recommended BVH as the most appropriate merger partner. Bluffton's board accepted their consultant's recommendation. Board members at BVH and the BVHA extended an invitation to Bluffton's board to join either the hospital or parent organization. Both Blanchard Valley governing boards expanded to provide places for their Bluffton colleagues. BCH thus became a subsidiary of BVHA in 1995.

Additional alliances were established with two large hospital systems, including the Ohio Health System based in Columbus, Ohio and ProMedica Health System based in Toledo, Ohio. The alliance with the Ohio Health System provided BVHA with significant savings on supplies and services, plus the services of a cardiologist who helped establish BVH's cardiac catheterization lab. To support the hospital's growing oncology services, BVHA constructed a radiation therapy center and entered into an agreement with the ProMedica System to provide the services of a radiation oncologist and dosimetrist. Further internal growth occurred with the building and opening of a new building dedicated solely to diagnostic studies. Since hospital lengths of stay were shortening and more care was moving to an outpatient setting, the new Center for Diagnostic Studies provided an ambulatory site for lab, x-ray, mammography services, cardiology, neurology, nuclear medicine, and an array of doctors' offices.

Winning confidence through the respect of governing boards and community members was again illustrated in BVHA's purchase of a part interest in Lima Memorial Hospital (LMH) in partnership with the ProMedica Health System. LMH, once a thriving 300-bed hospital, had fallen on difficult times. The city of the Lima had lost much of its manufacturing base and its population had declined significantly. Moreover, the second hospital in town, St. Rita's Hospital, an affiliate of the Mercy Healthcare System, had gained significant market share at the expense of LMH. Furthermore, LMH had experienced a strike by its nursing staff resulting in closure of its obstetrical unit.

As a result of these events, LMH considered a series of alternatives, including merging with its competitor, selling to a for-profit hospital chain, or partnering with a non-profit hospital system. The first option, merging with its competitor, St. Rita's, was soundly rejected by LMH's association membership, which held a veto power over any change in ownership. The membership was concerned that LMH would become part of a Catholic health system.

In the meantime, the BVHA approached the ProMedica Health System about the possibility of obtaining a joint interest in LMH. Both the BVHA and ProMedica were non-profit healthcare systems. Although the BVHA had a close working relationship with the management of LMH at that time, it was not large enough to consider partnering with LMH without another financially strong partner. With the approval of their respective boards of trustees, the BVHA and the ProMedica senior managements formed a partnership that provided the legal framework for making a proposal to LMH's board. The final proposal included the following provisions:

- Each partner would contribute $250,000 in cash to LMH.
- The partnership would guarantee up to $25 million in LMH debt.
- Each partner would acquire a 25% ownership in LMH.

- It was contemplated that ownership would be permanent; however, provisions were added that allowed for an unwinding at the end of seven years.
- Both the BVHA and ProMedica would obtain three seats on the LMH board (thus constituting 50% of total board membership).

While LMH was considering the partnership's offer, it was also entertaining an offer by Quorum, a large national hospital chain that managed and owned hospitals in several states. Quorum's initial purchase offer of $85 million was subsequently increased to well over $100 million. For-profit or non-profit—that was the dilemma that faced LMH. A series of debates were held in Lima's Civic Center, with nearly 1,000 people in attendance. Shortly after the final debate presentation, LMH's governing board and association members voted to accept the BVHA–ProMedica partnership's proposal.

Embracing partnerships with other healthcare providers in the county and throughout Northwestern and Central Ohio allowed the BVHA to flourish and sustain planned change and organizational growth from its humble inception. Many of the initial partners were small healthcare providers known for the quality of care they provided and for the personal empathy provided to each client. Another common trait of these early partners was the struggle to stay financially viable. To assure financial stability, the partners soon became wholly-owned subsidiaries of the system. In keeping with Darling and Heller's (2009) fourth leadership strategy, confidence through respect, BVHA's legal Management Agreement (1983) allowed its many partners to retain their own governing boards, with the system having certain reservations of rights, including approvals of the following:

- adoption of operating and capital budgets
- expenditures for non-budgeted and budgeted items in excess of certain thresholds
- submissions of any certificates of need
- execution of any contract with a term in excess of one year
- appointment of auditors and/or accountants
- adoption of long-range plans, including any agreement with consortia, alliances, et cetera
- sale or lease of real or personal property that comprised a significant part of the corporation's assets

Using the above approach to system expansion, organizations joining BVHA included home health and hospice agencies, a durable medical equipment company, and an Alzheimer's association. Doctors' offices and clinics that each included a physician and nurse(s) as well as lab and x-ray services were established in rural areas throughout Northwest Ohio.

Partnerships with large and with small health organizations characterized BVHA's planned change and expansion over the years.

STRATEGIC PLANNING AND ORGANIZATION DEVELOPMENT

Characterized by planned change, OD is closely linked to the strategic planning process. Strategic planning and OD often require a choice between competing alternatives. In the text, *Cases in Health Services Management,* Rakich, Longest, and Darr (2004) suggest five questions to ask when choosing among alternatives:

- Which alternative provides the greatest benefit?
- What is the relative cost of alternatives?
- Are internal capabilities to implement alternatives equal?
- Will external influences constrain or support implementation of the alternatives differentially?
- How consistent are the alternatives with organizational philosophy, culture, and objectives?

To grow and prosper, health services organizations must consider alternative courses for the future when planning for the present. The last case study vignettes provide examples of how BVHA reviewed the alternative directions for growth and proceeded in concordance with strategic planning as a guide for its planned actions.

Case Study: Growth and Diversification: Budgeting and Strategic Planning

When the BVHA developed its strategic plans in the 1990s, senior management and the governing board reviewed alternative courses for the future and recognized the potential of entering the long-term care market. Nursing homes in the county were running at nearly full capacity. This meant that hospital patients who were ready for discharge to a nursing home often had to stay in the hospital until a bed was available. Because Ohio's CON law decreed that no new nursing homes could be built, providers desiring to enter the nursing home market had to either lease or purchase an existing nursing home or nursing home beds within their county. Inquiries with existing for-profit long-term care providers indicated that a purchase in the near future was unlikely.

Having determined the costs and benefits (as well as the lack of current internal capabilities to offer long-term care services), the BVHA's executive board decided to diversify its holdings as part of its strategic planning approach. Consistent with this organizational objective was the purchase of the Winebrenner long-term care complex in June 1997. Winebrenner Village and Winebrenner Haven were located in Findlay's north side, adjacent to the campus of the University of Findlay. Owned by the Churches of God, the Village was a 172-bed nursing home, while the Haven was a 47-bed residential facility. In addition, 10 cottages provided housing for independent living residents. The Winebrenner complex was overseen by a board that had recently reorganized. Formerly consisting entirely of church members, the new board included a blend of church members and other community members.

Under the leadership of the new board and its management team, fundraising success increased dramatically; but the complex still struggled to be financially viable. It was at this juncture that discussions between the BVHA and the Churches of God commenced. Although the BVHA was interested in leasing the Winebrenner complex, it soon became apparent that the church preferred to sell Winebrenner. Following prolonged negotiations, the BVHA purchased the Winebrenner complex for slightly over six million dollars, and the church agreed to fund a chaplain's position from the earnings on the purchase price.

The BVHA now had a long-term care complex; however, expansion would be difficult because the Winebrenner complex would be competing with the university for land in a heavily residential neighborhood. The BVHA's president met with the president of the University of Findlay and suggested that the university consider purchasing the Winebrenner complex, which would be ideally suited for offices and student dormitories. Shortly thereafter, the BVHA sold the Winebrenner facilities to the university, with a delayed two-year closing that would allow time to build a new long-term care complex. Proceeds from the sale provided sufficient funds so that, today, the BVHA continuing care division is located on a 130-acre tract of land east of Findlay that includes a nursing home, exercise facilities and pool, a lodge for social gatherings, condominiums, apartments, a cancer and radiation center, a women's center, and medical offices. Moreover, the win–win strategic move meant that the university obtained much-needed dormitory rooms, facilities for its new hospitality management program, and additional administrative office space.

As the 21st century dawned, the BVHA continued to expand through the acquisition of additional lines of business and the building of new facilities. Thus, from its humble beginnings, BVH grew into a regional health system. This growth ensued from its ongoing commitment to OD, strategic planning, attention to budgeting, and consideration of long-term needs while meeting short-term objectives. Serving as an exemplary managerial leader and primary change agent, one of the authors was the CEO of the case study hospital and subsequent health system for 36 years. The Blanchard Valley

Health System is now one of the largest employers in the area, with 2,200 associates providing services for eight counties in Northwest Ohio (BVHS, 2009). As the health system reaches its mature years, continuity into the future will require organizational renewal through improved effectiveness and growth to avoid decline and eventual closure. According to Cummings and Worley (2009), "organization development is a system wide application and transfer of behavioral science knowledge to the planned development, improvement, and reinforcement of the strategies, structures, and processes that lead to organizational effectiveness" (pp. 1–2). This case study demonstrated that in order for healthcare organizations to achieve sustainable growth and success, they inevitably undergo periods of significant change guided by strategic planning and visionary leadership.

Thus, the organization development process at BVHA has involved all four of Darling and Heller's (2009) leadership strategies, and the first strategy, *attention to vision*, continues to be a key aspect of managerial leaders in the present healthcare organization. The second strategy, to provide *meaning through communication*, is particularly relevant for internal stakeholders in OD who experience increased uncertainty and anxiety as the impact of healthcare reform efforts, regulatory policies, and budgetary pressures in the external environment percolate through the organization. To this effect, healthcare executives at a recent conference (AHCLA, 2009) mentioned that transparency and town hall meetings with staff were essential measures for promoting organizational cohesiveness in times of environmental uncertainty. Likewise, the third strategy's focus on *trust through positioning* is a major determinant of how the healthcare organization survives and thrives through such environmental change and relative instability created by factors beyond an organization's control. Last, but not least, the fourth strategy of *achieving confidence through respect* will foster internal cooperation, external collaboration, and effective change processes in the Blanchard Valley Health System's ongoing organization development.

CONCLUSION

Recent proposals to reform the U.S. healthcare system have undergone contentious national debates as policymakers attempt to control rising healthcare costs using advances in technology, payment alterations, and changes in healthcare delivery. Expenditures continue to rise as the federal stimulus package passed in February, 2009 allocated a significant amount to health care (PL 111-5 The American Recovery and Reinvestment Act of 2009). According to the renowned Kaiser Foundation (2009),

Successfully improving the efficiency and quality with which care is delivered is an enormous challenge, one that will require substantial investment in research, new information systems, performance incentives, and education, with the hope of transforming how health care is delivered by thousands and thousands of providers dispersed across our largely disaggregated health care system.

This chapter's case study focused on guiding health system change by discussing leadership strategies for OD. Additionally, the authors discussed the approaches and lessons learned from guiding the organizational change process in a healthcare delivery system: what worked and what did not work when implementing and managing changes ranging from relatively minor internal modifications to launching major capital expenditures and maneuvering strategic expansions. Lastly, the burgeoning regulatory, technological, and medical–industrial environments affecting the broad healthcare market were reviewed in light of their influence on leadership decisions.

Using the tools of OD, managerial leaders of healthcare organizations will be at the vanguard of implementing changes resulting from current reform efforts. Through its focus on Darling and Heller's (2009) framework of attention through vision, meaning through communication, trust through positioning, and confidence through respect as well as strategic planning, this case study provided a historical case study for analysis of leadership strategies that impact OD and guide health system change. Whatever shape the health reforms may eventually take, today's managerial leaders will be pulled in numerous directions as they endeavor to meet organizational objectives, manage with limited resources, and navigate the tumultuous changes in the U.S. healthcare system. Creativity in investments and timely innovation with transparency and integrity must be coupled with effective strategic planning and OD in order for healthcare organizations to achieve success.

NOTE

1. Mr. Ruse served as President and CEO of Blanchard Valley Hospital from 1963 until 1997 and as President and CEO of the Blanchard Valley Health Association from formation in 1983 until his retirement in 2000.

REFERENCES

Asian Health Care Leadership Association Conference. (2009, November). "Bridging a Legacy, Forging a New Vision." Chicago, IL.

Beckhard, R. (1969). *Organization development: Strategies and models*. Reading, MA: Addison Wesley.

Bierly, P, Kessler, E, & Christensen, E. (2000). Organizational learning, knowledge, and wisdom. *Journal of Organizational Change Management, 13*(6), 595–618.

Blanchard Valley Health Association. (1983, February 1). *Corporate reorganization of the Blanchard Valley Health Association*, Legal Documents, Sec. 8., Management agreement.

Blanchard Valley Health System (2009). *Significant events in the history and "pre-history" of BVHS*. Retrieved from http://www.bvhealthsystem.org/upload/docs/History/BVHS%20History%202009.pdf

Coy, P. (2008, November 3). Surviving the storm. *Business Week*, pp. 48–50.

Cummings, T., & Worley, C. (2009). *Organization development and change*. Mason, OH: South-Western Cengage Learning.

Darling, J., Gabrielsson, M., & Serist, H. (2007, Winter). Enhancing contemporary entrepreneurship: A focus on management leadership. *European Business Review*, pp. 4–22.

Darling, J., & Heller, V. (2009, Summer). Organization development in an era of socioeconomic change: A focus on the key to successful management leadership. *Organization Development Journal*. Retrieved from http://findarticles.com/p/articles/mi_qa5427/is_200907/ai_n32127541/

Drucker, P. (1999). *Management challenges for the 21st century*. New York: Harper Collins.

Farris, G., Senner, E., & Butterfield, D. (1973). Trust, culture, and organizational behavior. *Industrial Relations, 12*(2), 144–157. Retrieved from Business Source Complete at http://search.ebscohost.com/login.aspx?direct=true&db=bth&AN=4553575&site=ehost-live

French, W., & Bell, C. (1990). *Organizational development: Behavioral science interventions for organization improvement*. Englewood Cliffs, NJ: Prentice Hall.

Gabrielsson, M., Serist, H., & Darling, J. (2009). Developing the global management team: A new paradigm of key leadership perspectives. *Team Performance Management: An International Journal, 15*(7/8), 308–325.

Graf, T. (2009). The future of OD: Developing an effective virtual organization for the OD network. *OD Practitioner, 41*(3), 30–36. Retrieved from Business Source Complete at http://search.ebscohost.com/login.aspx?direct=true&db=bth&AN=42309497&site=ehost-live

Hackman, J. (1983). *A normative model of work team effectiveness*. New Haven, CT: Yale University School of Organization and Management.

Heath, C., & Heath, D. (2007). *Made to stick*. New York: Random House.

Hughes, R, Ginnett, R., & Curphy, G. (2009). *Leadership*. Boston: McGraw-Hill Irwin.

Kaiser Foundation. (2009). *Health care costs: A primer: Key information on health care costs and their impact*. Retrieved from http://www.kff.org/insurance/upload/7670_02.pdf

Koivisto, J., Vataja, K., & Seppanen-Jarvela, R. (2008). Relational evaluation of organizational development activities. *International Journal of Public Administration, 31* (10/11), 1167–1181. doi:10.1080/01900690801973261

Laszlo, A., Laszlo, K., & Johnsen, C. (2009). From high performance teams to evolutionary learning communities: New pathways in organizational development. *Journal of Organisational Transformation & Social Change, 6*(1), 21–48. doi:10.1386/jots.6.1.29_1

The American Recovery and Reinvestment Act of 2009, Pub. L. No. 111-5 (February 17, 2009).

Rakich, J., Longest, B., & Darr, K. (2004). *Cases in health services management.* Baltimore, MD: Health Professions Press.

Rouda, R., & Kusy, M. (1995). Organizational development: The management of change. Technical Association of the Pulp and Paper Industry. Retrieved from http://alumnus.caltech.edu/~rouda/T3_OD.html

Vandermerwe, S. (2000). How increasing value to customers improves business results. *Sloan Management Review, 42,* 27–37.

PART II

LEADERSHIP

THE STRATEGIC ROLE OF ORGANIZATION DEVELOPMENT IN TALENT MANAGEMENT AND TRANSFORMING LEADERSHIP

CEO and OD Executive Perspective

Rosa M. Colon-Kolacko

ABSTRACT

Christiana Care Health System, headquartered in Wilmington, Delaware, is one of the largest health systems in the country and is committed to "transformational change." This type of change is not evolutionary; it does not occur in small, incremental steps. It is intended to produce dramatic results through breakthrough thinking. All of our leaders will be at the front lines of this transformation by listening, collaborating, and building a learning organization. To reach our ambitious goals, we need to build the capability of our leadership team. This chapter will describe our "Transforming Leadership" strategy, which was introduced to build organizational capabilities and equip

Organization Development in Health Care, pages 63–88

our leaders with a set of competencies and skills to embrace and demonstrate leadership behaviors that will enable our transformation. Doing so, we will help our health system to make significant and sustainable changes in care delivery processes and systems to improve patient outcomes. We will then meet the constant challenges placed on healthcare systems today and serve our community. Developing new organizational capabilities is emerging as one of the major challenges that are faced by healthcare leaders. We recognize that people are our greatest asset. We need to have the ability to get the right people with the right skills into the right jobs in a cost-effective way, preparing our future leaders while making it possible to achieve excellence and continuously "transform" the care we give.

The purpose of this chapter is to introduce an integrated framework for the development of healthcare leaders successfully employing key processes: talent management, succession planning, coaching, and leadership development to accelerate clinical transformation and develop a great place to work. We will also introduce a strategic approach to the OD function so that it can play a vital role in the macro dialogue on systemic and cultural change in health care, while at the same time playing a critical role in supporting the day-to-day organizational learning needs of hospitals, nurses, clinical professionals, support staff, and doctors to develop and create learning capability to provide the best healthcare solutions to our patients and community. We share reflections and lessons learned from our CEO and myself (an OD executive).

INTRODUCTION

Christiana Care Health System is a leading nonprofit, teaching health care provider serving Delaware and neighboring areas of Maryland, Pennsylvania, and New Jersey. This 1,100-bed hospital system is one of the largest not-for-profit teaching health systems in the country. With more than 10,000 employees, it is the largest private employer in Delaware and the 10th largest employer in the Philadelphia region, ranking by volume compared to other U.S. Hospitals as 14th in admissions, 28th in births, 24th in emergency visits, and 17th in total surgeries.

Christiana Care exists to take care of its neighbors and community. In 2008 we provided $37.7 million in free care and medicine to those who could not afford to pay. The generous support of our partners in business, government, and the community helps us expand and enhance the care we provide to all community members.

The ability to deliver this promise is embodied in the extraordinary talent and dedication of our physicians, surgeons, nurses, healthcare professionals, community outreach coordinators, and administrative staff members. A growing national reputation enables us to attract some of the best healthcare specialists in the country.

Christiana Care Health System recently embarked on a journey of "transformational change" to reach new levels of clinical and workplace excellence, develop a great place to work, and provide the best quality safety environment and patient experience. Our system is already ranked among the elite of America's hospitals, appearing on such lists as *U.S. News and World Report's* "America's Best Hospitals" and Thomson Reuters' "100 Top Hospitals."

The purpose of this chapter is to present the systemic approach to talent management (TM) and leadership development that we have introduced at Christiana Care Health System to accelerate transformation and build leadership capability. This program reflects the integration of key human capital processes needed to build leadership capability.

In this chapter, we will share our story of working together through conversations to define leadership within health care for both clinicians (including physicians) and administrators. We will introduce our leadership strategy and tools and supporting structure: a system learning function where OD is working at a strategic level in an organization supporting the CEO. We will discuss ways in which the new emergent Dialogic OD (Bushe & Marshak, 2009) is applied in a health system. Dialogic OD tends to rest on an opportunistic-centric approach, social constructionism that starts from common aspirations and shared visions, making engagement in the change process more appealing. In Dialogic OD, change comes from changes in meaning-making and new, associated decisions and actions that people can and will take as a result of those changes in meaning. It moves away from the traditional OD Diagnostic approaches, which focus more on behavior and a problem-centric approach, toward action research, where the assumption is that the organization is broken and needs fixing.

To move toward a more dialogic model, we commissioned a more strategic approach for OD, renamed the "System Learning Function," to enable more cross-functional learning and to grow the leadership bench and the management of talent learning and development across the system. The System Learning team developed a "Transforming Leadership" model that linked self-awareness, setting expectations, behaviors in action, and learning. This, we believed, would enable the organization to more effectively identify and develop leaders in both clinical and nonclinical settings. We discuss here key factors and challenges that we experienced during the design and implementation of our strategy.

BACKGROUND

Effective leadership in organizations can have a great impact on organizational health and performance, as has been demonstrated across industry sectors. Given the enormous number of books already written on leader-

ship, one might be forgiven for asking, "Do we have a consensus on definition and approach?" There is even more diversity of opinion on how leadership can be applied in different industries. Of course, it could be that
some of the leadership authors and researchers are right and the rest are
wrong, but the difficulty is deciding which are which. We could have simply
read all the books to evaluate their utility and then implemented whichever
we thought most appropriate. But at the rate of one book a day it could
take us many years, and we would not be in a position to implement "the"
answer because leadership studies do not appear to be getting closer to an
agreed-upon formula. We also recognize that in almost every case where
organizations fail, whether that organization be a surgical team, a hospital
unit, a company, or a country, it is rarely the consequence of one leader's
actions, but may well be that the overwhelming issue is the power of leadership and the hierarchy of leaders. We can also argue that each leadership
situation is so unique that we require more than one alternative model to
explain them all. According to John Kotter (2001), "Leaders don't make
plans, they don't solve problems, and they don't even organize people; what
leaders really do is to prepare organizations to change and help them cope
when they struggle through it" (p. 3).

Grint (2003) also argues that "leadership is not a position at all but a
process, not a noun but a verb. And the 'doing' of leadership is manifest
by the behavior of many people in organizations, and not just formal leaders" (p. ix). We can conclude that leadership is critical but it may have little
to do with (formal) leaders. We should pay attention not only to who the
leader is, or which model has the answer, but to ensuring that our own
responsibilities for leadership, whether we are in the role of follower or
leader, maximize the possibilities of collective success.

We do not want to end the discussion on leadership without emphasizing the complex-nature of this role in the healthcare industry. Leadership
in the medical domain has many flavors and levels. On one hand, salaried
doctors (employed primary care and specialty physicians) are members of
organizational hierarchies, while other non-salaried service line specialty
doctors, such as those in a cancer program or a joint replacement program,
typically have as their top-level leaders members of professional networks.
These networks usually include local and national organizations for professional registration; quality and ethical control; education; and negotiations
with government, payers, and also policy makers. Their leadership control
may well be mediated through senior medical administrators (medical/
dental staff and medical chairs).

On the other hand, many allied health, nursing, and clinical professions
come together to improve the health and wellbeing of everyone in our
community through innovative programs. Providing care on a daily basis
to our patients is a team effort and requires the dedication and hard work

of many healthcare professionals. These professionals come to our system in many cases to continue their education, conduct research, and develop new ways to deliver care.

Emphasis on talent and leadership development was precipitated by Christiana Care's desire to achieve its Focus on Excellence goals in the areas of *Safety First, Clinical Excellence, Great Place to Work, Think of Yourself as a Patient,* and *Financial Strength,* and also to continuously transform the care we provide to our patients. Working toward these goals has taught us many lessons. Prime among them are the ways we care for our neighbors, shaped by complex processes that form our "system of care." Radical improvement can only come from redesign of our work—a "transformational" change. This *Transformation of Patient Care* is a key theme for Christiana Care Health System in 2009 and beyond. Our commitment to transformation, as opposed to gradual, small changes, has been deliberate and significant. With the healthcare industry in a constant and rapid state of change and with mounting pressures impacting health systems around the country, Christiana Care Health System knew it could not continually reach new goals by taking slow, incremental steps. It realized that breakthrough results in a challenging environment require radical thinking and dramatic change. To get there, it would have to harness the best thinking, the most productive collaborations, and the active engagement of every employee. And it would have to start with the people on the front line of the transformation: its leaders.

"The leader's behavior inspires the team's commitment to excellence and innovative thinking and encourages personal growth for the individual team members," comments our Vice President of Pathology and Laboratory Services. Leaders will have to pave the way for transformation through their own motivation and behavior, as well as by drawing on heightened interpersonal skills; being able to listen effectively; promoting collaboration; developing high-performance teams; and inspiring big, bold change.

Christiana Care's senior leadership team, including our CEO, recognized that all of our leaders will be at the front lines of our transformation, listening, promoting collaboration, and building a learning organization. For this reason, the organization chartered the System Learning Team to launch a comprehensive leadership development program, "Transforming Leadership," and a new set of leadership behaviors, tools, and programs that would facilitate transformation at the leadership level and, ultimately, throughout the system.

Christiana Care Health System is committed to *transformational change.* This type of change is not evolutionary; it does not occur in small, incremental steps. It is intended to produce dramatic, breakthrough results through radical thinking and *big* changes. To reach their ambitious goals, every member of our leadership team must embrace and demonstrate certain leadership behaviors. Doing so will help us to make significant and sustainable changes in our processes to improve our patient outcomes and to meet the continual challenges placed on our healthcare system.

SYSTEM LEARNING STRATEGIC APPROACH FOR ORGANIZATION

Development: CEO Perspective

Christiana Care Health System CEO Dr. Robert J. Laskowski provided his rationale for the creation of the "System Learning" function as follows. At Christiana Care Health System, we developed the "system learning" function because of some simple observations. First, after considerable self-reflection, we realized that as a service organization we need to be acutely attuned to the needs of those we serve. While this would seem obvious, our assessment of many organizations (including our own) concluded that too often the "worldview of organizations" is "inside out" (serving the needs of its members) as opposed to "outside in" (serving those whom it is one's mission to serve). Second, we noted that while we at CHHS excelled in the adoption of new technology and in its application, the ultimate usefulness of that technology depended on how it was deployed in generally very complex systems of care. We were giving relatively less thought to issues of technology deployment, assuming that these were self-evident. Clearly, upon closer scrutiny, they were not. Rather, the good that technology was able to deliver depended largely on the "system" of human interactions—generally very complex. When we had done this well (e.g., in our Cancer Program and Joint Replacement Program), we excelled in our ability to care for others. Third, we realized that the development of good systems of care requires leadership, teamwork, creativity, and an ability to change what we are accustomed to (and very comfortable with) doing. These are well-worn concepts honored by their being glibly named in many vision statements, but generally dishonored by their lack of application. We thought that the broadly applied moniker "Learning Organization" (defined too little in operational terms) should embody these concepts as critical parts of its culture. Finally, we did not believe that traditional OD functions, with their emphasis on data collection and classroom work and their didactic orientation, were likely to help us to develop ourselves as a true "learning organization" imbued with creativity and ability to change in the service of others.

From these observations, the idea of a systems learning function developed. What one can say is that for most organizations, systems learning is a strategic function. With that in mind, it should be located within an organization in a formal place that highlights this strategic role. For us at

Christiana Care Health System, this is reporting directly to the CEO. The CEO at Christiana Care Health System is the "chief strategy officer" and "the chief learning officer." The Christiana Care Health System Systems Learning Department is a key enabler of the development of strategies of service and sets the tone for an organizational culture of learning.

In this time of considering healthcare reform, the "systems" issues of healthcare have become ever more evident. To deliver "value" to the people healthcare organizations serve demands systematic approaches to meeting individual human needs. These are not matters of engineering or technology or technical prowess, but rather of all those things linked by the human behavior of dedicated professionals. If we are truly to reform health care, we need to develop new systems of care. The precepts and functions of system learning will be critical to accomplishing this vital social goal.

The idea of systems learning is to first focus on the mission of the organization. In the instance of Christiana Care Health System, that mission is to help the people we serve—people who count on us for our expertise and value their relationship with us. We do this by delivering the very best healthcare services that we can organize, based on our assessment of the best scientific evidence and customized to meet individual needs. This requires us to think always with the patient in mind ("as if we were patients"). This very simple focus demands that we think broadly. The delivery of care, while it should be perceived as simple when received by the patient, is anything but simple. The "system" of how we organize ourselves is often extraordinarily complex. OD thinking that focuses on the development of organizational capacity as the only focus may miss the point. Organizational capacity is developed by challenging colleagues to think broadly, engaging them in critically reflecting on their own roles, and helping them learn to be comfortable in creating ever-improving ways of working with others to bring the very best care to an individual who is relying on them. So, the focus is not on the "organization" but on how the people who comprise the organization think of themselves, their work, their colleagues, their colleagues' work, and—most importantly—structuring their work to meet a patient's individual needs.

Leaders in a learning organization lead through learning and helping others to learn. This leadership, while not without its hierarchical aspects, is fundamentally an act of service. The assumption is that by helping others to learn about themselves, their capabilities, and the capabilities and passions of other colleagues, they will develop better ways to deliver care—better *systems of care*. This is not an exercise in management engineering, but rather a discipline of self- and collective discovery. And, while it is informed by analysis, it is fundamentally creative in its essence. In summary, a *dialogic OD* approach is one where organizations are meaning-making systems, where through individual dialogues change can be encouraged and the emphasis is on changing mindsets about what learning and organization capacity really mean. This continuous dialogue can enable new definitions to emerge that can enable growth and transformation. The system learning function was created to apply a dialogic OD approach in the design and implementation of learning and talent management strategies.

"System Learning" Has a Purpose, Vision, and Mission in its Charter

System Learning Purpose

System learning at Christiana Care helps advance our *Great Place to Work* culture and facilitate the delivery of our Focus on Excellence goals. Our purpose is to enable personal growth and organization transformation through learning to achieve higher levels of performance.

System Learning Vision

We strive to be recognized as an inclusive, "people developer" learning organization and as a culturally competent healthcare leader that provides ongoing growth opportunities to our colleagues and excellent service and care to our patients and community.

System Learning Mission

- Grow leadership capacity to deliver our Focus on Excellence goals and foster a Great Place to Work
- Implement strategies and programs that will continue evolving our culture to accelerate transformation in the areas of change, learning, and coaching
- Develop our colleagues at all levels to be the best they can be while implementing a system-wide learning strategy
- Create an inclusive culture that respects and leverages the diversity of our colleagues to enhance innovation, quality of care, teamwork, and value so that we can deliver the best care for our patients as individuals

Figure 4.1 describes the Service model being implemented by the System Learning Team as a process to provide consulting solutions to their internal customers. This model focuses on identified individual and organizational needs that were validated with appropriate OD and learning expertise and aligned with the Christiana Care Health System focus on excellence goals.

The System Learning function operationalized its mission and purpose, implementing two key priorities. The first priority, Talent Management or, more specifically, Transforming Leadership, will be further discussed in the

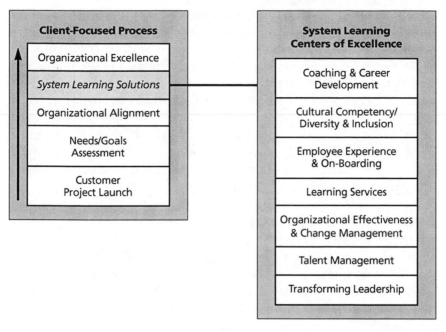

Figure 4.1 Transforming leadership as a key pillar of talent management.

course of this chapter. Our second priority is to continue implementing processes to enable a learning organization. The System Learning VP chairs a system-wide Education and Learning Council that is in the process of implementing a vision of accelerating transformation through experiential, continuous, interactive, innovative, and informal experiences to promote thinking and growth at all levels of the organization. The Council also sets the system-wide strategic direction, priorities, measurements, and learning models for education and staff development.

The Talent Management center of excellence is to enable Christiana Care to achieve its Focus on Excellence goals, recognizing that the most important challenge faced by virtually all of our colleagues is the need to respond quickly to changes in our healthcare industry. As in many organizations, people are the largest component of costs and also the primary providers of service to our patients. We need to have the ability to get the right people with the right skills into the right jobs in a cost-effective way, making it possible for us to achieve excellence and continuously "transform" the care we give.

According to a recent research report by Josh Bersin (2007), high impact talent management has become one of the most pressing topics and priorities in organizations today. With a recession in progress, ever-increasing pressure to cut costs, and the impending shortage of executives and directors, organizations are challenged to get the most out of every employee. *Talent management* is not just a new buzzword applied to old HR processes, but a significant transformation in strategically integrating processes and systems such as career development, competency management, performance management, leadership development, and succession planning. Another highlight of this report is the revelation that the number two problem facing organizations across industries today is a shortage of potential leaders, otherwise known as "gaps in the leadership pipeline." What this means is that organizations are struggling to hire, develop, coach, and build managers. Companies are spending more money than ever on leadership development programs (more than 30 percent of training spending in learning and development).

We can say that this challenge is also recognized at Christiana Care, and for that reason the first strategy launched by the System Learning function was the Transforming Leadership Strategy. There was also a need to create a common language and definitions for talent management. It was found that the majority of our healthcare professionals did not gravitate to this label in defining the growth of people in organizations. Therefore, the following definitions were introduced:

1. Talent Management: The process of facilitating the development and career progress of highly talented and skilled individuals for the future of the organization.
2. Replacement Planning: Planning the potential replacement of current leadership positions.
3. Succession Planning: The processes of looking at the leadership competencies and structures that will be needed for the future and ensuring the development of successors to meet future needs.
4. Coaching: "Shape the understanding, development, and learning of team members so they can act both independently and in concert with the goals of the whole organization" (Wright, 2004, pp. 1–2).

Goals

In concert with our theme of transforming patient care, all Christiana Care leaders will be at the front lines of this transformation, and they will need to draw on skills such as listening, promoting collaboration, developing people, and building high-performance teams. Christiana Care's talent management strategy is therefore focused on the following goals:

- Build strong leaders who have the qualities needed to meet our Focus on Excellence goals and work together as a community to transform our organization.
- Address the anticipated shortages of top talent in health care in the light of demographic shifts and the economic downturn.
- Continue the implementation of an integrated talent management process, aligning leadership behaviors, performance management, succession planning, and career planning/development as a seamless process.
- Identify Christiana Care professionals who are interested in growing their leadership competencies and taking on leadership roles.
- Prepare internal candidates, by developing current leaders and identifying potential future leaders, to fill upcoming leadership vacancies.
- Implement talent management programs by increasing the number and range of education and development opportunities for high-potential employees, managers, nurse managers, executives, and physician leaders.

CHRISTIANA CARE'S TRANSFORMING LEADERSHIP STRATEGY

Christiana Care is committed to *transformational change*. To prepare our leaders for this transformation, we introduced our "Transforming Leadership" strategy in 2008. Our goal is to nurture and develop our colleagues while providing practical processes and programs to ensure the identification, development, and inspiration of our current and future leaders in order to drive learning and transformation. This strategy is based upon the principles of "Servant Leadership" proposed by Robert Greenleaf (1991):

> Servant-Leaders seek not to be served, but rather to serve. They view leadership positions as opportunities to help, support, and aid other people. Servant-Leaders create trusting work environments in which people are highly appreciated. Servant-Leaders visibly model appropriate behavior and function as effective mentors. They have a high degree of credibility because of their honesty, integrity, and competence. Such persons have a clear leadership vision and implement pioneering approaches to work. (p.)

We introduced this philosophy to our new leaders by having a dialogue every quarter with newly appointed leaders and our CEO.

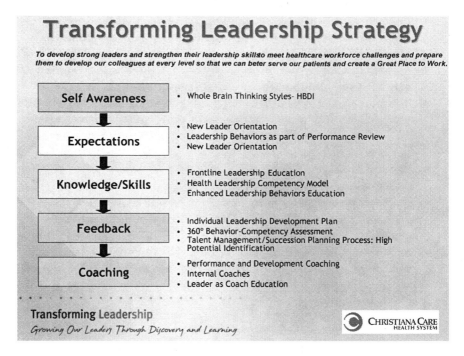

Figure 4.2 Transforming leadership strategy.

There are five key components to our strategy, as shown in the diagram in Figure 4.2.

Component 1: Leadership Thinking Style: Self-awareness

Support Our Leaders in Discovering Their Thinking Styles

We introduced the *Whole Brain® Thinking*–Herrmann Brain Dominance Instrument® (HBDI®), by Ned Herrmann (1996), for personal and team development for greater engagement and productivity.

Through assessments of the existing leadership development program offerings and review of patient satisfaction surveys, the Systems Learning Team was able to identify several interrelated gaps in the formalized development and growth of its leaders.

Patient satisfaction surveys revealed that communication was a key opportunity area that leaders could improve upon, given the right knowledge and skills. Effective communication is vital not just in direct interactions with patients, but in ensuring that team members interact with each other in the most productive way to reach better decisions and better outcomes.

In the high-stress environment of a large health system, successful communication can lead to more efficient, focused teams and minimize the distractions and misunderstandings that can potentially impact the quality of care delivered. However, we realized that our current development offerings were limited in equipping leaders with the necessary background and competencies they would need to address this critical issue. Research has shown that individuals can enhance their communication, productivity, problem-solving, creativity, and other interpersonal development by understanding their own and others' thinking preferences (Herrmann, 1996). This knowledge, grounded in self-awareness, can help people become more effective leaders, educators, and team members. Yet very few personal development and self-awareness programs were being offered to leaders at Christiana Care Health System on an ongoing basis.

Additionally, while a personal assessment instrument was available to anyone who requested it, participation was low, and feedback suggested that many struggled with understanding, retaining, and applying its concepts. Furthermore, there was no instrument available as part of the new leader orientation process to help new leaders learn how to integrate their personal thinking styles with those of their new team members.

These findings indicated a need for:

- A validated, research-backed assessment instrument that would provide the baseline of knowledge about an individual's thinking preferences
- A model and approach that would be easy to understand, remember, and apply
- A method and common language to help leaders integrate their thinking styles with those of other team members for more effective communication
- An approach that demonstrated how thinking styles impact communication, productivity, and teamwork, and as a result, patient satisfaction

A Brain-Based Self-Awareness Solution

The System Learning function identified Herrmann International's Whole Brain® Technology, which includes the Herrmann Brain Dominance Instrument® (HBDI®), as a possible solution to address these needs.

The HBDI® is the instrument at the core of Herrmann International's Whole Brain® model, which is based on decades of research on the brain and thinking. Of particular interest to Christiana Care, the HBDI® is a strongly validated assessment tool; it has been researched and studied for over 12 years, and all of the validation studies have been positive, considered by experts to be a rarity in this field.

*758:
use the text ¶
Disc + ref-
clarification w/o
taking the test?*

c/ DISc

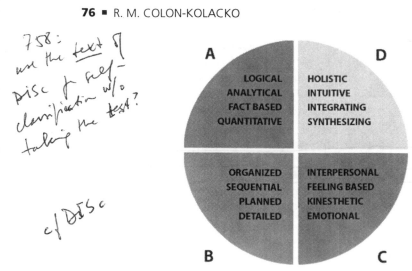

Figure 4.3 The Whole Brain® model.

The Whole Brain® model, which was developed by Ned Herrmann (1996), a physicist who headed Management Education at General Electric before founding Herrmann International, goes beyond left-brain/right-brain studies to reveal four distinct thinking preferences: *analytical, organized, strategic,* and *interpersonal.*

Herrmann's research showed that everyone is capable of flexing to less preferred thinking styles and learning the necessary skills to diagnose and adapt to the thinking preferences of others. He found that presenting information in a way that recognizes, respects, and is compatible with different preferences is critical to effectively communicating with and meeting the needs and expectations of those one interacts with in the work environment. The model's basis both in solid research and in practical use indicated that it could appeal to our leaders on a scientific as well as an application level.

pilot

To evaluate the approach, a pilot "Whole Brain Thinking®" program was conducted with the Senior Management Team and System Leadership Committee. With the busy schedules of everyone in a hospital environment, there was some initial resistance to spending time on the program, but the pilot quickly alleviated concerns. Seeing the HBDI® data and experiencing the pilot session immediately demonstrated the value of the Whole Brain® model and how better thinking could be leveraged to increase leadership effectiveness.

Following this pilot, 350 leaders completed the HBDI® and learned about their thinking preferences and the application of Whole Brain® Thinking at their Leadership Planning Meeting in December of 2007. A post-meeting survey of participants revealed that a large majority of the leaders strongly recommended sharing the program with all leaders throughout the system to enhance not just communication but interpersonal understanding, creativity, and team effectiveness.

As a result, in 2008, Christiana Care introduced Whole Brain® Thinking as a key component and as a key foundation of our "Transforming Leadership" strategy, designed to give current and future leaders the skills to drive and inspire learning and transformation. Whole Brain® Thinking principles would serve as the framework to continue the leadership education process on self-awareness, communication, engagement, and creativity.

Whole Brain® Thinking as a Framework for Transformation

Under the umbrella of its Talent Management strategy, The System Learning function moved forward with implementing the HBDI®/Whole Brain® model solution throughout the ranks of the organization's leaders, using Herrmann International's four-stage model of transformation as a planning tool.

In keeping with its philosophy of pursuing dramatic change and breakthrough results, we applied an accelerated example of the transformation model:

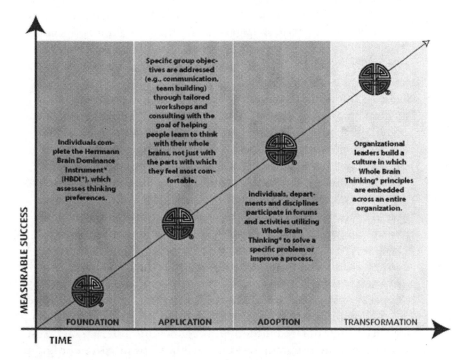

Figure 4.4   Four-stage model of transformation.

- Stage 1 – Foundation: Between February and April of 2008, the HBDI® assessment and one-hour overview was delivered to 601 managers and supervisors, comprising all leaders who had not participated in the December Leadership Meeting.
- Stage 2 – Application: System Learning team members consulted with department leaders to create customized programs aimed at meeting the individual learning needs of each participating department. From these discussions, the team developed educational sessions drawing on Whole Brain® Thinking concepts to enhance team engagement, communication, effectiveness, and creativity throughout the Christiana Care Health System. In total, 40 customized Whole Brain® Thinking team sessions, including physician retreats, were conducted between March and July of 2008. In these sessions, participants learned how to leverage their preferred modes of thinking at both the individual and team levels. As the VP of System Learning notes, "I would start sessions by saying, 'I know you're going to wonder why I'm talking about the brain,' but as soon as they saw their HBDI® data, they started to see the value. They appreciate the insights it gives them into relationships and the practical ways the Whole Brain® model helps them communicate more effectively." She adds that the departmental workshops and retreats have been very beneficial for managers at all levels, including physicians: "They have achieved a greater understanding about how colleagues process information. This will improve working relationships, camaraderie, and collaboration."
- Stage 3 – Adoption: A Creativity and Innovation Forum was held in February, 2008 to explore how Whole Brain® Thinking could be used to promote system-wide creativity and innovation. In addition, an educational program aimed at strengthening communication and relationships between "blue/green" (representative of many physician profiles) and "red/yellow" (representative of many nurse profiles) thinkers was conducted in April, 2008. This program was useful in offering insights and approaches for bridging the communication gap that often exists between physicians and nurses. Whole Brain® Thinking demonstrated how team members can leverage differences in thinking styles and actually use them to the team's advantage. It also underscored the fact that no one is strictly a "type"; everyone has the ability to flex beyond their comfort zones and think in different ways. The HBDI® and Whole Brain® Thinking have been incorporated into the Emergency and Internal Medicine resident training programs as well. Facilitated by physician program directors, these programs give residents the necessary context and

motivation as well as the tools to optimize their communication with nurses, patients, staff members, and others.

- Stage 4 – Transformation: To ensure the ongoing application of the Whole Brain® model as a tool for transformational change, we found a number of ways to embed the language and approach of Whole Brain® Thinking into the culture. Among them, the System Learning function is providing a variety of resources via the organization's online Leadership Knowledge Center. These on-demand resources not only help to keep Whole Brain® Thinking front-of-mind for the leaders, but they also fulfill an identified need for ongoing leadership development and support. The resources cover all areas of leadership responsibility through the lens of Whole Brain® Thinking, from job design to performance management conversations to project management.

Better Thinking Transforms Leadership ... and More

In all, 1,048 employees—including nurse leaders, physicians, and other professionals—participated in Whole Brain® Thinking programs during the second quarter to fourth quarter of 2008. Many more employees participated in the program as well at the request of department leaders who wanted to extend the educational opportunity to others beyond their leadership team. Physician leaders and residents have also embraced the use of the HBDI® at their annual retreats to promote improved nurse–physician collaboration.

Based on the results of an HR Customer Satisfaction Survey, 78% of the leaders responding indicated that they would be able to use the information and skills they learned in the program back on the job. In overall feedback about the program, participants say that they have gained an enhanced understanding of their own and others' preferred thinking styles, which has resulted in improved communication, working relationships, and creativity within their teams.

With improvements in patient satisfaction levels a constant priority, we are finding that Whole Brain® Thinking provides the necessary framework to help people communicate more effectively in order to better meet the needs of patients. According to the Director of Respiratory Care, "Whole Brain® Thinking has helped us improve communication because now we understand how each other needs to receive information. This knowledge helps us to rearrange *how* we communicate to be more effective."

"The Whole Brain® Thinking program has helped me better understand how I think under stress versus how I normally think," says the Director of Cancer Care Management, noting that these new insights have already been put to good use in her department.

As a tool for furthering system-wide transformational change, the impact of Whole Brain® Thinking is being felt even in unexpected places, as people find that the applications are broader than just interpersonal communication and self-awareness. "Whole Brain® Thinking has allowed us to fine tune processes we use as a group when conducting everyday business or when approaching new projects," the Director of Respiratory Care says.

It is also playing a role in the mentoring process, a critical component of development in a healthcare environment. "Nurse managers require both 'red' and 'green' qualities," says the VP of System Learning. "Nursing teams are now encouraging their strong 'green thinkers' to mentor those who wish to develop those skills." This new knowledge of thinking styles is changing the way Christiana Care approaches team development, self-assessment, and identification of individual strengths and opportunities.

The framework of Whole Brain® Thinking now permeates the system and has become integrated into New Leader Orientation programs, regular employee communications, and the everyday language of staff members. Regular workshops are provided to departments on an ongoing basis, and physician leaders continue to use Whole Brain® Thinking in strategic retreats to promote collaboration among colleagues.

Physician leaders are also exploring opportunities to incorporate the HBDI® into residency training throughout the system. The program director for Internal Medicine sees great potential for its use in medical education by helping residents learn how to interact more effectively with patients, staff, nurses, and others.

For a Christiana Care Health System committed to accelerating change to reach breakthrough results, Whole Brain® Thinking has become the foundation for transforming leadership, and it continues to push the organization to leading-edge excellence—for the people it employs as well as for the patients and communities it serves.

Component 2: Introduction of the Christiana Care Leadership Behaviors Expected of All Leaders

The Leadership Behaviors provide direction for leaders to bring our Core Values to life in their daily work. We followed a four-step process to develop our Leadership Behaviors to create noticeable and lasting improvements in our organization—behaviors that will result in our patients receiving the best care:

1. Benchmarked leadership competencies and performance models at other healthcare and pharmaceutical organizations.
2. Gained insight and recommendations from a cross-section of leaders, including the System Leadership Committee (SLC), President's

Cabinet, the Human Resources Advisory Committee, role model leaders, the Learning and Education Council, and physician leaders.

3. Partnered with the National Center for Healthcare Leadership (NCHL) to use their extensive research into strategic healthcare leadership development in validating our leadership behaviors. The NCHL and GE Healthcare have joined to form the Institute for Transformational Leadership, aiming to improve health status and health system performance nationwide. NCHL's mission is to be an industry-wide catalyst to assure that high-quality, relevant, and accountable health management leadership is available to meet the needs of 21st-century health care. This unique competency model was developed to support the different professions in the healthcare industry (physicians, nurses, and administrators). The Model provides a guide for reorienting leadership development to stimulate the capabilities that make the most difference to performance.

4. Applied the model from Ulrich and Smallwood's (2007) philosophy of leadership brand in order to prioritize key behavioral areas that will make the bigger impact in delivering our Focus on Excellence goals: "Organizations can strengthen their leadership brands by working hard to translate what they stand for in the marketplace into a set of managerial behaviors" (p. 3). The primary goal was to create a unique set of behaviors that will create a unique healthcare leadership brand for Christiana Care Health System to promote as a visible recognition of our leadership capability within our employee and patient population. This will help us accomplish our mission of caring for our patients and community, provide the best patient experience, and enable organization transformation.

Christiana Care Leadership Behaviors

Christiana Care Health System Leadership Behaviors bring our Core Values to life by defining the way we expect all of our leaders (vice presidents, directors, physician leaders, and managers) to carry out their roles on a consistent basis, and *these behaviors are expected of all leaders.* There are five categories of Leadership Behaviors:

- Develops people and creates high-performance teams
- Collaborates and builds relationships
- Enables learning and innovation
- Leads and promotes change
- Creates value

Strong leadership is at the heart of any organization's transformation. To help our strong leaders further develop and to ensure consistency in our

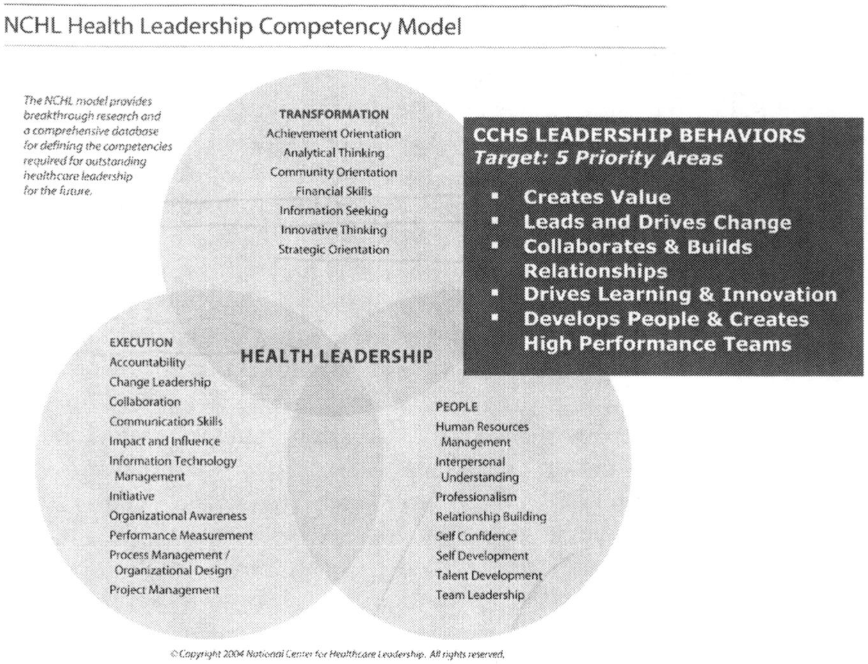
NCHL Health Leadership Competency Model
The NCHL model provides breakthrough research and a comprehensive database for defining the competencies required for outstanding healthcare leadership for the future.
TRANSFORMATION
Achievement Orientation
Analytical Thinking
Community Orientation
Financial Skills
Information Seeking
Innovative Thinking
Strategic Orientation
CCHS LEADERSHIP BEHAVIORS
Target: 5 Priority Areas
Creates Value
Leads and Drives Change
Collaborates & Builds Relationships
Drives Learning & Innovation
Develops People & Creates High Performance Teams
HEALTH LEADERSHIP
EXECUTION
Accountability
Change Leadership
Collaboration
Communication Skills
Impact and Influence
Information Technology Management
Initiative
Organizational Awareness
Performance Measurement
Process Management / Organizational Design
Project Management
PEOPLE
Human Resources Management
Interpersonal Understanding
Professionalism
Relationship Building
Self Confidence
Self Development
Talent Development
Team Leadership
© Copyright 2004 National Center for Healthcare Leadership. All rights reserved.

Figure 4.5 NCHL leadership competency model (2006).

actions throughout our system, the Leadership Behaviors will be used as a benchmark in future performance management and leadership development processes.

Leadership Behaviors differ from the Competency Model used in the Health Leadership Assessment. While we are not expecting leaders to be

TABLE 4.1 Example Christiana Care Health System Leadership Behavior and Corresponding NCHL Competencies

DEVELOPS PEOPLE AND CREATES HIGH-PERFORMANCE TEAMS

Creates a "Great Place to Work" environment, encouraging camaraderie and pride in the service we provide, engaging colleagues and developing high-performing teams.

• Attracts and selects outstanding individuals from diverse backgrounds to grow the Christiana Care Health System team.	• Talent Development • Team Leadership
• Identifies team members with growth potential and offers challenging developmental assignments.	• Talent Development • Team Leadership
• Develops team members by giving timely, honest, and constructive performance feedback, including coaching, mentoring, and recognizing/rewarding accomplishments that add value.	• Talent Development • Team Leadership
• Seeks and acknowledges input and feedback from staff and colleagues.	• Collaboration • Self-Development

---

TABLE 4.2   Additional Leadership Behavior Definitions

COLLABORATES AND BUILDS RELATIONSHIPS
Develops trust by practicing credibility, respect, and fairness to enable the accomplishment of our focus on excellence vision.

ENABLES LEARNING AND INNOVATION
Promotes, supports, and participates in learning practices and disciplines that enable colleagues and the system as a whole to continuously learn, adapt, develop creative solutions, and expand their capacity to achieve desired results.

LEADS AND PROMOTES CHANGE
Challenges and improves the way we do things.

CREATES VALUE
Maximizes benefits/value for our patients, families, and colleagues.

---

experts in all applicable competency areas, we do expect that our leaders demonstrate the key actions described for each behavior on a daily basis. The new set of behaviors is part of our leadership performance management process and is used to assess role model or key contributor rankings.

Table 4.1 shows an example of one of the Christiana Care Health System Leadership Behaviors and the corresponding NCHL competencies. Each Leadership Behavior includes two components: (1) a one-sentence definition and (2) four actions expected from each leader in each particular area of expertise in our organization.

There are four other leadership behavior definitions, as outlined in Table 4.2.

Component 3: Introduction of the Health Leadership Competency Model

It is our goal to drive excellence in leadership within Christiana Care. We launched a 360° feedback process aligned with our Leadership Behaviors to drive leadership excellence within Christiana Care. The 360° feedback process, which started with the CEO, executives, and physicians and nurse leaders, has now been expanded. A total of 154 leaders at the vice-president, director, and middle-management levels have participated to date. The data collected showed the following strengths: Goal Oriented, Analytical, Technical/Functional Expertise, Quality Focused, Mission/Values Centered, and Involving/Engaging Others; and also the following opportunities: Collaboration across Teams, Change Leadership, Aligning Activities to Organizational Priorities, Coaching and Feedback, Prioritization and Driving Accountability, Communications/Conflict Management, and Talent Management. The findings in the 360° assessment instrument correlate with other learning needs assessments with employees at all levels (with the participation of 658 individuals) and a physician leadership development survey (171 participants) in the following learning opportunities: Change Leadership, Communications/Conflict Management, and Coaching and Feedback.

Component 4: Leadership Learning Opportunities for All Levels

It is our goal to offer leadership learning opportunities for all levels of leaders, professionals, and high-potentials, including developmental assignments, projects, lateral and/or promotional moves, and internal and external education. Also, we intend to implement a targeted leadership education curriculum to address competency and skill gaps identified in the Leadership Behaviors self-assessment, the Individual Leadership Development plans, and the 360° feedback process, including leveraging the online Leadership Knowledge Center and other online and classroom education. The following tactics have been part of this component:

- Transforming Leadership Forums: Quarterly forums promote ongoing exploration and understanding of our new Leadership Behaviors. The Winter, 2008 forum focused on the "Creates Value" Leadership Behavior, and our forum in April explored the "Develops People and Creates High Performance Teams" Behavior.
- Nurse Leadership Development Forum: Launched in April, 2008 with the objective of providing a forum for Nursing Directors to share ideas and learn together, with the focus on "transforming leadership" in a rapidly changing environment. Agenda topics were chosen based on input from the Nursing Directors, the Chief Nursing Officer, the VP Professional Excellence/Associate CNO, and development areas identified as part of the 360° feedback process. The forum represented a departure from traditional training approaches, in that it was largely discussion-based and the eight participants shared in the facilitation roles. The objectives of this program are to provide Nurse Directors and Managers with a forum for sharing ideas and learning together within the framework of the Christiana Care Leadership Behaviors. One of the most powerful elements of the program was Peer Coaching, in which the Directors paired up to discuss the program, what they were learning, and how they could most effectively apply the learning, and gave each other coaching on related "just in time" situations. Over the course of the program, each Director had an opportunity to pair with each other Director at least once. More than 40 participants have benefited from this program.

- Physician Leadership Development Committee: This committee, chaired by our Chair of Internal Medicine and the VP of System Learning, was established to enhance offerings to our physicians in leadership development. A survey was conducted to identify education requirements with the participation of 171 physicians representing the medical/dental staff community. Their major interests were: Management Skills, Technology Implementation, Clinical Quality Improvement, Financial Management, and Communication Skills. We have launched a Physician Leadership Boot Camp and Physician Leadership Academy for physicians with leadership potential, and started a Physician Leadership Forum with 20 high-potential physician leaders. This strategy will support both our talent management and physician engagement goals.
- Transforming Leadership Behaviors Education: Implementation of a new six-session leadership education action learning series, providing practical skills for implementing our Leadership Behaviors. This education also includes the introduction of the leadership behaviors to medical residents.
- Leadership Knowledge Center™: The Christiana Care Leadership Knowledge Center™ is an online learning portal made available to all Health System leaders in March, 2008. Since its inception, 377 current leaders have used the Leadership Knowledge Center to obtain access to Christiana Care Featured Topics and online e-learning courses, as well as an online library of full-text leadership books via Books24x7®.

Component 5: Increase Coaching Capability Among Our Leaders and Create a Network of Internal Coaches

We have been implementing an internal coaching strategy to support leadership development. This will affect visible changes in the execution of our Leadership Behaviors. It is our goal to grow the coaching capabilities of our leaders, enhancing their communication skills and their ability to implement "coachable" moments with their teams to support our focus on transformational change and promote a Great Place to Work. We also strive to develop a coaching culture within Christiana Care in which leaders learn from on-the-job challenges through supportive, learning-oriented coaching relationships. This includes the identification and education of internal coaches who are promoting a culture of feedback and coaching. We have implemented group and team coaching as part of the 360° competency assessment process and have launched specialized coaching for targeting the behavior of "Developing People and Creat-

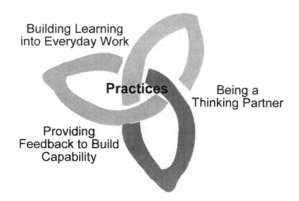

Figure 4.6 Internal coaching framework.

ing High-performance Teams." The following is our Internal Coaching framework, which we developed in partnership with The Forum Corporation, to promote learning and equip our leaders to become thinking partners in daily interactions.

We offer three sessions as part of our coaching education curriculum to educate our internal coaches:

- Session #1: Trust and Feedback
  - Identify opportunities to build and sustain trust
  - Advocacy and Inquiry: "Ladder of Inference" exercise
  - Develop coaching relationships
  - Improve individual and team engagement through coaching
- Session #2: Challenging Conversations
  - Describe different types of diversity
  - Identify ways to leverage diversity
  - Develop personal best practices for addressing diversity
  - Apply an understanding of diversity issues to challenging conversations
- Session #3: Synthesizing Learning
  - Action learning: moving forward as a team
  - Sustaining progress
  - Coaching next steps

INTEGRATED TALENT MANAGEMENT PROCESS

In addition to the Transforming Leadership Strategy, another key component of our Talent Management Strategy is the introduction of an integrated process to identify and develop talent across the system. As part of this strategy, we have added an online succession planning function to our online performance management system, designed to support the identification of high-potential employees at all levels of the organization. The strategy is to identify those individuals whose talents and career interests are aligned with Christiana Care's future needs, create development plans, and track progress through the use of Talent Pools. We encourage individual development plans for employees at all levels. As part of the enhancements to our Performance Management system, leaders will enter their Individual Leadership Development Plans and Career Aspirations into the online system.

We have also established a Talent Management Committee. The Office of the President, chaired by the President and CEO, serves as the talent management committee for the health system. This committee meets bi-monthly to review the talent management and succession planning needs of our health system. In 2009, the Succession Planning process focused on the top 45 leadership positions, including physician chairs and nursing leaders. Also, this committee has reviewed the nominations of more than 130 high-potential candidates for key positions. We have also introduced a definition for "High Potentials" and as part of our strategy are planning to introduce talent reviews to identify high-potential colleagues and future leaders so that appropriate developmental activities can be designed and provided for them.

BENEFITS

Christiana Care Health System's Talent Management and Transforming Leadership Strategy will enable our system to continue to be proactive in addressing our leadership development needs so that we can meet the future growth needs of our health system. It will also allow us to get the right people with the right skills into the right jobs in a cost-effective way so that we can achieve excellence and continuously "transform" care to our patients and community.

CONCLUSION

How do we know that our leadership strategy is making an impact in the organization? First, there is a clear definition in the organization of what is expected from our leaders. Second, the Whole Brain® Thinking methodology, introduced as a self-awareness tool, has created a culture in which healthcare professionals are encouraged to understand, respect, and leverage diversity of thinking to enhance communications and better collaboration among nurses, physicians, and the patients we serve. Thirdly, we are investing time on a quarterly basis to continue to learn new concepts and principles targeting the leadership behaviors. This is allowing us to create a community of leaders that can meet not only to solve problems but to learn and encourage the appropriate dialogue—a community in which change can be encouraged and where the emphasis is on changing mindsets, learning in action, and helping others to learn. Fourthly, the Transforming Leadership Strategy has introduced a more concrete language and definition of leadership for residents and physicians. Finally, we have created a learning road map for all employees interested in leadership roles and have provided a framework to support leadership recruitment and promotion efforts and have started to introduce a common language for talent development and management for employees at all levels. This is also driving accountability of managing as well as motivating and growing our talent to meet the needs of our community, patients, and the 21st century of healthcare challenges. Finally, positioning the role of OD as a function that works in partnership with the CEO and Senior Executives, including physicians, has elevated the conversation of leadership and learning at the right level of the health system, allowing the right conversation to take place to enable change and transformation.

REFERENCES

Bersin, J. (2007). *High-impact talent management: State of the market and executive overview.* Bersin & Associates Industry Report, V1.0.

Bushe, G. R., & Marshak, R. J. (2009). Revisioning organization development: Diagnostic and dialogic premises and patterns of practice. *Journal of Applied Behaviors Science, 45*(3), 358–363.

Dopson, S., & Mark, A. L. (2003). *Leading health care organizations.* Great Britain: Palgrave Macmillan.

Greenleaf, R. K. (1991). *The servant leadership: A journey into the nature of legitimate power and greatness.* Robert K. Greenleaf Center, Inc., Paulist Press.

Hermann, N. (1996). *The Whole Brain® business book: Unlocking the power of whole brain thinking in individuals and organizations.* New York: McGraw-Hill.

Kotter, J. P. (2001). *What leaders really do.* Best of HBR, Harvard Business School Publishing Corporation, 3.

Ulrich, D., & Smallwood, N. (2007, July/August). Building a leadership brand. *Harvard Business Review.*

Wright, S. (2004). The leader as coach: Creating high performance in change. *Leadership Compass*, The Bass Centre, pp. 1–2.

CHAPTER 5

THE MULTIDISCIPLINARY HEALTHCARE LEADERSHIP MODEL

Charlotte D. Lofton and Howard O. Straker

ABSTRACT

Healthcare delivery teams are viewed as complex adaptive systems (CAS), and therefore traditional management approaches are not ideal in these settings. Leadership is the result of the interactions of the team of healthcare practitioners from various disciplines. The Multidisciplinary Healthcare Leadership Model (MHCLM) is grounded in complexity leadership theory and has three major components, which are *group dynamics*, *team culture*, and *discipline-specific assumptions*. MHCLM presents a dynamic, multidisciplinary, multilevel perspective of leadership that emerges from within the team. It provides the OD practitioner with a tool for the diagnosis and intervention for leadership emergence in healthcare teams.

INTRODUCTION

Throughout our combined 40+ years of professional experience, it has become more and more clear that the healthcare system, as it is today, is not

Organization Development in Health Care, pages 89–106

working. Rising costs and substandard quality of care are impacting this delivery system. Healthcare reform is being controversially enacted in the United States. Regardless of party affiliations, one thing that is certain is that the current health system in the U.S. is not optimal, and something must be done in order to prevent the system from completely collapsing. For practitioners, not only understanding the phenomena is necessary, but understanding how to effectively function in such an environment is critical in order to build an optimal 21st-century model health system.

As scientific medical information and technologies are rapidly changing, we believe that organizationally a major culprit is the assumption that decision-making processes within these organizations rest within a select few individuals. Historically, healthcare delivery organizations and teams have been viewed from the traditional mechanistic organizational perspective (Porter-O'Grady & Malloch, 2007). Such traditional organizations have bureaucratic hierarchical structures functioning for control, stability, and equilibrium as opposed to structures that support growth, change, and innovation. Leadership under this perspective focuses on the traits and behaviors of one person or a select few for decision making and action initiation. As a result, leadership for healthcare teams has traditionally focused specifically on the role of a person for hierarchy, control and management.

We feel that the hierarchical management approach to multidisciplinary healthcare teams negatively impacts healthcare delivery. It fails to build on the potential dynamic complexity of the team or to produce creative solutions to delivering patient care. The Institute of Medicine's report, *Crossing the Quality Chasm* (Committee on Quality Health Care in America, 2001), noted the healthcare system's failure to recognize that the interdependence of the organization or team compromises patient care.

For example, most medical institutions presume and communicate that the physician is the highest authority in the unit (Sangvai, Lynn, & Michener, 2008). Most medical schools do not offer or incorporate leadership training for the medical students, thus leaving physicians to try to assume hierarchical roles to control the team (Crites, Ebert, & Schuster, 2008; Pawlina et al., 2006). Nursing schools may provide some information about leadership, but much of it comes from the mechanistic viewpoint and focuses on uni-disciplinary teams of nurses (Moody, Horton-Deutsch, & Pesut, 2007; Long, 2004). Health discipline training begins the socialization of health professionals. Yet it lacks formal leadership development training, which promotes utilizing the leadership capacity of the team by helping the team member to utilize her or his acquired knowledge and to reflect and understand the dynamics and complexities of each situation. This view of healthcare leadership is incompatible with the complexities of today's changing healthcare technology and environment.

Our proposition is that health care is a CAS that requires a different approach in order to effectively enhance the performance of multidisciplinary teams. Our chapter will focus on this dilemma and showcase how an effective relationship between group dynamics, team culture, and professional/discipline-specific assumptions promotes the leadership emergence that is necessary in order to enhance delivery of health care. This chapter will use the terms *discipline* and *profession(al)* synonymously.

Using the multidisciplinary bedside healthcare delivery team as a model for complex adaptive decision making, this chapter introduces the Multidisciplinary Healthcare Leadership Model (MHCLM). This model has three major components and is grounded in complexity leadership theory. The components are *group dynamics, team culture,* and *discipline-specific assumptions.* MHCLM presents a dynamic, multidisciplinary, multilevel perspective of leadership that emerges from within the team. This is followed by a presentation of leadership emergence and the interactions that create it. The chapter continues by providing the OD practitioner with a perspective for the diagnosis and intervention for leadership emergence in healthcare teams. The chapter closes by discussing potential methods to research our theoretical model, some limitations of our model, implications for practice, and a conclusion.

HEALTH CARE AS A COMPLEX ADAPTIVE SYSTEM

A more dynamic way to view a healthcare organization is as a complex adaptive system (CAS). "The focus of complex systems is on how systems of interacting agents can lead to emergent phenomena" (Miller & Page, 2007, p. 44). According to Uhl-Bien, Marion, and McKelvey (2007), "Dooley (1996) describes a Complex Adaptive System (CAS) as an aggregate of interacting agents that 'behaves/evolves according to three key principles: order is emergent as opposed to predetermined, the system's history is irreversible, and the system's future is often unpredictable'" (p. 302). Plowman and Duchon (2008) further define a CAS as being made up "of numerous interdependent agents, who, in parallel, purposely pursue individual plans based on local knowledge or rules and adapt to feedback about the behavior of others in the system" (p. 131). They have an ability to learn and adapt from numerous interactions that are occurring simultaneously. This is quite common in the healthcare industry, especially during the course of delivering care in a multidisciplinary healthcare team approach.

The interaction between the individual and discipline-specific agents in a constantly changing environment supports our position that bedside healthcare delivery is a CAS. Healthcare teams are dynamic units where individuals of varying disciplines function within their own rules, assumptions, and priorities. They approach patients from their discipline's perspectives and ultimately may or may not adapt to the feedback of the other team members. Sometimes this is done directly in the multidisciplinary team setting (team meetings or "rounds") while other times it occurs through interactions with the patient, individual team member sub groupings, or through documentation in the patient's chart.

Health care is a continuously changing environment. Each patient presents a unique problem with unique history that should be considered in order to optimize the care that will best help the patient. For example, a hospital emergency department may have multiple patients to manage simultaneously. The staff is unable to predict the types of patient problems that will come in that day. Each patient's problem is unique, even though it may seem similar to prior cases.

In addition to the needs of the patient varying, the bedside team may be composed of different individuals working at varying time shifts. Teams may consist of varying disciplines and subspecialties that will see the patient at the clinician's availability. Nurses, physicians, physician assistants, and subspecialty physicians (e.g., neurosurgeons, radiographers, and cardiologists) may have to see the patient at various times, making assessments, decisions, and giving plans of care. Even though two patients may present with similar symptoms, their health histories, genetics, social, and environmental differences make each patient's problem unique. They may have different diagnoses. Even if they have the same diagnosis, they may respond to the same treatment differently due to a variety of factors (i.e., family history, body chemistry, allergies, etc.). Thus, health care meets the principles of future unpredictability and history irreversibility as defined by CAS.

CAS has the ability to adapt to the environment rapidly and creatively. Instead of viewing leadership as a person, it views it as a process that emerges and grows out of the interactions and tensions of the team members (Uhl-Bien et al., 2007), the patient's problem, and the hospital environment. The uniqueness of the patient causes the team's problem-solving process and outcome not to be predestined.

Although other scholars have recognized healthcare delivery as CAS (Tan, Wen, & Awad, 2005; Porter-O'Grady & Malloch, 2007), it has not been fully embraced. There is a need for continued research and application. Attempting to function in a routine manner and not adapting to the continuously changing environment means that an organization fails to embrace its attributes as a CAS. Just as it is impossible to place a square peg in a round hole without manipulating its structure, attempting to force a CAS to operate under the constraints of a traditional management model leads to outcomes of suboptimal patient care as the organization loses some of its structure in order to "fit" into the traditional model. For the healthcare OD practitioner, it is important to not only recognize this phenomenon but to develop systems that will promote the ability of agents to effectively interact and reflect in order to promote this emergence process.

THE MULTIDISCIPLINARY HEALTHCARE LEADERSHIP MODEL

The Multidisciplinary Healthcare Leadership Model (MHCLM) approaches the multidisciplinary healthcare team as a CAS, thus it requires leadership to be viewed from a new perspective. Our model is designed specifically for hospital bedside teams; however, it is applicable for any multidisciplinary team where the differing educational training and expectations of team members potentially hinders the emergence process. It is a dynamic, multilevel, and multidiscipline model that is grounded in the CAS process of emergence. Instead of leadership residing in a person as a trait or behavior, leadership is viewed as the process of influence that occurs in the interactions of the team members working together. It can be embedded in an individual through their pattern of interactions.

The MHCLM acknowledges the interactions between the discipline-specific assumptions of team members, the team or group dynamics, and the team culture (Figure 5.1). Each team member brings the assumptions of their professional discipline and its approach to the patient problem-solving process. As Schon (1987) notes, "Practitioners of a profession differ from one another, of course, in their subspecialties, the particular experiences and perspectives they bring to their work and their styles of operation" (p. 33). They approach patient care through their lenses and their own specific perspectives based on their educations and experiences. This phenomenon, called *knowing-in-action* (Schön, 1987), contributes to understanding how individuals are able to skillfully execute based solely on their knowledge and experience (See letter B in Figure 5.1).

Yet, to function as a team, the members must learn to not only work with each other but to gain a deeper understanding of the group's priorities and assumptions. Thus, the importance of transitioning from individual assumptions to thinking as part of the collective is the essence of being part of a team. It involves group dynamics. Having the ability to reflect on issues facilitates the members relating to and with each other. Teams each have their own culture that has collective assumptions and values. This also contributes to how the team operates collaboratively toward the team goal of providing quality patient care. The team members' individual discipline assumptions interact with both the team culture and the group dynamics. Likewise, group dynamics and team culture interact with each other. This

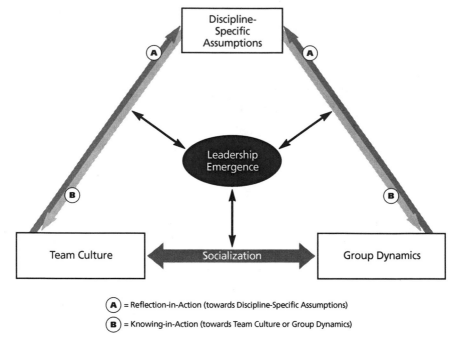

Figure 5.1   The Multidisciplinary Healthcare Leadership Model (MHCLM).

creates a complex set of interactions that allows the team to adapt to work-ing on each patient's problem(s).

Leadership emerges in the interactions of the discipline-specific assump-tions, group dynamics, and the team culture. *Adaptive leadership* emerges from the "spaces between" the team members working together (Uhl-Bien et al., 2007). We use this adaptive leadership as the definition of leadership emergence. It is an emergent characteristic of the team members' relation-ships as they creatively work (adapt) to solve the unique situation of the patient. It is also an emergent characteristic of the interactions of the mem-bers' ideas. Thus, leadership can identify a strategy, catalyze the other inter-actions, organize choices to navigate the complexity of the situation, and form a distinct output for the group (Hazy, 2008). Leadership can emerge throughout the group's interactions, changing from moment to moment.

Leadership emergence is the reformulation of assumptions and practices of the team and its members. It is a non-hierarchical interactive social pro-cess of team members that allows different pieces of problem-solving knowl-edge to come together to make a significant impact or solution. It is also the spontaneous self-organizing process of the team (Uhl-Bien et al., 2007).

Leadership emergence in a bedside healthcare team creates the collective mind that delivers distinctive care for each patient. It also moves members from thinking solely based on their discipline-specific assumptions to thinking in kind, with the collective team assumptions and goals in mind.

Leadership emergence is a function of team interactions. It occurs at the team level. In order for it to successfully occur, a hospital multidisciplinary team must be supported by the hospital administration. When organizational structures promote and encourage interactions among individuals, they tend to develop enduring and stronger relations and group affiliations (Emerson 1972a, 1972b; Homans, 1950). The arrows in the model represent interactions between the major constructs. The perimeter arrows (arrows A and B) connect the major phenomena. Individual knowing–in-action (Schön, 1983) is represented by the two downward B perimeter arrows to both the group dynamics and team culture constructs. In the reverse direction (A arrows) from these constructs is reflection-in-action (Schön, 1987). In addition, interaction of socialization is represented by the arrows between group dynamics and team culture. Leadership emergence rises from the interactions in the "spaces between" which is represented by the emergence arrows connecting to the perimeter arrows. Leadership emergence also influences those perimeter arrow interactions. Failure to adequately employ knowing-in-action and/or reflection-in-action during either of these interactions has a direct impact on leadership emergence within the multidisciplinary team.

Group Dynamics

Today, hospital-based health care is delivered in teams that can be composed of various interacting agents or individuals from multiple professions. Therefore it is important to understand the role that group dynamics have in delivery of health care. We define *group dynamics* as the interactions of the individual team members. These interactions are shaped by the *knowledge, skills,* and *attitudes* of each team member (Burke, Stagl, Salas, Pierce, & Kendall, 2006). They are influenced by the professional cultural lens of individual members as well as the culture of the team (Burke, Priest, Wooten, DiazGranados, & Salas, 2009). Each individual group member brings to the team the assumptions and rules of practice of their respective professional disciplines. This tints the way he or she views the patient encounter, and this becomes part of the interactions of the group. Interactions within these groups are the processes that shift focus from that of an individual toward that of the team, thus aiding the team as it merges into its own specific entity. Burke et al. (2009) describe this as part of the process of team adaption.

Knowledge is the cognition that one brings to the group in three major areas: *mental models, task expertise,* and *team expertise* (Burke, Stagl, Salas, Pierce, & Kendall, 2006). Mental models are "dynamic, simplified, cognitive representations of reality that team members use to describe, explain, and predict events" (Burke et al., 2006, p. 1199). *Mental models* provide frameworks that guide the team members' interactions and systems of operation. This includes their professional rules and practices. Burke et al. (2006) define *task expertise* as the knowledge that a team member commands about the task and their role in the task. It is technical knowledge that is acquired through their experience and training in their specific profession. This is a type of cultural lens, which the person uses to view each situation. Each team member brings their professional expertise to the patient encounter. *Team expertise* is the individual team member's knowledge of the other team members and team operations; this is the ways in which teams function (Burke et al., 2006). This area of knowledge is based on the team member's training in group or team functioning and their personal experience.

These three knowledge areas play off each other. The mental models from the professional disciplines may impact the way each member views patient encounters as well. The way a team member views the other disciplines represented on the team may also be involved. Task expertise may reinforce this, but it also provides a unique set of knowledge to the team. Knowledge of team expertise promotes team facilitation and team adaptation. Team members have various degrees of knowledge in these areas. (Burke et al., 2009; Burke et al., 2006).

Attitude (team orientation) is a perspective brought to the group toward operating in a team. *Team orientation* is the members' openness and feelings toward this specific group and its operation (Burke et al., 2006). The more positive team members' feelings are toward the group and teamwork in general, the more likely they are to contribute to group functioning.

Skills are the capabilities that individual members have toward the team adaptation. Three major areas compose this category: *perspective taking, negotiation,* and *emotional competence. Perspective taking* is the ability to take on the perspective of other; to "walk a mile in their shoes" (Galinsky, Ku, & Wang, 2005). It is a way of creating empathy. Nursing teams trained in perspective taking have been shown to view conflict as task-oriented, which allows for easier group decision making than viewing conflict as a social or personal issue (Sessa, 1996). Discipline-specific assumptions can broaden a team's perspective, but it can narrow an individual's perspective. If a team member can only see things through her or his discipline, then the possibility for the emergence of a new solution is limited. Hoff (2010) noted that some negative assumptions that operate on experience-based schemas of physician teams limited opportunities for learning and participation. On the other hand, a discipline's assumptions or perspective may help the team see the problem and solution in a new way. It is important for team members of various disciplines with different assumptions and rules to be able to view the patient encounter from another team member's perspective as well as from the patient's perspective.

Emotional competence is "the awareness of one's own and others' feelings, and using that awareness to manage feelings as a constructive resource in achieving work objectives" (Wasylyshyn, Gronsky, & Hass, 2004, p. 7). It is based on the emotional intelligence literature, which Goleman, Boyatzis, and McKee (2004) identify as self-awareness, self-management, social awareness, and relationship management. This competency relates to both the individuals and the group. Emotional competency is needed by the individual team member to interact with the other members. The team also needs emotional competence to function as a group. Emotional competence at the team level, which is based on the competence of the individual team members, has been shown to correlate positively with team cohesiveness and performance (Rapisarda, 2002).

Negotiation is the process by which two or more team members communicate with one another and try to come to a mutually acceptable agreement on some matter (Lomuscio, Wooldridge, & Jennings, 2003). Negotiation is a skill of both the individual team member and the team. The individual holds the skills to communicate with other members. This skill is used to create compromise in values and assumptions of the team. It helps in formation of the hybrid team culture. Over time, through the interactions of the members with each other, the team builds experience in negotiation among members. These skills, attitudes, and knowledge are individual-level functions; that is, they operate within individuals. Group dynamics are primarily at the individual level of analysis.

Together, the knowledge, skills, and attitudes of individual bedside team members contribute to the overall interactions within the group. Each member brings her or his discipline's assumptions and practices along with her or his skills and understandings of team functioning. As the team members work with each other in the care of a patient, reflection-in-action helps provide them the opportunity to revise their own discipline-specific assumptions. Reflection-in-action for the individual team member occurs as a result of interactions between the discipline-specific assumptions and group dynamics. As the members work together, their interactions also mold the group culture as well as influence their individual impressions of their discipline assumptions. Comprehending the other members' ideas and assumptions impacts how they work together. Socialization, the interaction of group dynamics and team cultures, is pivotal in transitioning individuals from their individual priorities to thinking in terms of the collective team. The team culture socializes the members to reformulate the dynamics of the group. Likewise, the group dynamics socialize the members into the team culture.

Team Culture

Schein (2004) defines the culture of a group as

> a pattern of shared basic assumptions that was learned by a group as it solved its problems of external adaptation and internal integration, that has worked well enough to be considered valid and, therefore, to be taught to new members as the correct way to perceive, think, and feel in relation to those problems. (p. 17)

Using this as the foundation and definition of culture, we focus specifically on the external adaptation and internal integration. These, according to Schein, assist with culture formation by establishing boundaries and group norms.

Spontaneous interaction in an unstructured group gradually leads to patterns and norms of behavior that become the culture of the group (Schein, 2004). The need for established norms is important, and ground rules set the tone for the team's ability to function and develop. The team culture is influenced through the interaction with the embedded discipline-specific assumptions of the team members. It is also influenced by the interaction of the group dynamics. The integration of these interactions shapes the behavior, values, and assumptions of the team as a collective culture. It is how the team self-organizes for problem solving the patient's care. The patient's problem is part of the external environment that the team must adapt to, while the integration of the interactions is the *internal integration* of Schein's definition of culture.

Socialization is a key component of the development and transition from functioning as a group made up of individuals to a team having a unified culture. According to Lawler, Thye, and Yoon (2008), individuals are bound together by interpersonal and common social ties. Through interactions that occur between group dynamics and the team culture, socialization aids in developing and further promoting the culture of the team. As the team culture is formed, socialization reformulates the team members' knowledge, skills, and attitudes. The interaction of socialization is a reciprocal, back-and-forth dynamic between the members as individuals and as a collective.

The interaction of team culture with discipline-specific assumptions presents an opportunity for professionals to review assumptions through reflection-in-action. It is the collective reflective process of the team that reformulates, modifies, or reinforces the discipline-specific assumptions of the members for the future. In the reverse direction, these discipline assumptions are brought to the bedside health team where members of different professions and sub-professions (subspecialties) interact. This interaction from the discipline-specific assumptions is knowledge-in-action. It is the professional discipline knowledge, including the assumptions, used by the team members in the moment of problem solving that is influencing the team's culture in behavior, values, and underlying assumptions.

Health Discipline-Specific Assumptions

Davis defined professional culture as "the pattern of shared beliefs and values that give the members of an institution meaning, and provide them with the rules for behavior in their organization" (as cited in Alexander, 2003). Underlying the shared beliefs, values, and practices are basic professional assumptions. Each health profession has its own values, rules, and beliefs that are held by the individual members of that profession or discipline. These discipline-specific assumptions create a mental model for the members of the discipline. Though discipline-specific assumptions are usually considered an institutional construct, their manifestation is in the individual member. Healthcare professionals are taught in discipline-specific training programs, forming the foundation of their discipline-specific assumptions. Experience builds on the initial training. Even within multidisciplinary healthcare teams, where individuals are from different disciplines, individual professionals maintain their discipline assumptions. Physicians and nurses working within the same hospital units have been shown to have different cultures. Broom, Adams, and Tovey (2008) found that hematology/oncology physicians and nurses differed in their beliefs regarding evidence-based practice. Nurses saw evidence as a continuum that includes qualitative and quantitative evidence, while physicians believed evidence as only being quantitative, having a clear "black and white" characteristic. The physicians also differed by subspecialty regarding the level of evidence (quantitative) that they believed necessary to make clinical decisions. Oncologists were more conservative, requiring higher levels (randomized trials) for clinical decisions on individual patients, while hematologists used lower levels (case reports) in making their decisions.

In another study of physicians, nurses, and hospital administrators, Degeling et al. (2006) found nurses to be family-centered, physicians to be individual patient-centered, and administrators falling in between. Dougherty and Tripp-Reimer (1985) described medicine as "primarily (and properly) concerned with disease, its etiology, pathophysiology, and treatment" (p. 220) through models of normal and abnormal conditions. They described nursing as "the diagnosis and treatment of human responses to actual or potential health problems," which is "less discrete than medical diagnostic categories" (p. 220). Physicians' and nurses' beliefs and assumptions about human disease and the role of their professions indicate the distinct differences of their professions.

Nurses and physicians are the most studied health professions noted in our review of the health, organizational, and social sciences literature. Myerson (1994) applied institutional theory to professional manifestations of culture and demonstrated differences in basic beliefs, assumptions, and practices of medicine and social workers within hospital systems. She also found that dominant professional culture could influence the members of non-dominant professions. Thus, the interactions of the professions can have reciprocal influence. Applying the institutional cultural perspective, there is more cultural variance across institutions than within them (Chatman & Jehn, 1994). Applying this to the health professions, there is more variance in cultures and their assumptions across professions than within them.

The team members' particular discipline-specific assumptions interact with both the team culture and the group dynamics. The interaction of the discipline-specific assumptions with group dynamics is knowing-in-action; it is the use of a team member's discipline-specific assumptions and practices in problem solving simultaneously along with the other team members. The reverse interaction, reflection-in-action, is the individual's possibility of reformulating how the discipline-specific assumptions will be used in the future with the team. Similar interactions of knowing-in-action and reflection-in-action occur with team culture.

Leadership Emergence

The complexity leadership theory proposed by Uhl-Bien et al. (2007) describes three types of leadership: *administrative, adaptive,* and *enabling* leadership. Leadership emergence of the MHCLM is adaptive leadership. It is "an emergent, interactive dynamic that produces outcomes in a social system" (Uhl-Bien et al., 2007, p. 302). It emanates from the interactions of the agents as they work together in a CAS. Its emergent quality means that it occurs spontaneously and not in a predetermined manner. It influences a change. "The essence of leadership is influence, and influence can occur anywhere at any time in a system, particularly outside the formal boundaries of hierarchical roles" (Plowman & Duchon, 2007, p. 115). Leadership does not rest on a function or a single person, but is the dynamic process of interactions between individuals, groups, teams, and operates through the tensions of relationships, ideas, technologies, or actions (Uhl-Bien et al., 2007).

The MHCLM model is a model of group-level leadership. The emergence leadership is a group- or team-level process that does not have a "team leader." Teams benefit from leadership emerging spontaneously as the team is working. In order for emergence leadership to function in a hospital situation, the hospital's administrative leadership must provide supports that will encourage and assist teams to self-organize and self-manage.

For the MHCLM, leadership emergence comes forth as the multidisciplinary care team is problem solving as a team. Group dynamics, team culture, and discipline-specific assumptions interact with each other. Leadership emerges from these interactions. The interactions of knowledge-in-action and reflection-in-action can create leadership emergence. The socialization interactions have the same potential. Likewise the interaction of leadership emergence with any or all of these interactions can reformulate into new leadership emergence. (The arrows in Figure 5.1 indicate this process.)

This emergence is multifaceted, multidisciplinary, and multilevel. The emergence of leadership occurs across the individual and collective levels. Discipline-specific assumptions are an institutional-level dynamic, though they are manifested in the individual team member. Team culture is a group-level dynamic, and group dynamics occur primarily at the individual level.

DISCUSSION

Implications for Practice

The need to improve delivery and quality of health care is essential. An even greater need is to develop a mechanism to improve the functionality of multidisciplinary health teams. Viewing the healthcare team as a CAS can be an important step in serving this need. Our model can serve as a guide for existing healthcare organizations to identify areas of training and development for current team members and new team members. We believe that the paradigm shift from traditional hierarchical management to leadership emergence in a multidisciplinary healthcare team is needed for the future sustainability of health care in America.

The MHCLM is a tool that provides a perspective that healthcare OD practitioners, including change agents, can utilize in order to assess the level of interactions within teams. The strength of the model is that it focuses the practitioner on the leadership capacity of the team and not just one particular individual. This allows them to work on ways to facilitate leadership emergence. We feel that the MHCLM can assist the practitioner by identifying the level of analysis where there are breaks or problems in the system (i.e., individual, team, or organizational) level. Is it a problem with individual team members' knowledge, skills, or attitudes toward functioning on a multidisciplinary team? Or is it a problem of the team member limiting her/himself to her or his discipline's assumptions? Once the source of the problem is identified, the OD practitioner can make the necessary changes to incorporate training, education, facilitation, or coaching to promote improvement of these interactions. In essence, the MHCLM can aid in developing systems for improving overall organizational effectiveness.

The MHCLM has training implications for health professionals as they enter new teams and oversee new teams. Viewing the healthcare delivery team as a CAS calls for change in what health professionals are taught as well as how they are taught. Group dynamic skills, including negotiating skills and understanding of other professions and their assumptions or perspectives, should be part of the curriculum. This also requires experience using this knowledge and these skills. In addition, our model will allow the ability to transform the training curriculum for the next generation of health professionals by incorporating group dynamics training during their discipline-specific education.

Although there has been some research that reviews healthcare group dynamics, it appears that researchers have not looked specifically at the role of training and education of multidisciplinary team members. Kerosuo and Engestrom's (2003) empirical work on boundary crossing among physicians of various specialties demonstrates the potential of our model. Their work focused on the organizational learning in the creation of a patient care tool. Doctors and nurses from primary care and other specialties crossed boundaries of beliefs and norms in the creation of the tool. Because their focus is on tool creation and learning, they do not analyze the process of leadership, although a dynamic leadership process is implied in their work. This appears to be an area that warrants further investigation and review.

Limitations

This model is in the early stages of development and has several limitations. This theoretical framework has not been empirically tested. The lack of empirical testing makes it challenging to justify and support our proposition. Although there definitely appears to be a need to research such topics, the lack of research does serve as a potential weakness in our theory building. Although we believe knowing-in-action, reflection-in-action, and socialization are important components to the interaction and development of leadership emergence in multidisciplinary healthcare teams, we do not believe that they are the only factors. There is a need to identify other interactions occurring in the model, such as sensemaking, sensegiving, and structuring. In addition, as CAS are learning systems, it may also be beneficial to research other factors such as learning, freezing, and unlearning in order to gain a deeper understanding of the learning process in teams. The model isolates the clinical bedside healthcare team without discussing its existence within a hospital, which is a larger organization or institution.

Future Research

Much of the current complexity leadership theory literature does not focus in-depth on the role of group dynamics, team culture, and professional culture/competence. The MHCLM addresses this by looking at leadership emergence in the multidisciplinary healthcare team environment. Because teams are composed of individuals, there is a need to research how the emergence of leadership occurs in teams where individual priorities take precedence.

We propose that this new model might be examined through both qualitative and quantitative research methods like case studies of several hospital bedside teams—specifically, cardiac critical care, emergency room, and a geriatric inpatient teams. These teams should include multiple healthcare disciplines, such as nurses, physicians (multiple specialties), social workers, pharmacists, physical therapists, occupational therapists, psychologists, and hospital chaplains. These teams deal with optimizing patient care with possible outcomes of patients ranging from restored health to death.

As stated earlier, many healthcare teams are functioning from a conventional leadership model and do not recognize themselves as CAS. The hospital bedside teams proposed are probably operating in this capacity with an authoritarian type of leader, which may stifle the potential emergent interactions. Research can be done with highly interactive teams or with pilot teams versed in this new model.

CONCLUSION

Leader emergence in the bedside healthcare team is created by a complex dynamic set of interactions that allow the team to adapt to working on the problem of the patient. The MHCLM is grounded in CAS theory and complexity leadership theory. Using the concepts of complex adaptive systems and emergent (adaptive) leadership from Uhl-Bien et al. (2007), the model was derived to focus on group dynamics and team culture interacting with individual and collective components. It integrates institutional theory and organizational culture of healthcare professions by using healthcare professions as institutional fields. This brings organizational theory and complexity leadership into the arena of the healthcare clinical team. It provides OD practitioners a new way to perceive healthcare organizations and teams. We propose that having such a strong understanding of the complex nature of health systems will promote leadership emergence in multidisciplinary teams. This will result in better team performance and will ultimately improve the quality of care delivered to patients.

REFERENCES

Alexander, L. M., (2003). *Variations of professional identity over time: A study of physician assistants* (Doctoral dissertation, The George Washington University, 2003). Available from Dissertation Express database (UMI No. 3083788).

Broom, A., Adams, J., Tovey, P. (2009). Evidence-based health care in practice: A study of clinician resistance, professional de-skilling, and inter-specialty differentiation in oncology. *Social Science & Medicine, 68*(1), pp. 192–200.

Burke, C. S., Priest, H. A., Wooten II, S. R., DiazGranados, D., & Salas, E. (2009). Understanding the cognitive processes in adaptive multicultural teams: A framework. In E. Salas, G. F. Goodwin, & C. S. Burke (Eds.), *Team effectiveness in complex organizations: Cross-disciplinary perspectives and approaches* (pp. 209–240). NY: Routledge.

Burke, C. S., Stagl, K. C., Salas, E., Pierce, L., & Kendall, D. (2006). Understanding team adaption: Conceptual analysis and model. *Journal of Applied Psychology, 91*(6), 1189–1207.

Committee on Quality Health Care in America, Institute of Medicine (2001). *Crossing the quality chasm: A new health system for the 21st century.* Washington, DC: National Academy Press.

Chatman, J. A., & Jehn, K. A. (1994). Assessing the relationship between industry characteristics and organizational culture: How different can you be? *Academy of Management Journal, 37*(3), 522–553.

Crites, G. E., Ebert, J. R., & Schuster, R. J. (2008). Beyond the dual degree: Development of a five-year program in leadership for medical undergraduates. *Academic Medicine, 83*(1), 53–58.

Degeling, P., Zhang, K., Coyle, B., Xu, L., Meng, Q., Qu, J., & Hill, M. (2006). Clinicians and the governance of hospitals: A cross-cultural perspective on relations between profession and management. *Social Science & Medicine, 63*(3), 757–775.

Dougherty, M. C., & Tripp-Reimer, T. (1985). The interface of nursing and anthropology. *Annual Review of Anthropology, 14*, 219–241.

Emerson, R. (1972a). Exchange theory part I: A psychological basis for social exchange. In J. Berger, M. Zelditch, Jr., & B. Anderson (Eds.), *Sociological theories in progress* (pp. 38–57). Boston, MA: Houghton Mifflin.

Emerson, R. (1972b). Exchange Theory part II: exchange relations and networks. In J. Berger, M. Zelditch, Jr., & B. Anderson (Eds.), *Sociological theories in progress* (pp. 58–87). Boston, MA: Houghton Mifflin.

Galinsky, A. D., Ku, G., & Wang, C. S. (2005). Perspective-taking and self–other type overlap: Fostering social bond and facilitating social coordination. *Group Process and Intergroup Relations, 8*(2), 109–124.

Goleman, D., Boyatzis, R., & McKee, A. (2004). *Primal leadership: Learning to lead with emotional intelligence.* Boston: Harvard Business School Press.

Hazy, J. K. (2008). Toward a theory of leadership in complex systems: Computational modeling explorations. *Nonlinear Dynamics, Psychology, and Life Sciences, 12(3), 281–310.*

Hoff, T. (2010). Managing the negatives of experience in physician teams. *Health Care Management Review, 35*(1), 65–76.

Homans, G. C. (1950). The human group. New Brunswick, NJ. Transaction Publishers.

Kerosuo, H., & Engestrom, Y. (2003), Boundary crossing and learning in creation of new work practice. *Journal of Workplace Learning, 15*(7/8), 345–351.

Lawler, E., Thye, S., and Yoon, J. (2008). Social exchange and micro social order. *American Sociological Review, 73*(4), 519–542.

Lomuscio, A. R., Woolridge, M., & Jennings, N. R. (2003). A classification scheme for negotiation in electronic commerce. *Group Decision and Negotiation, 12*(1), 31–56.

Long, K. A., (2007). Preparing nurses for the 21st century: Revisioning nursing education and practice, *Journal of Nursing Education 20*(2), 82–88.

Meyerson, D. (1994). Interpretations of stress in institutions: The cultural production of ambiguity and burnout. *Administrative Science Quarterly, 39*(4), 628–653.

Miller, J., & Page, S. (2007). *Complex adaptive systems.* Princeton, NJ: Princeton University Press.

Moody, R.C., Horton-Deutsch S., & Pesut, D. J. (2007). Appreciative inquiry for leading in complex systems: Supporting the transformation of academic nursing culture. *Journal of Nursing Education, 46*(7), 319–24.

Pawlina, W., Hromanik, M. J., Milanese, T. R. Dierkhising, R., Viggiano, T. R., & Carmichael, S. W. (2006). Leadership and professionalism curriculum in the gross anatomy course. *Annals of the Academy of Medicine, 35*(9), 609–14.

Plowman, D., A., & Duchon, D. (2008). Dispelling the myths about leadership: From cybernetics to emergence. In M. Uhl-Bien & R. Marion (Eds.), *Complexity leadership: Part I: Conceptual foundations* (pp. 129–153). Charlotte, NC: Information Age Publishing.

Plowman, D. A., & Duchon, D. (2007). Emergent leadership: Getting beyond heroes and scapegoats. In J. K. Hazy, J. A. Goldstein, & B. B. Lichtenstein (Eds.), *Complex systems leadership theory, volume 1* (pp. 109–123). Mansfield, MA: ISCE Publishing.

Porter-O'Grady, T., & Malloch, K. (2007). *Quantum leadership: A resource for health care innovation* (2nd ed.). Boston: Jones and Bartlett Publishers.

Rapisarda, B. A. (2002). Impact of emotional intelligence on work team cohesiveness and performance. *International Journal of Organizational Analysis, 10*(4), 363–380.

Sangvai, D., Lynn, M., & Michener, L. (2008). Defining high-performance teams and physician leadership. *Physician Executive, 34*(2), 44–51.

Schein, E. (2004). *Organizational culture and leadership* (3rd ed.). San Francisco, CA: Jossey-Bass Publications.

Schön, D. (1983). *The reflective practitioner.* New York: Basic Books.

Schön, D. (1987). *Educating the reflective practitioner.* San Francisco: Jossey-Bass Publications.

Sessa, V. I. (1996). Using perspective taking to manage conflict and affect in teams. *The Journal of Behavioral Science, 32*(1), 101–116.

Tan J. H., Wen, J., & Awad, N. (2005). Health care and services delivery systems as complex adaptive systems. *Communications of the ACM, 48*(5), 36–44.

Uhl-Bien, M, Marion, R., & McKelvey, B. (2007). Complexity leadership theory: Shifting leadership from the industrial age to the knowledge era. *The Leadership Quarterly, 18*(4), 298–318.

Wasylyshyn, K. M., Gronsky, B., Hass, W. (2004). Emotional competence: Preliminary results of a coaching program commissioned by Rohm and Hass Company. *Human Resource Planning, 27*(4), 7–12.

Weick, K., & Quinn, R. (1999). Organizational change and development. *Annual Review of Psychology, 50,* 361–386.

CHAPTER 6

COLLABORATION IN HEALTHCARE

A Complex Proposition for One Leadership Team

Daniel J. Dangler and Susan Burns-Tisdale

ABSTRACT

Because of its complexity and inherent challenges, the healthcare system in the U.S. offers deep and potentially "oceanic" insights into what teaming, teamwork, or collaboration can really mean in the current and future healthcare environment (for purposes of this article, *teaming, collaboration,* and *teamwork* are used synonymously). This article will present, discuss, analyze, and reflect on the efforts of a leadership team for a New England healthcare system in its struggle to apply and achieve a significant degree of success through the application of collaborative OD methodology and insights. The committed and long tenured group of executives was able to move from an entrenched, hierarchical structure to a broad-based, collaborative work approach, having a significant impact on patient care and performance outcomes.

On its own merits, teaming is a complex proposition. But in health care, complexity is the norm and is unmatched in comparison to that of other

Organization Development in Health Care, pages 107–129

industries. To even attempt to standardize collaboration or teaming efforts in health care would be somewhat like making baseball, football, and hockey into one game that plays at the same time with the same set of rules. The inherent complexity would not allow it, just as it does not in a healthcare environment. In order for successful collaboration to occur in health care, a very different set of assumptions must first be applied, requiring people to stretch beyond their own belief systems and assumptions about processes, themselves, and others. OD is uniquely qualified to usher the next chapter of human collaborative technology in to health care, not as a one-size-fits-all, but as a broad-based, customized methodology. This case explores how an OD consultant applied a research-based methodology for collaboration, and how the leader, and subsequently the team, took these insights and learning and applied them first between themselves and then throughout the organization with impressive results. The first half of the case is told from the voice of the client, and the second half is in the voice of the consultant.

THE ENVIRONMENT AND THE BUSINESS NEED FOR CHANGE

There is great uncertainty about the future of health care, and there is much rhetoric regarding the reform imperative to increase access and slow the rate of spending. For healthcare systems, this means a rethinking of decades of assumptions about what constitutes success. Specifically, healthcare systems are considering and engaged in redesign to include more alignment and inclusion of the component parts of health care: hospitals, physician practices, and post-acute services such as skilled nursing and home health and hospice services. In this way, organizations are prepared for potential bundled payments, accountability for collective care outcomes, and potentially a more rational approach to the delivery of services (Fischer, Berwick, & Davis, 2009).

THE VIEW OF THE CLIENT: SARAH

Background: The Organization

Our visionary CEO had been readying our New England-based healthcare system for these changes for the past decade and a half. The nexus of our organization had been the 100-bed community hospital. As with most healthcare systems in New England, our system started with a cottage hospital in the late 1890s. The hospital soon added a school of nursing that continued for the next thirty years. In the seventies, the hospital acquired a local nursing home. This was followed by the launch of a physician organization and the acquisition of a home health hospice organization in the nineties. With the component parts in place, a healthcare system was born.

Currently, our healthcare system oversees the care of 80,000 primary care patients who receive the vast majority of their care within our system. Additionally, we have a significant number of patients who receive primary care elsewhere but come to our organizations for specialty care, emergency care, procedural and diagnostic services, and home health/hospice services.

The physician organization, with over 90 primary and specialty physicians, now has the potential to serve as the new organizational nexus. In particular, with the move toward Accountable Care Organizations (Glass & Stensland, 2008), a focal point for managing the components of health care will be required; and given the longer-term relationships between patients and their primary care doctors, the physician organization is viewed as the most logical place for this to occur.

The Need for a Clinical Operations Vice President

As one of several steps toward readying the organization toward this outcome, the CEO determined that a leadership position, specifically a Senior Vice President for Clinical Operations, was required to bring together the component parts and agendas of the hospital, the skilled nursing facility that had been significantly reduced in its number of beds in recent years, and the home health hospice organization. It was expected that this restructure would serve as an impetus for greater organizational alignment and flexibility for future care delivery models. The physician organization would not fall within the scope of the new role, but the expectation was that this new leader would work closely with the physician organization President to identify and advance, in collaboration with the CEO, an agenda for greater system integration.

A major driver of this alignment was the patient's experience across the services of the organization. In other words, the CEO viewed the *patient experience* (internal document) as the totality of the patient and family's experience throughout every part of the organization, including:

- Care and support processes
- Interactions between the patient and organizational staff from the moment they walk through the door to the moment they leave
- Physical environment in which care is rendered
- Health outcomes
- Access to information
- Respect and control

The New Senior Vice President of Clinical Operations and Her Team

The realignment was expected to be accomplished within a cost-conscious and efficiency-oriented paradigm. As the first leader to be hired for this role, I had great optimism about my ability to work with four individual operational Vice Presidents (VPs) as direct reports and a VP for system quality who had a matrix relationship with this role to create a team to forge this agenda. I had experience in each of the healthcare venues overseen by the VP group and arrived eager to share this experience and a viewpoint that included experience as an executive director for continuum of care for a large system. For me, the idea of bringing together our various perspectives to create a whole that would advance the CEO's agenda and my agenda of a patient experience that included an integrated view of care delivery, including rational coordination of care on behalf of patients and their families, made perfect sense.

The organization had long been successful in several ways. It had a sound financial basis, a competitive view to offer the best in services and facilities, a well-defined strategic planning process, and a focus on improving the health of the community. Ironically, this success provided little in the way of a compelling reason to change for my direct reports, given their association with a high-functioning organization. However, with the potential change in definitions for success, and the visionary perspective of the CEO, there were clearly many reasons for the group to restructure their current approach to achieve future goals.

On reflection, I realized that I often entered organizations that were less successful and my arrival generally filled a leadership void. This was not the case in this organization. There was no immediate crisis, so it was difficult to galvanize this group to advance the larger organizational agenda of integration.

Each VP operated in a semi-autonomous way, with significant accountability and latitude for their respective part of the organization. These roles included a VP for acute care (who had a dual role as the Chief Nurse Executive); a VP for ambulatory, emergency, and perioperative services; a VP for the skilled nursing facility who had oversight for the hospital's case management program; and finally a VP for the growing cancer center that includes medical and radiation oncology and the home health hospice program. The newest recruit in the group had been in the organization for seven years, and the longest had thirty-year tenure.

The Team and Its Challenge

In my first year in the organization, I focused on forging relationships. The VP for System Quality, who had a less hierarchal matrix reporting re-

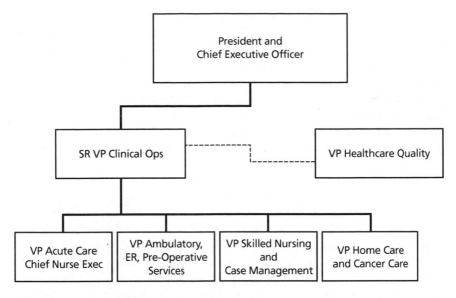

Figure 6.1 Organization of the healthcare system.

lationship with me, was welcoming. In truth, I had so much to do within operations, I had little time to consider and potentially influence the quality program during the first year. My direct reports were less welcoming. In fact, in my early days in the organization, two of my four reports appeared to dismiss me; a third report was continually stressed by my expectations, while the fourth was welcoming and supportive. The group had not functioned historically within the context of a single team, though they were members of the CEO's larger team. They might work on initiatives together and coordinate elements of a specific project, but they appeared to see little reason for integrating their work and resources.

Much good work was occurring within the VPs' individual areas, but not as a collective. My challenge was to first gain the group's trust and then expand their view of the work from that of their respective programs and services to a more expansive view of the larger organization as an integrated system. I observed opportunities for improvement in clinical care delivery and in how we interacted with patients and families, and I began to share my observations.

Over the course of most of the first year, I tried to draw on over twenty-five years of leadership experience to forge a team and to partner as the senior member of the team. I met with the group weekly and with individual participants biweekly. I spent time observing on units and gaining the perspective of administrative and physician colleagues. However, regardless of what I learned in these meetings, my orientation, or my travels through the organization, I did not believe that I was making the kind of impact that I had expected to make, and I felt tension when offering recommendations. In short, many of my recommendations seemed to be viewed as criticisms, resulting in a fair amount of defensiveness. This was a new experience for me, in that in the past I was able to build credibility and gain trust early on.

I spent time trying to analyze what I could do differently to gain trust. I tried not to change too much too soon, thinking it more important to allow significant time for assessment. It was clear to me that my coming to the organization was a significant change for the team and that this was creating stress for the team members.

The group had been part of a larger leadership team meeting with the CEO. Upon my arrival, these meetings morphed and I chaired a clinical operations meeting with the four VPs and leaders of the support departments, including quality, finance, human resources, and information systems. We had a full agenda discussing issues relevant to both operations and the support departments. What I did not appreciate at the time was that the new structure created less direct interaction between the clinical VPs and the CEO. Having worked with the CEO since they began in the organization, this represented a significant loss to the VPs.

These meetings were transactional in nature and did not include a thoughtful dialogue about our collective work and its impact on our patients. A member would bring an item forward, and within the context of a sometimes uncomfortable environment we would address the issue. We might be successful at addressing the issue at that moment, but I generally felt that much was unsaid and it was unclear whether consensus existed. It was clear the operational VPs did not share an identity as a team. It was therefore difficult to discuss issues within a broader context: *Is it the right item? Is it really a symptom of a more systemic issue or topic? Is this the right time to address it? Are we the right group?* I changed the format over time to include a VP-centric meeting for every other operational meeting. It was in these meetings that themes about our collective work began to emerge. This work included patient satisfaction scores and opportunities for improving patient safety based on what we learned in staff surveys and case reviews (meetings where care regarding a specific patient situation is reviewed in a safe, confidential manner). At times, I had some sense of optimism about the discussions at these meetings because these topics clearly mattered to the team. However, this was not enough to move the group forward, and I continued to struggle because I perceived myself as unsuccessful in building a team ready to take on the diverse and complex issues of integration of the patient care experience across the continuum.

This lack of teaming troubled me. In general, I have been viewed as a supportive leader who creates teams and, although interested in the detail, provides the latitude for reports to manage their respective departments and programs. Additionally, as the new recruit in this new role, I felt compelled to deliver outcomes immediately. I had not had VPs as reports in the past and thought perhaps this could explain some part of my reception, believing that VPs expected even more latitude in their roles. I worked to incorporate their perspectives, while reining in my sense of urgency about change and the expectations of this new Senior VP role. I began to experience an overwhelming sense of being irrelevant, despite the CEO's positive feedback related to my accomplishments.

Seven months into this role, I realized that I had not succeeded in building the team that I needed. I had pulled out every tool in my leadership bag of tricks and, at this point, decided that I needed help. It was within this context that I sought outside help from an OD consultant.

THE VIEW OF THE CONSULTANT: DAN

Step One: The Presenting Problem

Client Entry Meeting. As I drove to meet with Carol that morning for our entry meeting (Block, 1999), I reflected on our phone conversation the prior week. We had not spoken for at least a year, and though the small facilitation project I did for her three years prior was a success, this project sounded quite different. Back then, as the VP for Operations and Chief Nurse for a small subsidiary hospital of a large academic healthcare system, Carol was perceived to be an effective and respected leader. This raised my own assumptions that after 7 months on the job Carol's new staff would also see her as a highly competent, seasoned healthcare professional, both administratively and technically, since she was a nurse with extensive experience in a very successful hospital. Unconsciously, I also assumed Carol would be skilled in building a new team. Though most of my perceptions of Carol were accurate, I recognized that I needed to be careful in assuming that her new staff would perceive her the same way. If the appropriate intervention was going to be a team development effort, these assumptions would not only skew the data during the diagnostic phase, but could undermine trust between her staff and myself, which was going to be essential, especially since Carol brought me in as someone she had previously worked with.

Upon my arrival, Carol had insightfully invited the VP of Quality to be in our meeting, since she had been in the system for three years and was able to provide helpful historical facts and objective information on both the organization and Carol's staff. Since she had a "dotted line" relationship with Carol, in a role that was not operational, she was not a member of the operations team.

Our discussion focused on one primary question: *What did they see as the problem with this team and what did they believe was the source of their performance problems?* The primary challenges presented came down mostly to the fact that these clinical VPs operated and behaved as if they were functional islands. Moreover, it was Carol's view that the source of their problems were that these VPs acted as if the larger healthcare environment was the same now as it had been 20 years ago. They believed they could control it as long as they held their functional ground. According to Carol, any attempts she made to address and change these views and behaviors were met by fierce resistance. Though this brief explanation was helpful, I still lacked an understanding of how the team's behavior had an adverse affect on the patient (Reddy, 1994).

Carol was able to easily provide specific examples since these were the very changes she was hired to make. Carol described the problems within the context of "the continuum of care," which is defined as "an integrated system of care that guides and tracks patients over time through a comprehensive array of health services spanning all levels of intensity of care" (Evashwick, 1989, pp. 4–6). In simple terms, the problems existed at the handoff points between functions. The lack of collaboration at these transition points presented the following challenges:

1. There is a lack of integration of the care experience between the Emergency Department (ED) and the Inpatient Unit (each area is under a different VP) when the patient moves from one setting to another.
    a. The receiving unit (Inpatient Unit) had a different view of expectations related to transition of the patient and their information than the sending unit (ED) and in the definition of timing as to when patients would be transitioned. This resulted in struggles between the unit, blame-placing, and a lack of focus on the patient and her or his needs during this transition.
    b. The ED and the post-anesthesia care unit both want to transfer patients to the inpatient unit at similar times, resulting in a need to manage competing priorities from the Inpatient Unit. Collaborative processes across functions could anticipate this challenge.
2. Lack of timely and complete information as the patient moves from one setting to another (a challenge for all healthcare organizations), causing angst for patients and families as they repeat their story time and time again, believing that it is not known to the care system.
    a. The timing and handoff of home care referrals at the end of the day on Friday is appropriate for inpatient work flow but creates havoc for the receiving home health and hospice organization that has to deploy limited resources when an early referral

might have meant the availability of additional staff to address patient needs.

  b. The handoff and discharge from the Inpatient Unit to Skilled Nursing lacks adequate information considered essential to the Skilled Nursing unit but superfluous to the Inpatient Unit, creating stress between these groups and potentially resulting in a delay of transfer for the patient.

3. A lack of partnership at the VP level to get to outcomes, creating winners and losers based on the specific initiatives and the strongest voice instead of placing the patient in the center and working from this perspective.

  a. Policy changes are created with the belief that the policy is consistently implemented in all respective clinical areas, without actually testing this assumption. However, a problem pops up because the VPs over each area do not understand the interdependency related to policy implementation for consistent care and care processes.

  b. Palliative Care views their role in relation to the patient differently than Case Management, creating conflict as to who owns what aspect of the patient's care.

Figure 6.2 depicts the interdependencies and the flow of information required between each of the VPs.

Step Two: The Goal of the Work

The primary implication of all these challenges for this leadership team was that if there is inadequate cross-functional collaboration at the top, the "disconnects" will undoubtedly be revealed and evident to the patient as they cross over each of the VPs' functional areas on their "continuum of care" journey (Hansen, 2009).

Many of the examples (or, more accurately, *symptoms*) were significant enough that the implications of this team acting differently could have a far-reaching affect on the organization. What was unclear, though, was how exactly the team needed to act differently in order for these broader systemic changes to occur. This, in fact, was the problem needing to be assessed and solved, resulting in the defined goal of the work: *Help develop an integrated, collaborative leadership team, capable of leading (and modeling) an organizational alignment and collaboration that would prepare the organization for future care delivery models.*

The work was two-fold: First, the team needed a mental model for collaboration that they could rely on to improve their collaborative practices.

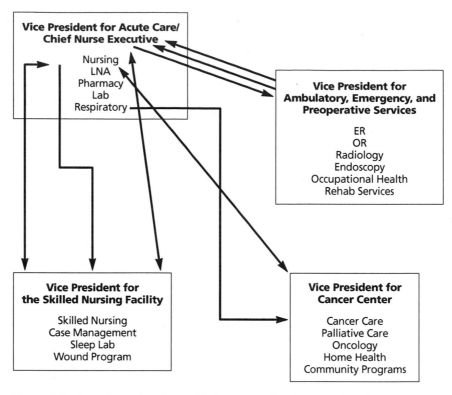

Figure 6.2 Interdependencies and information flow between functions.

Second, they needed a sustainable process for change so that the work this team began together could naturally continue through the continuum of care. I had no illusions that this team could make these changes overnight, but I expected (and was betting on) that once the team began addressing their own narrow, collaborative challenges, the cultural forces that kept this team at the status quo in the first place would surface. My hope was that this would create the opportunity for the team to discover and coalesce around their true mission, which, in my view, was nothing short of changing the underlying operating assumptions of how patient care was delivered in their system. Although that outcome seemed a long way off based on Carol's current description of the team, the broader and longer implications of this work could not be underestimated (Cope, 2003).

Step Three: Contracting With the Client

Our contracting conversation focused around expectations, commitment, buy-in, roles, boundaries, and the goals of the assessment process

(Block, 1999). We agreed that the team should provide input into crafting the diagnosis process based on the assumption that the team would have to give up something for this change to occur and that the increased involvement during the front end of the process would increase potential buy-in to required changes as well as trust in me and the process (Block, 1999).

To that end, I first met with Carol and the team collectively. After explaining the project and its goals, I invited their input and collective agreement and commitment to those goals. This enabled me to gain consensus from the VPs on who should be interviewed for the assessment, and it provided me a brief opportunity to view the team "in action." Each VP provided a list of their stakeholders that included their direct reports, VP peers, and the CEO.

In addition, I also explained the model I was going to use for the assessment and why. The team agreed that this work could have broader implications if successful and that by having a strong mental model (Gentner & Stevens, 1983) it would (1) provide ongoing direction to the leaders on a new collaborative approach within a complex healthcare system, (2) identify broad data points of the organizational culture and, (3) gather specific data on the team itself.

This meeting with the whole team was important in gaining their commitment to the project both as a collective and as individuals. The final step of the meeting was agreeing on what I was committed to providing them and what commitments they were making to the process, which resulted in the writing and signing of the contract. As well as being an important component of any OD project, the collective team sign-off on the contract played an important symbolic role in beginning this project.

Step Four: The Assessment Process

The assessment process began by building an approach based on a viable model that could look not just at this team but at broader organizational context. The model used was an amalgamation of several teaming models, developed over the past 10 years through other collaboration projects. I combined three mental models or frameworks that could isolate a team's collaborative "sweet spots" based on the needs of the patients. These work well for encouraging the appropriate interdependent group of people to reach towards, what I call collaborative intelligence. Using the definitions of teams and teamwork by Katzenback & Smith (1992) along with the discussion by Arthur Himmelman (2001) on collaboration, I define the term "collaborative intelligence," as "a collaboration that taps into the collective wisdom and skills of the team through the group's ability to have respectful, yet open disagreements and dissent in the process of sharing information, in order to make meaningful and sustainable decisions together."

For any collaborative model to be useful, the team's performance outcomes must be practical and linked to the model. In this case, the long-term outcomes were defined early on, making the application of this model appropriate. This model can be used for any kind of team at any level of the organization, assuming there is a commitment to collaboration as previously defined.

Model: Framework One

One must always be suspicious when a client states they want "better teamwork" or more "collaboration." What do they exactly mean by this? Is there really an actual business need and process need that necessitates collaboration, or is it just their perception that they "should" work better together? The underlying question that must first be answered is: To what degree do these people need to "work together" to meet the business needs of the organization? Or, put another way, how inherently interrelated is this group of people, such that if they did not work well together it would adversely affect the business?

To answer this question, I use a model that defines 3 modes of "working together." In his article, "Collaboration for Change Definitions: Decision-making Models, Roles, and Collaboration Process Guide," Arthur T. Himmelman (2001) defines three modes of working together: *coordinating, cooperating,* and *collaborating.* In all three modes, a group will always need *to exchange information* for mutual benefit. When *coordinating,* the individuals in the group will need to *alter their activities* to achieve a common purpose; and when *cooperating* they will need to *alter their activities and share resources.* But to *collaborate* requires team members to not only *exchange information, alter their activities,* and *share resources,* but also *enhance the capacity of each other.* This is a critical difference from the other two modes, and if a team knows how to practically enhance the capacity of each other, they may be able to leverage that critical power of collaboration, which can be easily measured.

Model: Framework Two

To better understand how exactly the team can go about enhancing each other's capacity, it is important to understand the surrounding complexity that can have bearing on their performance. I use a second assessment framework to mine the team's organizational context by exploring some of the following (Kotter & Heskett, 1992):

- A linking strategy between team and organization
- A supportive organizational culture
- Consistent organizational processes
- Effective leadership

Model: Framework Three

The definition of *collaborative intelligence* assumes that the success of a team is related directly to how open, honest, and willing they are to discuss and deal with differences—differences of opinions, thoughts, personalities, and approaches. This piece of the overall model is used to encourage collaborative intelligence and is based on the work developed by Druskat and Wolff (2001). It looks at three internal aspects of an effective team by asking: *Does a team have the right people doing the right things in the right way?*

1. Efficacy ("the right people"): Efficacy is when there is a shared feeling on the team that they have a highly competent, capable, and unique group of people that can accomplish anything together. This means that the team has an unstated certainty that they have the collective power to produce a desired outcome. According to Lencioni (2002), several indicators for this are:
   - The team has a high commitment to success.
   - There is an ability to maintain a shared accountability.
   - The team possesses a high degree of resilience to change.
2. Identity ("doing the right things"): Identity is when a team has an explicit agreement, clarity, and confidence about the mission, strategy, goals, and outcomes required to be successful. This includes:
   - Having a cohesive strategy (Nash, 1999)
   - Focus on their collective results (Lencioni, 2002)
   - Sound cross-functional roles and responsibilities (Nash, 1999)
   - An effective decision-making process (Katzenbach & Smith, 1992)
3. Trust ("in the right way"): Trust is when the right people are doing the right things *the right way*, meaning that the team has a high regard for their collaborative process and there is a core belief that team members have each other's and the team's best interests in mind. The behavioral indicators of trust are the team's ability to:
   - Have spirited and respectful disagreement via dynamic communication (Nash, 1999)
   - Explicit value differences
   - Possess mutual respect
   - Demonstrate capable leadership

Step Five: Summarize Findings and Make Recommendations

The twenty individuals interviewed provided a considerable amount of information on each of the elements described above. Themes were identified from the collated data and used to establish a diagnosis and to present recommendations (Block, 1999). After speaking with each team member individually, it was clear they were willing to invest energy to address their performance as a team. I recommended a two-day retreat (subsequently conducted) focusing on addressing the findings described below. The following provides an overview of the data findings consistent with the assessment model described above and then what was done to address them.

Data Framework One: Findings

During my discussion with the CEO, prior to beginning the assessment interviews, he stated, "There needs to be a high level of synchronicity between functions to achieve operational excellence, including putting in place the structures and processes that will provide exquisite continuity across the continuum of care." These kinds of outcomes would certainly require each VP to *enhance the capacity* of the functional areas of their fellow VPs, implying that the CEO had a clear idea of what collaboration must look like. Though this requires a sophisticated level of interaction, the CEO knew that the business benefits of collaboration would far outweigh the difficulty in getting there.

In addition, during each assessment interview, individuals were asked to identify which definition (*coordination, cooperation,* or *collaboration*) most closely reflected the current functioning of the Operational Leadership Team and where they thought the team should be to succeed. This provided additional data on the collective perception of how this team was currently performing. In all 20 interviews, every person stated, including each team member, that the team was somewhere between *coordinating* and *cooperating,* but never *collaborating.* This data was presented to the team so that they could see how they were viewed by others and to self-identify new activities that could enable them to improve their collaboration.

Data Framework Two: Findings and Interventions

Linking Organizational Strategy/Effective Leadership: Findings.   In order to understand the functioning of the team, it was important to understand the context in which it operates. The evidence of a *linking organizational strategy* in the work of this team was evident from the start. After all, this was why Carol was hired and why I was called in to assist with the performance of this team. The CEO provided a clear strategic charge to this team in order for them to fulfill the strategy of the hospital. It was now up to them to come together and translate their own approach to fulfilling this linking strategy. In addition to a linking strategy, there was little question as to *effectiveness of the leadership* surrounding this team. Though there were plenty of opportunities for ongoing leadership development throughout the organization, this had little bearing on the team's current performance. The team had a significant amount of support from a variety of leaders, including the CEO, CFO, and key doctors in leadership positions, and their future was in their own hands.

Supportive Organizational Culture: Findings. The culture of the organization was often described as intense, driven, competitive, and at times unforgiving. At the director and manager levels, individuals felt that the culture provided little encouragement in the way of cross-functional collaboration. Individuals felt that they lacked the autonomy and incentives to innovate and collaborate. And though this was a long-standing aspect of this organization's culture, there were some assertions that this could be traced back to the leadership practices. Though upper management was trusted and respected, some data suggested that leaders needed to find better ways to share information with each other and the organization, which would contribute to eliciting a greater degree of autonomy and empowerment.

Consistent Organizational Processes: Findings. This showed up in the data as being an ongoing clinical problem pointing directly to this team's inability to collaborate cross-functionally. Some of the representative comments are: "The organization doesn't have efficient processes, which results in wasted resources"; "There are too many procedural formalities to fulfill, which affects the quality of patient care"; "Outpatient procedure and protocol decisions are based on Inpatient norms"; and finally, "There's a need for more efficient scheduling processes across the functions."

Consistent Organizational Processes: Intervention. A significant portion of day two of the retreat was spent looking at the consistent organizational processes data. I arranged the data on flip charts according to the specific organizational processes and provided a process for the team members to review, respond to, discuss, and begin to address these organizational process challenges (Reddy, 1994). The team had a significant "awakening" simply by viewing this information, as it became clear that these problems led directly back to their lack of cross-functional collaboration. Throughout the afternoon of the second day, the team identified a number of discussions, action steps, and long-term projects needed to begin resolving the process inefficiencies.

At the heart of these inefficiencies, data was identified while exploring the team's efficacy around *clear cross-functional roles*. This revealed the fact that the team had never even analyzed their cross-functional interdependencies. Among others, this became a critical long-term project owned by several team members who would assemble a project team to address this.

Data Framework Three: Findings and Interventions

Efficacy: Findings. Though most stakeholders viewed all of the VPs as being committed, driven, intelligent, and competent individuals, they were not viewed as a team who understood or was committed to their collective mission. They were committed to their own functional silos, serving only to isolate and at times even create competition among them.

The team members were also perceived as being "significant obstacles for change" by their stakeholders, and with their collective total of almost 60 years of tenure at the hospital (one member was even born there), major change was not something they had had to wrestle with. This change was the first generation of major change, and using statements such as "shock," "disbelief," and "betrayal by the CEO who just handed us off" (the CEO had also been there for 25 years), it was clear that they were going through significant turmoil regarding their roles. Though their stakeholders viewed these changes as a positive step in building a strong clinical operational leadership team, the team members felt "left in the dark" with little understanding of why the change was needed (Mauer, 2009). In order for Carol to establish herself as their leader, she would need to find a way to address this immediately and move through this resistance.

Efficacy: Intervention. Since there was never a "formal" reporting changeover from the CEO to Carol, I asked the CEO to spend several hours with the team prior to the retreat. My main goal was to unfreeze the team (Lewin, 1947) and begin to develop the competency of resilience to change. Prepared by reviewing the data, he acknowledged to the VPs how difficult this change was for them and admitted some of the mistakes made. He reassured them of the vital role they played in the organization and asked them to consider what it would take for them to lead this new strategy. Once stating this, he and Carol turned the rest of the meeting over to the team, giving them the opportunity to ask questions, express feelings and thoughts, and to respond in an honest, yet respectful manner. Both the CEO and Carol mostly listened, acknowledging the team's struggle, even pain. After spending a significant amount of time just listening, he closed the meeting by reiterating the importance of both Carol's role and the team's role in leading the organization to delivering healthcare in a new way, thereby reaffirming their importance to the long-term success of the system. The team described these two hours as a "cathartic experience" and felt prepared and even "excited" for the team retreat to have a meaningful discussion with Carol about her role and what was needed from both parties to succeed.

Identity: Findings. Though Carol had a strong cohesive strategy, the data suggested a lack of buy-in from the team, as they felt "left in the dark." And, as already discussed, the data showed clear functional roles, but undefined cross-functional roles and responsibilities. This was at the heart of their inability to actually implement collaborative team practices. They also came to the team from their years in the organization with a hierarchical view of decision making, yet at the same time, they resented Carol when she made decisions. So the group needed to redefine their decision-making process, and Carol needed to help them make the right decisions at the right time.

Identity: Intervention. Gaining buy-in to the strategy required relatively little effort, other than presenting the team with their goals and allowing them to wrestle with what needed revision. The key however, was to do this after addressing issues of trust. And surprisingly, their process of discussing the strategy actually brought up how decisions were being made and how they should be making which decisions when. There were also several critical conversations between Carol and team members about what was needed from each other regarding how which decisions were made when. Again, the key to this conversation was to first address the issues of mistrust, making this conversation relatively easy.

Trust: Findings. The data showed considerable issues of trust between the team and Carol and amongst most members of the team. However, the issues of trust had mostly to do with history and their collective assumption that they had been marginalized and had lost power under their new reporting relationship to Carol. The team needed to learn to bring these perceptions into the open with each other and with Carol in order to flush out which were accurate and which were false.

Trust: Intervention. The intervention with the greatest impact on the team was the use of the Myers-Briggs Type Indicator (MBTI). Though the conversation with the CEO laid the groundwork for softening the team's resistance, the MBTI enabled the team to address specifics and helped create norms around team discussions and decision making (Nash, 1999). There were several challenges regarding communication problems that surfaced. After learning about type theory, I had the team members analyze specific cross-functional challenges. During these discussions, the team was able to isolate and stop action on a variety of communication challenges using type preferences as a lens. Specifically, issues around conversational pacing arising from the introvert/extrovert functions and important issues of misinterpretation about cross-functional problems could be traced back to the MBTI perceiving functions of *Intuition* and *Sensing* (Nash, 1999).

As the team continued through the afternoon of day one exploring their individual and collective team preferences, they were able to normalize their challenges and point to and identify a variety of past problem interactions, realizing how their personality differences led to differing perspectives. The team watched themselves with "amazement" discuss past events that they had labeled as irreconcilable differences. As one team member described, "It took the personal out of the professional, so that we no longer viewed our differences as a personal affront but rather as a collaborative opportunity."

The paradox is that this team wanted to work well together and their statements often reflected a belief that they should be working well together, but they never quite understood why they were not. As a team of four seemingly homogeneous women and one man, there seemed to be an unconscious assumption that they had enough in common to be able to achieve their collective goals. This subtle, yet powerful assumption seemed to stand in the way of their being able to even acknowledge their differences, which they saw as a threat. Many times on a team, the combination of the human need for inclusion with a weak ability to negotiate differences can override willingness to acknowledge and address differences. As a result, the differences go "underground," having a disastrous effect on team performance. The strongest competency of a team's collaborative intelligence is the members' ability to differentiate from each other and have rich and respectful discussions around those differences.

Though it remains a simple tool, and it does not solve all team problems, the MBTI did provide a way for this team to eliminate the finger pointing and turn the focus on ownership and personal responsibility. The team stated that out of all the work done those two days, this was the most "helpful exercise," because it established a much needed foundation for trust and gave them the "tools to figure out how to talk about differences without blaming the other."

Carol was a capable leader, yet the team's classic signs of resistance with outward displays of anger, even denying she was their leader, revealed she had more work to do (Bridges, 2003). The stakeholders saw Carol as a "sorely needed, no-nonsense, competent, action-oriented leader inpatient with slowness or inefficiencies." Yet they also felt that Carol needed a different strategy with this group since they had not had a consistent advocate for a long time. Though she tried to be careful in how she approached the team in their shortcomings, her restrained directness was still viewed as more "grist for the resistance mill." The data revealed to Carol how vital coaching would be and, frankly, that she needed to model what collaboration and partnering with others should look like.

Carol will now describe her view of the long-term impact from this work.

THE LONG-TERM IMPACT
(THE VOICE OF THE CLIENT: SARAH)

The primary result of the work done at the retreat was that it provided the team with a solid foundation along with some tools to begin to create (and model) a collaborative, flexible healthcare system. During the retreat, the team identified and soon after began to implement a variety of projects that would create momentum toward achieving the identified long-term outcomes.

The first major change of the consultant's work was that the group gained an identity as a team, kindred spirits, trying to advance an agenda related to patient care. We recast our group as the Patient Care Executive Team (instead of Clinical Operations). This communicated to stakeholders, colleagues, and direct reports that the patient is the primary mission of this group's work. This in no way minimizes our work in other areas such as finance, IT, strategic planning, human resources, and the like, but it makes clear the centricity of the patient as our core focus.

As the group's leader, I felt that a weight had been lifted as a result of the work we had undertaken with the consultant. It validated my role as the team's leader. For me, an important lesson learned was that I needed to articulate my vision for this team. I had been reluctant to provide this clarity because of the group dynamic, and yet, once stated, this seemed to provide some relief for the group and a greater sense of collective purpose. This purpose has helped us move forward as a team, identifying and addressing issues related to the patient experience in our organization and building strategies together. With this as a platform, VPs have advanced significantly in taking accountability for cross-organization outcomes. Some achievements include:

1. We are planning for a model for chronic care, involving collaboration from all parts of the organization.
2. We continue to identify ways to ensure effective handoff between clinical programs and units, outpatient and inpatient. This continues to be work in progress.
3. We are in the early stages of developing a nursing practice model, both at the hospital and home care hospice levels, which will connect each horizontal care unit with a consistent set of care practices and values.
4. Consolidation of the rehabilitation program under one system director, who reports to one of the VPs, instead of four VPs having a rehab report.
5. Integration of a palliative care program across three entities.
6. The early stages of developing a cross-system view of the management of patients with wounds.
7. Teaming and sharing resources with regards to effective management of our FTEs (full time equivalents) and making reductions where necessary.
8. The early stages of exploring the role of the manager (VPs' direct reports) to create a shared vision of this role across the organization, which the group believes will support integration of a shared vision for the patient experience and facilitate implementation (where relevant) of the organization's strategic plan at the unit level.

In addition, this process has helped us recognize the need to be more inclusive of physicians in our operational work. From this insight, the group has led the development of a hospital best practice committee, chaired by a physician and with the Senior VP serving as the administrative partner. The purpose of this group is to ensure the integration of best practice in care delivery, continuing to affirm our mission of patient-centric planning, implementation, and evaluation.

Finally, the clarity gained through this retreat helped the group to work more effectively with colleagues in support departments, particularly Quality. The need to expand the notion of team to others (support departments) has begun to take hold, and we are beginning to consider more fully our interdependence across the organization beyond the delivery of clinical care services.

It goes without saying that collaboration is not the answer to every problem. However, in today's very complex healthcare environment, a healthcare system and its leaders must be able to understand how to analyze and leverage their wide net of interdependencies. The only way to wade through and build upon these complex interdependencies is through customized and sophisticated collaborative strategies that tolerate and build upon the complexity of human difference.

PRIMARY LEARNING

In any kind of organization, collaboration can be a messy business and is not just a matter of increased competence. Particularly in healthcare, with the many levels of complexity and differences, collaboration is a fine balance of science and art. It requires a team to track valid data to know how best to move themselves forward, while also calling upon their collective intuition and emotional intelligence (Goleman, 1998) to navigate the more challenging times together.

At the most fundamental level, if a group is clear and explicit about its inherent interdependence and about how this intertwining affects the business, then they are beginning with a strong foundation. It seems that we human beings, more so in the Western Hemisphere, struggle with our need to depend on others and our desire for independence. Placing this struggle at the center of collaboration, a group will either deny their interdependence, undermining any attempt to understand how their behaviors have anything to do with one another, or they will assume that they need each other more than they actually do, thereby creating a pseudo-team of bland performers incapable of moving any deeper business challenges forward. If a group can collectively, explicitly, and constructively understand their interdependence from the perspective of having to either coordinate, cooperate, or collaborate, they will save themselves a great deal of time, and maybe even pain, in reaching their desired end state.

An important competence of a high-performing team is its ability to self-reflect on its own process. Many attempted collaborations can be rife with interpersonal conflicts, leaving the individuals assuming that those people should not be working together. Yet it has often been stated that one can put a great person into a bad system and the bad system will win out every time. This is also true with collaborations. No matter how strong the individuals working together are, if they live in a system not set up for cross-disciplinary or cross-functional collaboration, they will be set up for failure. In today's healthcare environment, collaboration is a given, but it is not necessarily in the organizational DNA. If the system is unconscious about how it encourages collaboration, a good team can easily fail. Teams should learn how to reflect upon and understand their interpersonal conflicts not just as personal differences, but possibly as a symptom of broader systemic problems.

Strong mission, vision, values, norms, and goals are all "givens" for great collaborations. However, if a team lacks a foundation for trust, the quality of its mission, vision, and goals makes little difference. When it comes to trust, it seems that many teams unconsciously undermine collaboration by trying hard to get along. The problem with trying to get along is that differences go underground, leaving little authenticity and honesty in their interactions. Outstanding collaborations are born from honest and respectful discussion of and struggle with differences. Therefore, one of the primary tasks of any group wanting a strong collaboration is to identify and discuss how the members are different, not how they are alike. This seems counterintuitive, as every group wants discussions and decisions to go smoothly. We often hear individual stories of the nightmare team someone worked on and how nothing ever got done because of differences. But when explored further, there is a consistent theme that these nightmare teams had an inability to acknowledge and navigate natural and useful differences. Again, it seems that humans desire harmony to such a strong degree that we are willing to smooth over vital and life-giving differences that are the seeds of extraordinary collaborations. Use tools such as the MBTI to explore, acknowledge, and integrate the wonderful human differences in which many innovations have been born. Create agreements on how your team will navigate differences and what kinds of behaviors are acceptable and unacceptable.

Finally, the primary role of a team leader is to enable the team to do all of the things discussed above. This requires a leader to be not only a boss, but to be a coach, a facilitator, an intervener, and even a consultant. Leading a team toward satisfying and productive collaboration requires the leader to know when to step in and when not to, but most of the time, it requires the leader to create a space for the team members to have their differences, to hold each accountable, to learn how to be resilient, and to help the members learn how to lead their own teams. Most of the time, a team learns these competencies by the leader's modeling of these behaviors through authentic honesty, making mistakes and taking risks by challenging people to live from their souls. It is then that one will begin to witness the sparks of deep and lasting collaboration, which cannot be manufactured by will alone, but only by creating a container where the seeds of human relationship can be nurtured and grown.

REFERENCES

Block, P. (1999). *Flawless consulting* (2nd ed.). San Diego, CA: Pfeiffer & Company.

Bridges, W. (2003). *Managing transitions: Making the most of change.* Cambridge, MA: De Capo Press.

Cope, N. (2003). *The seven C's of consulting: The definitive guide to the consulting process* (2nd ed.). London, U.K.: Pearson Education Ltd.

Druskat, V. U., & Wolff, S. B. (2001). Building the emotional intelligence of groups. *Harvard Business Review, 79*(3), 81–90.

Evashwick, C. (1989). Creating the continuum of care. *Health Matrix, 7*(1), 30–39. Retrieved from http://www.ncbi.nlm.nih.gov/pubmed/10293297?ordinalpos= 11&itool= EntrezSystem2

Fischer, E., Berwick, D., & Davis, K. (2009). Achieving health care reform: How physicians can help. *New England Journal of Medicine, 360*, 2495–2497.

Gentner, D., & Stevens, A. L. (Eds.). (1983). *Mental models.* Hillsdale, NJ: Lawrence Erlbaum Associates.

Glass, D., & Stensland, J. (April 9, 2008) *Accountable care organizations.* Retrieved from http://www.medpac.gov/about.cfm

Goleman, D. (1998). *Working with emotional intelligence.* New York: Bantam Books.

Hansen, M. (2009) *Collaboration: How leaders avoid the traps, create unity, and reap big results.* Cambridge, MA: Harvard Business Press.

Himmelman, A. T. (2001). *Collaboration defined: A developmental continuum of change strategies.* Retrieved from http://depts.washington.edu/ccph/pdf_files/4achange.pdf.

Katzenbach, J. R., & Smith, D. K. (1992). *Wisdom of teams.* Boston: Harvard Business School Press.

Kotter, J., & Heskett, L. (1992). *Corporate culture and performance.* New York: Macmillan.

Lencioni, P. (2002). *The five dysfunctions of a team.* San Francisco, CA: Jossey-Bass Publishers.

Lewin, K. (1947, November 1). Frontiers of Group Dynamics, *Human Relations, 1*, 5–41.

Mauer, R. (1996). *Beyond the wall of resistance: Unconventional strategies that build support for change.* Austin, TX: Bard Press.

Nash, S. (1999). *Turning team performance inside out: Team types and temperament for high-impact results.* Palo Alto, CA: Davies-Black Publishing.

Reddy, B. R. (1994). *Intervention skills: Process consultation for small groups and teams.* San Diego, CA: Pfeiffer & Company.

Sorensen, J. (2002, March). The strength of corporate culture and the reliability of firm performance. *Administrative Science Quarterly.* Retrieved from www .findarticles.com/p/articles/mi_m4035/is_1_47/ai_87918557/pg_9

PART III

ENGAGEMENT

CHAPTER 7

PROMOTING EMPLOYEE ENGAGEMENT

Tabitha Moore

ABSTRACT

This chapter is a case study of a Denver hospital that entered into a partnership with ARAMARK Healthcare in 2007. This 565-bed facility is the largest private teaching hospital in Denver and cares for more patients on an inpatient basis than any other hospital in the area. Eager to improve employee satisfaction and to reduce employee turnover within its support services departments, the hospital partnered with ARAMARK Healthcare to support this objective. The author of this chapter facilitated the implementation of I-Impact as an Organizational Effectiveness Manager with ARAMARK Healthcare. Within a year, the hospital began to realize results, which continue to accrue into the present.

INTRODUCTION

Sitting down with a group of housekeepers in a Denver, Colorado hospital, I asked them how they have been able to help their patients recently. All of them had stories to tell and big smiles on their faces. One of them spoke up and said, "I cleaned a room for a patient and we became really good friends

Organization Development in Health Care, pages 133–145
Copyright © 2011 by Information Age Publishing
All rights of reproduction in any form reserved.

and talked about our families." Another housekeeper beamed, reporting, "I cleaned a room for a patient for two months, and I ran into her a couple of weeks ago. She introduced me to her family and talked about how nice I was to her and how clean I kept the room." It was inspiring to be in that room with people filled with such pride and joy for the work they were doing. Another housekeeper exclaimed, "A patient received some bad news from the doctors. When they left, I made a little joke, and the patient said I made his day." On their feet 8 to 10 hours a day, cleaning the same thirty to forty rooms, it became obvious to me that these employees were highly engaged in their work and that they felt like they were making a difference in their patients' lives.

The healthcare industry is unique. For those working in clinical environments, there are daily opportunities to realize their vision of improving people's lives. Health care attracts passionate individuals who are dedicated to this vision and are committed to making a difference. In health care, it is not about how to motivate employees; it is about how leadership can stop unintentionally de-motivating employees from doing their very best for every patient (Studer, 2003).

The challenge for leadership in health care is to promote employee engagement and to minimize the barriers that cause miscommunication, apathy, and burnout in this difficult but rewarding profession. This chapter is a case study that follows the implementation of I-Impact, an employee engagement management system, within the support services departments at a Denver hospital. The purpose of this initiative was to give leadership the tools and structure needed to establish a collaborative relationship with the hospital's employees; to encourage their input, ownership, and creativity; and to bring out the inherent compassion that led them to this line of work.

EMPLOYEE SATISFACTION AND ENGAGEMENT

Support services are an often-overlooked resource in health care. Support services include facility services, clinical technology services, equipment distribution, patient transport, patient and retail food, and environmental services. These services are a major contributing factor toward the creation of a positive, healing environment for patients. Research has shown that patients have a better chance of getting well when they are treated in a hospital with a positive culture (Stubblefield, 2005). Also, it has been demonstrated that employee satisfaction is directly correlated with patient satisfaction (Atkins, Marshall, & Javalgi, 1996). In the case of support services, employees perform non-clinical duties so that nurses can focus on the clinical aspects of patient care. The more positive the relationship between nursing and support services, the better the care.

Several factors could affect this relationship, such as culture, language, role expectations, and power structures. In order to overcome these factors, it is important to base relationships on respect for one another as worthy, unique individuals (Gordon, 2001). This kind of relationship can only be built when employees engage with each other to attain the shared goals of increased patient satisfaction and quality clinical outcomes.

Such engagement is the subject of this case study. Employee engagement can be defined as the culmination of discretionary effort that employees put into their work (Orr & Matthews, 2008). This means that for employees to be considered actively engaged, they must be able to commit their hands, minds, and hearts to everything they do. Employees become actively engaged when they feel that their jobs have purpose, they are doing worthwhile work, and they are making a difference (Studer, 2003). As mentioned earlier, employees in health care have the opportunity to realize these values through the tangible difference they are making in the lives of the patients under their care. However, employees will only become engaged when leaders are able to clear the barriers that employees face in their work. Leaders can do this by creating a structured environment that allows for robust, two-way communication and effective collaboration. Such an environment promotes good relationships based on respect and appreciation, and efficient systems with the right tools, equipment, and training for the work (Studer, 2003). Employee engagement, then, is leadership-driven (Orr & Matthews, 2008).

In 2005, ARAMARK Healthcare, an industry leader in providing support services to hospitals and senior living facilities nationwide, partnered with the Studer Group, a healthcare consulting company that specializes in evidence-based tools and processes that foster a collaborative style of leadership. Together, they created I-Impact, an employee engagement management system that offers a focused approach to clearing the way for support services employees to make a difference in the lives of patients every day. ARAMARK Healthcare now implements this management system in their accounts, with the aim of improving productivity through the creation of a respectful and meaningful work environment for the staff.

This chapter is a case study of a Denver hospital that entered into a partnership with ARAMARK Healthcare in 2007. This 565-bed facility is the largest private teaching hospital in Denver and cares for more patients on an inpatient basis than any other hospital in the area. Eager to improve employee satisfaction and to reduce employee turnover within its support services departments, the hospital partnered with ARAMARK Healthcare to support this objective. Within a year, ARAMARK Healthcare was able to implement I-Impact and to realize results, which continue to accrue into the present.

I-IMPACT

I-Impact uses a set of tools to guide leadership in the creation of a positive work environment and to promote employee engagement. The tools reviewed in this chapter include employee rounding, thank-you notes, Stoplight Reports, AIDET, peer interviewing, and High-Middle-Low Conversations. These tools are based on the Appreciative Inquiry model (Cooperrider & Whitney, 2000), in that they bring out the positive potential in others through communication and relationship building. The questions asked with these tools are used to generate conversations about things that are going well and about things that could be even better. As concluded by Cooperrider and Whitney (2000), organizations grow in the direction of the questions they most persistently ask.

 AI

First-Round Implementation

Employee rounding is one of the most critical tools of I-Impact. Realizing that two-way communication is absolutely necessary to form positive relationships, leaders make a point to have a one-on-one rounding conversation with each employee at least once a quarter. These are structured conversations. Their purpose is to help leaders develop better relationships with staff, to get to know them on a more personal level, and to become more approachable. Front-line staff does the work every day; they know what needs to be fixed and how to fix it. Only through open, two-way communication can leaders find out what the true issues are and how best to solve them.

The employee rounding conversations start off with a personal question to build the relationship. Then, in asking about what is working well, leaders are able to celebrate successes with the employees and set a positive tone for the rest of the conversation. These conversations are also used to solicit peer recognition, which helps create and sustain teamwork. Toward the end of the conversation, they ask about what could be done better in order to learn about issues before they become major problems. They work with the employees to resolve those issues. Finally, employees are asked if they have all the tools and equipment they need to do their jobs. This last question makes a direct impact on the employees' work environment. When they make a request and receive the tools they asked for, it creates more trust within the relationship. These conversations go a long way toward removing existing or perceived barriers that employees may have in their work.

Leaders walk away from the conversation with useful knowledge that can be acted on. They now know whom to recognize for doing a great job. To follow up, they handwrite thank-you notes to those employees whom their peers recognized, and then they send these notes to the employees' homes.

This is a powerful form of recognition. Thank-you notes have the second greatest impact on employee retention and patient satisfaction after rounding conversations (Studer, 2003). When their families see the appreciation they have received, they understand the importance of their work. The employee also appreciates the leader and the peer who recognized them, creating better relationships.

With information collected on issues of employee concern, leaders are able to create a Stoplight Report that shows which issues have been remedied (green light), which are in the process of being resolved (yellow light), and which cannot be resolved (red light). Leaders then show the Stoplight Report to their staff in daily huddles, monthly staff meetings, and on communication boards, so that the staff is updated on the progress of their particular issues. This progress report goes a long way toward showing employees that they are being heard. Even for issues that cannot be resolved, there is a discussion as to why. This creates trust that the leaders are doing everything they can for the staff.

At the Denver hospital, these three tools were implemented within the first 90 days of the partnership startup. It was important to establish positive relationships and a sense of trust as quickly as possible. Though the tools were implemented quickly, it took over six months to hardwire them for every leader. Knowing that accountability is the backbone of hardwiring behaviors, scorecards were established to show how many roundings and thank-you notes each leader performed every month.

In the beginning, it felt awkward to write a prescribed number of thank-you notes per month. However, as leaders began shifting their thinking toward what was working well, they started discovering more and more opportunities for writing these notes. In addition, they received incredible responses from the employees who received them. The Food Services Director reported, "I have had at least three employees come into my office, with tears in their eyes, thanking me for the thank-you note. They said that they had never received one before in their lives." The leaders quickly realized how powerful these thank-you notes were and felt compelled to write them more often. Within three months of implementing thank-you notes, support services leaders were writing an average of 150% more thank-you notes than their goal every month. When asked why so many thank-you notes were being written every month, one of the managers of Environmental Services said, "The staff are all recognizing each other, so I don't want to pick and choose which thank-you note to write. I want them all to know that they have been recognized."

It was important to use these three tools from the beginning to establish trust and respect in the support services departments. One of the first issues that became clear was that the employees, particularly in Environmental Services (traditionally known as the Housekeeping Department), did not have the proper tools and equipment to do their jobs. So the leaders were able to collaborate with the employees to get the tools that would be the most effective for their work. By using I-Impact tools, and following up on the issues they uncovered, the leaders were able to establish a climate where the employees felt appreciated, valued, respected, and a part of the overall team.

Second-Round Implementation

With this mutual trust and respect established, leaders were able to work with employees to change how they did their work. One of the more significant changes was in how the employees within Environmental Services interacted with the patients. Many of the housekeepers did not feel confident engaging patients in conversation, citing such issues as language barriers and other socio-cultural discomforts. Conversation, however, is one of the most significant factors influencing patient satisfaction for Environmental Services (NRC Picker, 2009). After establishing trust and positive relationships with the staff, the leaders were able to work with them to adopt a communication tool called AIDET to structure their conversations with the patients. AIDET stands for *acknowledge, introduce, duration, explanation,* and *thank you.* The structured conversations helped the housekeepers to express the empathy that they already felt for their patients. Though it took time and patience to hardwire this change, it was possible because of the positive relationships between employees and leaders that had been built before the change occurred.

I-Impact includes several other tools, each designed to facilitate communication and build relationships. Peer interviewing had a profound effect on how employees worked with each other. With peer interviewing, leaders interview potential candidates and, if they want to hire them, they send them to a panel of high-performing employees who would become that candidate's peers. Before implementing peer interviewing, leaders found that when there was an open position, they felt tremendous pressure to fill it with a body. Employees, however, realized that not all the new hires were a good fit for the organization. Often, they could tell this within the first day of the new hire on the job. Once peer interviewing was put in place, employees were able to screen out candidates that did not fit in with the culture of the organization.

This simple tool helped tremendously with employee turnover. Not only did it decrease the number of employees that voluntarily left within the first year, but it also helped strengthen the bonds between the peer interviewers and the new employees. Within the Food Services department (which includes patient room service, catering, and the cafeteria), there was a tradition of placing new employees in difficult situations, without the typical support needed during on-boarding. Once peer interviewing was implemented, the peers took ownership of new employee on-boarding, because they knew that if new hires left, they would have to take responsibility for a bad decision. In addition, because only actively engaged employees were a part of the interviewing team, it was their positive influence that encouraged new employees to be engaged as well. Peer interviewing created a profoundly different way for people to work with each other to establish positive relationships and positive results. In the Food Services department alone, voluntary turnover went from 29% to 7% within a year and has continued to remain below 10%. In a department that typically has one of the highest turnover rates in hospitals, this was a significant decrease in turnover, indicating higher employee engagement.

Third-Round Implementation

Eleven months after starting I-Impact, most of the tools were in place and hardwired. As with any change initiative, there were still a few employees who remained unwilling to become engaged in their department. Their attitudes toward the leaders and toward their work remained poor. They were actively disengaged employees with whom leadership had not been successful in establishing positive relationships using the tools of I-Impact. They weighed down the rest of the department, talking negatively about it and about the hospital in general. It was time to implement the final tool, High-Middle-Low Conversations.

High-Middle-Low Conversations focus on employee performance, not only in regard to their jobs, but also their interactions with patients, peers, and leaders. High performer conversations start first. These are the employees who are actively engaged, and conversations with them revolve around showing appreciation and asking if there is anything that can be done to keep them around for a long time. Middle performer conversations come second. Middle performers are very solid employees, but have one or two opportunities for improvement. Middle-performer conversations use the sandwich method: showing appreciation first, then coaching on a specific issue, before ending with a final round of appreciation. Such conversations help these employees become more engaged because they feel appreciated for the things they are doing well and supported on the issues that still need work. Finally, leaders meet with low performers, or actively disengaged employees, who have been negatively impacting the department and contributing to lower patient and employee satisfaction. The purpose of these conversations is to move these employees toward engagement, or, failing that, out of the organization.

The tools of I-Impact are designed to be cumulative, to set up employees for success over time. When the Environmental Services department implemented the High-Middle-Low Conversations, they only had a handful of actively disengaged employees out of a staff of over one hundred. By using this final tool, they were able to convey the importance of engagement, and several of these conversations became breakthroughs. One employee in particular went from a low performer to a high performer after the initial low-performer conversation, reinforced by a series of follow-ups. Through this process, she realized that leadership cared about her as a person, not just an employee. Later, she said to one of the managers, "I started noticing that you were trying to make me successful, and I realized that it was me who had the issues." She was able to take ownership of her situation and become engaged. The Director of Environmental Services said, "She is one of our biggest success stories."

Six months after those conversations, this same employee was nominated for and won the hospital-wide employee-of-the-month award. In talking with one of the managers of Environmental Services, he said, "She really cares about her unit now. We had moved her to a new unit where she felt she could succeed. Within two weeks, she wanted to recognize the whole nursing staff for making her feel welcomed. I wrote that thank-you note, and it has created a very strong bond for her with nursing on that unit. She now feels like she is set up for success in her work environment." She has been on the unit for a year now and feels like part of the family. Her manager also added, "A few weeks ago, while mopping the floor, she noticed that one of the homeless patients had worn holes in his shoes. She decided to go down to the hospital gift shop and purchase a new pair of Crocs for him. She did this without telling anyone." This is a truly remarkable story of selflessness. After becoming an actively engaged employee, she was really able to shine. The Environmental Services department now regularly receives several positive letters every month from patients thanking her for her hospitality.

Employee Engagement Results

After hardwiring all the I-Impact tools, the support service departments have seen tremendous changes in the attitudes of their employees. These attitudes have been noticed by others outside these departments as well. The Chief Medical Officer of the hospital exclaimed, "The housekeepers have started looking me in the eye, and saying hi to me in the hallways!" Employees are taking more ownership in their work environment by bringing up issues and offering suggestions. They are more open about changes and willing to give ideas to make the changes stick. They trust their leaders and communicate openly to them about their feelings toward their jobs.

The employee satisfaction scores in Food Services increased from 50% to 70%, bringing them into the 70th percentile of organizations participating in this survey nationwide. The employee satisfaction scores in Environmental Services increased from 64% to 83% in a year, boosting them all the way into the 95th percentile. I-Impact had a profound impact on how employees felt about their jobs, their peers, and leadership. Once they felt cared about and respected as people, they were able to become more fully engaged.

Teamwork and camaraderie also improved between Nursing and Support Services. Support Services leadership formed positive, collaborative relationships with Nursing through the use of nurse-rounding conversations and thank-you notes. These tools went a long way in helping nurses and Support Services employees establish mutual respect. Many of the housekeepers have been welcomed into the units as part of the family, and housekeepers can be seen talking and laughing with nurses. Several units have bulletin boards up with pictures of the staff and their families; many of the housekeepers are on those boards. Nurses can also be seen helping housekeepers collect sheets or empty the trash when they see that the housekeepers are busy.

Financial Performance Results

The trust and respect established through I-Impact became important factors in navigating the changes necessary to improve the hospital's financial performance in 2009. With the deterioration of the U.S. economy, the hospital felt repercussions as the census fell below predictions, and the hospital suddenly found itself over budget. Senior leadership asked each department to come up with ways of modifying their budgets in order to keep the hospital financially stable. A climate of fear threatened the culture of the hospital. Several hospitals nationwide had already started letting employees go. Though senior leadership had expressly stated that they would do everything possible before considering that option, employees were still concerned about their jobs.

The Director of Environmental Services called a staff meeting to talk about ways in which the department could save money. Not knowing exactly how the staff would take the news, he could not have been more pleased with the outcome of the meeting. Staff members completely understood the struggles of the hospital and were very concerned with what they could do to help. During that meeting, the Director said that the staff was "very open to sharing their ideas on what they felt we could do to help save money." They came up with ways of centralizing equipment to save replacement costs. One of the employees mentioned the idea of working an hour less each day. Others said they would be willing to move from third shift to second shift. These last two ideas meant bringing home a smaller paycheck, but they were willing to do that to help the hospital. Within a month of the meeting, the department was able to implement several of their ideas and to realize a $45,000 savings, with full buy-in from the staff.

Patient Volume Results

Bed turnaround times have been one of the largest challenges the Environmental Services department has faced. Bed turnaround times—or the time it takes to prepare a bed for a new patient once the original patient has been discharged—directly affect the financial performance of a hospital. If beds are not turned around quickly enough, hospitals can be forced to send patients elsewhere. Bed turnaround times at the hospital averaged around 80 minutes in 2007. After I-Impact was implemented, leaders were able to work with the staff to bring down the average bed turnaround time to approximately 55 minutes. This, however, was still not good enough.

The leaders knew that it took 28 minutes to clean a room and prepare it for another patient. Staff was doing a great job staying within 28 minutes. The issue revolved around the time it took for them to get to the room. The hospital tended to discharge patients from 3:00 pm–5:00 pm. With this influx of beds to be cleaned, the Environmental Services department simply did not have enough staff during that period. To further complicate things, the first shift generally ended at 3:30 pm, so shifts were changing during one of the most critical times of the day. Leaders knew that they had to make a bold move to ensure that there were enough people during this critical time. They decided to change the hours of the first shift from 8- to 10-hour days so that first-shift employees could stay on to help.

Leaders knew they needed full buy-in from the staff in order for this change to work. They talked with staff members that would be affected by this change, one-on-one and in small huddles, in order to understand each person's concerns and to figure out how to address them. Knowing that this change would affect the employees' personal lives, they gave them time to prepare for it. Since they had built the positive relationships in advance of this change, they were able to receive frank and honest feedback from the employees and to get buy-in for the change through discussions with them. Within two months of making the switch to 10-hour days, the bed turnaround times dropped to an average of 42 minutes. This significant decrease in time resulted in increased patient volume at the hospital. With the mutual trust and respect that had been built, the employees were able to understand the reason behind the change, and the leaders were able to work with them to make it possible.

Collaborative Leadership

This chapter has shown I-Impact's effectiveness in the promotion of employee engagement and the results thereof. However, this effectiveness also depends upon leaders who are, themselves, actively engaged. In other words, leaders must be willing to collaborate with employees toward a positive work environment. This is a prerequisite for I-Impact's success.

Too often, leaders feel that in order to be effective they must sacrifice the needs of the employees to meet the needs of the organization. Such leaders tend to see these two sets of needs as dichotomous, and since their viewpoint naturally comes from the needs of the organization, they feel compelled to meet those organizational needs, often at the expense of their employees. When problems arise, these leaders try to solve them by themselves. They get into problem-solving mode, alienating employees, ignoring their input, experience, and needs.

Less often, leaders align themselves in the opposite manner, taking the side of employee needs over organizational needs. These leaders also see the two sets of needs as dichotomous; however, they tend to give in to the needs of employees in the name of having a happy and contented staff. In this kind of leadership style, employees are rarely inspired. Preoccupied with their own needs, they see little reason to modify their behavior to meet the organizational needs. This leads to a status-quo environment in which leaders are frustrated with their inability to influence, and staff is complacent, nonproductive, and disengaged from their environment.

Effective leaders are able to clear the way for employees, realizing the importance of meeting both employee needs and those of the organization. They recognize that these two sets of needs are not mutually exclusive. When effective leaders are faced with problems, they acknowledge that their perspective derives from organizational needs, and they also recognize that this is not the whole picture. They know they must have employee involvement because employees do the work on a day-to-day basis and are often more knowledgeable about operational intricacies. If leaders seek employee input from the beginning, then they will gain employee commitment to higher-quality solutions while also meeting employee needs. Effective leaders, then, consider themselves to be facilitators of problem solving, rather than problem solvers, and they use a collaborative style of leadership that clears the way for employees (for a further discussion of these leadership styles, see Gordon, 2001).

While it is true that an effective implementation of I-Impact requires a collaborative style of leadership in order to work, the tools of I-Impact are meant to help create a structure that supports such collaboration. I-Impact fosters open and honest communication between leaders and employees, encouraging both sides to speak up, make suggestions, participate actively in problem solving, and feel comfortable enough to constructively criticize each other's ideas. This type of collaborative engagement can be difficult at first, but it is mutually reinforcing. Both leaders and employees become more engaged the more they see the benefits of this positive, new relationship. So, while I-Impact does not, in itself, create collaborative leaders, it does provide the structure for this upward spiral.

CONCLUSION

Employee engagement is at the heart of organizational excellence for healthcare organizations. Employee engagement leads to service excellence, which in turn leads to higher patient satisfaction (Stubblefield, 2005). In other words, when employees feel that their jobs have purpose, that they are doing worthwhile work, and that they are making a difference, they will naturally go above and beyond to care for patients.

This chapter has offered a case study of I-Impact as it was implemented in a Denver, Colorado hospital. It has introduced a set of tools, including employee rounding, thank-you notes, Stoplight Reports, AIDET, peer interviewing, and High-Middle-Low Conversations—all of which are designed to promote employee engagement through the creation of a respectful and meaningful work environment. It has also shown the results of this implementation on employee satisfaction, financial performance, and patient volume.

More importantly, I-Impact has had a demonstrable affect on the lives of hospital employees. Tools like thank-you notes have helped to create a sense of worth for employees who have never been appreciated in that way before. One housekeeper was able to transform from a low performer to a high performer, winning a hospital-wide employee-of-the-month award. Others have been able to form more personal relationships with their patients, realizing the true meaningfulness of their work.

Healthcare employees tend to be individuals who are passionate and dedicated to making a difference in people's lives. That is why they are drawn to the healthcare profession in the first place. However, the stress of healthcare work can sometimes erode employee engagement and can ultimately lead to burnout if employees do not receive the support and appreciation they need. I-Impact is designed to help remedy this. It offers leadership a set of tools to provide employees with the support they need to give their best every day.

REFERENCES

Atkins P. M., Marshall B. S., & Javalgi R. G. (1996). Happy employees lead to loyal patients: Survey of nurses and patients shows a strong link between employee satisfaction and patient loyalty. *Journal of Health Care Marketing, 16*(4), 14–23.

Cooperrider, D. L., & Whitney, D. (2000). A positive revolution in change: appreciative inquiry. In D. L. Cooperrider, P. F. Sorensen, Jr., D. Whitney, & T. F. Yaeger (Eds.), *Appreciative inquiry: Rethinking human organization toward a positive theory of change* (pp. 3–27). Champaign, IL: Stipes Publishing.

Gordon, T. (2001). *Leader effectiveness training: Proven skills for leading today's business into tomorrow* (2nd ed.). New York: Berkley Publishing Group.

NRC Picker. (2009). *Always clean: Effective practices of performance leaders.* Retrieved from http://www.henrycountyhospital.org/pdf/Cleanliness_Case_Study.pdf

Orr, D., & Matthews, H. (2008). Employee engagement and OD strategies. *OD Practitioner, 40*(2), 18–23.

Stubblefield, A. (2005). *The Baptist Health Care journey to excellence: Creating a culture that wows!* Hoboken, NJ: John Wiley & Sons, Inc.

Studer, Q. (2003). *Hardwiring excellence.* Gulf Breeze, FL: Fire Starter Publishing.

CHAPTER 8

INTRINSIC

The Missing Link to Creating a Culture of Wellbeing and Employee Engagement

Rosalind Ward, Ph.D.

ABSTRACT

Employee engagement is an emotional attachment between an employee and his or her workplace. It is linked to several measures of organizational effectiveness, including higher levels of productivity, more innovation, greater customer satisfaction, and higher profitability. Engagement is also critical to the healthcare industry in fostering innovation and efficiency. This chapter addresses the OD issues with organizational wellbeing and performance too often addressed ineffectively with traditional behavior change approaches and the role leaders play in creating an effective organization. Literature and case studies will be explored to make the case for why a new perspective on organizational wellbeing and effectiveness is needed, and some practical tools for how leaders can put these concepts into practice in any healthcare organization will be provided.

Organization Development in Health Care, pages 147–170
Copyright © 2011 by Information Age Publishing
All rights of reproduction in any form reserved.

INTRODUCTION

Rising healthcare costs and the declining status of employee wellbeing are a major concern for most organizations today, including healthcare organizations. Numerous studies have demonstrated high levels of stress and burnout and low job motivation among nurses (Bégat, Ellefsen, & Severinsson, 2005; Butterworth, Carson, Jeacock, & White, 1999). In fact, it has been argued that consumers will not be able to receive the quality and safety of health care they deserve until healthcare organizations redesign and rethink how they deliver care and how they improve employee engagement (Mastal, Joshi, & Schulke, 2007). Furthermore, today's healthcare leaders must demonstrate leadership behaviors appropriate for the complex and constantly changing healthcare delivery system (Casida & Pinto-Zipp, 2008).

The Gallup Organization reports that lack of engagement costs American businesses more than $370 billion per year in lost productivity (Kruger & Kilham, 2006). Recent reports from the Gallup-Healthways Wellbeing Index™ initiative have shown a clear link between a negative work environment and missed days from work and reported wellbeing. Although an organization's culture is critical to engagement, the heart of engagement stems from individual intrinsic capacity and motivation.

Experts in multiple fields (e.g., worksite health promotion, OD, and psychology) all seem to arrive at a similar conclusion regarding the importance of having people who are intrinsically motivated and focusing on people's strengths. In fact, many argue that extensive use of extrinsic incentives for short-term behavior change actually hurts intrinsic motivation in the long term (Kohn, 1999; Anderson, 2002; O'Donnell, 2007). Furthermore, recent research also suggests that people will actively disengage at work when they feel that their intrinsic values are not supported (Ward, 2008). However, how to foster intrinsic motivation is not well understood.

It has been suggested that healthcare leaders need to move to transformational leadership through exercising "leading up" skills, which include a keen sense of self-awareness, practicing self-management, and balancing work and home life; in other words, it requires high levels of emotional intelligence (Mastal et al., 2007). In order to increase organizational effectiveness, research also supports the importance of increasing thought self-leadership (and, consequently, intrinsic motivation) by shifting cognitive thinking patterns (Manz & Neck, 1991). Additionally, studies have shown that improving communication skills among nurses so that they are collaborating with and empowering their patients improves the health for the client (Bégat et al., 2005).

Once again, guidance is lacking for how to best put these suggestions into practice. Too often, organizations try to create a culture of engagement and empowerment through making policy changes or applying a one-size-fits-all approach to their employees. However, empowering employees and increasing intrinsic motivation cannot be forced upon employees; it has to be elicited from within them by shifting how they *think* about their choices.

This chapter addresses the OD issues with organizational wellbeing and performance too often addressed ineffectively by traditional behavior change approaches and the role leaders play in creating an effective organization. Literature and case studies will be explored to make the case for why a new perspective on organizational wellbeing and effectiveness is needed and some practical tools for how leaders can put these concepts into practice in any healthcare organization will be provided. The first part will examine the critical role of engagement as a foundation to organizational effectiveness. The second part will expand on what is known about engagement to make a link to how the brain innately works and how thinking patterns impact engagement and whether or not people are able to make sustained changes. The third part will expand further to discuss the role of different types of motivation and why intrinsic motivation is critical to organizational effectiveness, yet so often misunderstood. The fourth part explores intrinsic motivation on a deeper level by addressing intrinsic capacity—a foundational way of thinking that is necessary for intrinsic motivation that can be measured with valid tools. Specifically, the benefits employees in healthcare organizations and their patients receive from increased intrinsic capacity will be discussed. The final part of this chapter will integrate each of the concepts explored to discuss how organizations can start to shift their culture to one that fosters increased intrinsic capacity and motivation and engagement, including a case study of a hospital shifting its culture to become an intrinsic organization.

ENGAGEMENT: THE FOUNDATION OF ORGANIZATIONAL EFFECTIVENESS

Employee engagement is an emotional attachment between an employee and his or her workplace. *Why should organizations care about engagement?* It is linked to several measures of organizational effectiveness, including higher levels of productivity, more innovation, greater customer satisfaction, and higher profitability. Engagement is also critical to the healthcare industry in fostering innovation and efficiency. A study of surgical teams implementing new technical procedures found that when leaders created an engaging environment, teams worked better; this resulted in creating a culture that streamlined implementation of complex new procedures (Edmonson, 2003). More importantly, improving employee engagement is essential for healthcare organizations to be able to provide the quality and safety of healthcare that consumers deserve (Mastal, Joshi, & Schulke, 2007). However, more than one in five healthcare workers are disengaged and are not inspired or motivated by their organizations or leaders (Towers Perrin, 2008).

Lack of engagement costs American businesses more than $370 billion per year in lost productivity (Kruger & Kilham, 2006). Engagement also plays an important role in the wellbeing and safety of employees. One study reported that the majority of engaged employees (62%) felt that their work lives positively affected their physical health, with 78% feeling that their work lives benefited them psychologically. However, 54% of actively disengaged employees felt that their work lives negatively affected their physical health, with 51% feeling that their work lives negatively affected their psychological wellbeing (Crabtree, 2005). Furthermore, a Gallup Consulting (2007) study found that individuals in workgroups in the bottom quartile of engagement average 62% more accidents than workgroups in the top quartile of engagement. These findings support the need to look beyond simple, medical-only explanations for poor levels of employee wellbeing and safety.

Doctors in New Zealand already recognize the importance of the complexities of what drives employee wellbeing. Consider these three questions: (1) *Would you describe your work as monotonous?* (2) *How satisfied are you with your job?* and (3) *How tense or anxious have you been in the past week?* When asked what these questions are assessing, most people think they are assessing stress or job satisfaction. In fact, these questions are part of a comprehensive back pain assessment used by doctors in New Zealand to predict with 83% accuracy who will be out of work more than 30 days due to low back pain (Accident Compensation Corporation, 2004). Of course, traditional medical questions are also part of the assessment, but job satisfaction and engagement play a significant role. Recognizing this provides opportunities for healthcare leaders to better effect change within their own organizations while also better supporting the needs of the patients.

Although on the surface it may seem "easier" to search for a quick solution to health and safety issues, most approaches that organizations use to improve employee wellbeing serve more as a temporary bandage and do not fully address the root cause of what impacts the business' bottom line—engagement. The good news is that senior leadership's actions and behaviors and the learning and development opportunities provided in an organization drive engagement (Towers Perrin, 2008). Since leaders set the tone for the organization, increasing engagement requires a *shift in thinking* for leaders regarding behavior change and a new approach to learning and development.

UNDERSTANDING THE BRAIN'S ROLE IN BEHAVIOR CHANGE: A FIRST STEP IN BUILDING ENGAGEMENT

Changing behavior is difficult for individuals, even when new habits can determine whether someone lives or dies. Change is also difficult at an organizational level; yet organizational success is not possible unless people within the company change their day-to-day behavior. Successful leaders wanting to effect change need to understand the physiological nature of the brain and how that impacts thinking.

The complexities of neuroscience research can help frame how change can be more effectively approached. For example, working memory is the brain's "holding area" where ideas and perceptions are first compared to other information and is frequently engaged when people encounter something new. This kind of memory activates the prefrontal cortex, a highly energetic part of the brain that supports higher intellectual functions. Deep in the core of the brain are the basal ganglia, which are stimulated by routine, familiar activities, forming and storing long-standing habits. In routine activity, the basal ganglia can function extremely well without conscious thought (e.g., riding a bike). Working memory, on the other hand, fatigues easily and can only store a small amount of information at any one time. However, as activities are repeated, they get pushed down to the habit center of the brain (the basal ganglia), thus freeing up processing resources in the prefrontal cortex (Rock & Schwartz, 2006).

The typical way people behave is deeply rooted in the basal ganglia. Additionally, when the human brain detects differences between expectation and actuality (i.e., being promised something only to receive something less desirable), another part of the brain is activated that stimulates fear and anger responses. When this part of the brain's circuitry is activated, it draws metabolic energy from the prefrontal region. The result is having animal instincts take over; people react more emotionally and impulsively. Therefore, changing hardwired habits requires great effort and attention and typically leads to feelings of discomfort. As a result, people naturally tend to avoid change (Rock & Schwartz, 2006).

In fact, one could argue that the brain is literally hardwired to resist change; it can behave like a 2-year-old and push back when it is told what to do. This is partly due to a function of homeostasis but is also reflective of the brain's innate desire to solve its own problems and create novel connections. When people work out their own solutions, the brain releases a rush of neurotransmitters like adrenaline. However, the more people try to get individuals to change or try to "fix" them, the more the brain sends out powerful signals that something is wrong; these signals readily overpower any rational thought.

Therefore, the change process works better when it starts with asking powerful questions of others designed to initiate new thoughts (Rock & Schwartz, 2006). Asking questions (as opposed to telling people what to do) allows people to initiate their own thoughts. This is a critical component to autonomy and, ultimately, engagement. However, these questions need to stem from a shift in perspective about motivation.

The Role of Motivation in Engagement

How do I motivate my employees? This is a common question asked by many leaders when trying to increase engagement. Before it can be answered, it is important to understand the two primary types of motivation. *Extrinsic motivation* is when one is driven to do something due to pressure or tangible rewards rather than for the fun or interest of it (Petri, 1991). *Intrinsic motivation* is doing an activity because it is interesting and the activity itself provides spontaneous satisfaction (Gagne & Deci, 2005). Essentially, extrinsic motivation uses a "carrot and stick" approach, where people do something because someone else is trying to get them to do it. Intrinsic motivation is when people do something because *they* want to do it. Research consistently shows that change efforts fail in the long run when based on "carrots and sticks" (e.g., Deci & Flaste, 1995; Gagne & Deci, 2005; Kohn, 1999; Pink, 2009), yet this approach is still predominant in organizations today. Ultimately, the key to effective healthcare organizations is moving away from extrinsic motivation toward intrinsic motivation.

The Pitfalls of Extrinsic Motivation

Human beings have a natural tendency to seek out new things and challenges and to explore and learn. Yet this natural tendency is stifled by the overuse of external rewards (Deci & Flaste, 1995). In his book, *Punished by Rewards,* Alfie Kohn (1999) cites numerous research studies to form his argument that, at best, rewards result in short-term behavior compliance— but at a great cost. Extrinsic motivation is not sustainable; once the reward is removed, the motivation vanishes. Furthermore, motivation will slowly decrease over time if the rewards stay at the same level; a bigger reward over time is required to get the same result. Contrary to popular belief, extrinsic rewards actually reduce intrinsic motivation; if a reward becomes the reason people are participating in an activity, that activity will be viewed as less enjoyable over time.

Extrinsic motivation can lead to participation but will not likely lead to engagement. It is important to note that engagement and participation are not the same. People can participate in an activity or initiative and simply go through the motions (especially with high external incentives), but it does not mean that there is commitment or that any behavior changes will continue outside of the program or incentive. Sustainable changes occur when people have high levels of engagement.

Therefore, if organizations ultimately want engagement, they must realize that it is not really possible to motivate other people; most attempts to motivate others fail and only result in compliance or participation. The *desire* to act cannot come from an external source; it can only come from within a person. All organizations can do is create conditions that maximize the likelihood that employees' needs, values, and interests will be met (Kohn, 1999). Unfortunately, most leaders and organizations operate from faulty and outdated assumptions about human potential and behavior. They continue to use various short-term incentive plans (i.e., a "carrot and stick" approach) to get employees to do what they want them to do. However, incentive plans and programs rarely work and are often harmful (Pink, 2009). Yet, even healthcare organizations are guilty of falling victim to such faulty assumptions.

The Failures of Negative Motivation

In health care, when the "carrot" approach does not work, the "stick" approach is frequently used, with attempts made to scare patients into making changes (e.g., "You must follow this treatment protocol or you will die."). Fear of punishment is also used within organizations to get employees to comply with rules and desired behaviors (including having healthcare workers take their own advice and make healthier choices). But does fear really work for long-term motivation and change? The evidence indicates that it does not.

Dr. Dean Ornish (2005) conducted research on heart patients who had double or quadruple bypass operations. These patients had a simple choice: They must make drastic lifestyle changes (i.e., eat healthy foods, stop smoking, reduce stress, exercise) or they would die. With avoiding death as the ultimate "motivator," only 10% were able to make sustainable lifestyle changes two years post operation. Dr. Ornish's program focused on teaching heart patients to appreciate life rather than fear death. The program included yoga, meditation, healthy diet, and stress counseling, all focused on having them enjoy life more; two years post operation, 70% of the patients made sustainable lifestyle changes. The difference is in the approach; having people look forward and build on what they wanted rather than looking back and simply trying to avoid a negative consequence ▪ resulted in greater success with long-term change.

Negative motivation also backfires at an organizational level. Focusing on short-term fixes through negative reinforcement may result in short-term behavior compliance that could temporarily help the organization financially; however, ownership and creativity of employees is reduced, thus limiting long-term benefits to the organization (Harter, Schmidt, & Keys, 2002). In the healthcare industry, patients are told daily to make drastic lifestyle changes or they will have serious medical complications; yet they still are not able to make changes. Behavior change is not as simple as finding a magic trick to motivate someone or telling them what to do in a different way. It requires a fundamental shift in how people think about their lives and their choices. It requires a shift to foster intrinsic motivation.

The Value of Intrinsic Motivation

The key to creativity, healthy behavior, and lasting change is intrinsic motivation (Deci & Flaste, 1995). Not surprisingly, the key to organizational effectiveness is having committed employees who are empowered and intrinsically motivated (Lahiry, 1994; Neck & Manz, 1992). In fact, people are most creative when they are primarily intrinsically motivated (Amabile, 1997); creativity marks the first step in innovation, which is critical for long-term organizational success in the healthcare industry. Organizations are able to enhance intrinsic motivation when they support and affirm people's perceived autonomy and competence (Deci & Flaste, 1995) and therefore foster self-leadership.

Self-leadership is another key to organizational effectiveness. It involves individuals redesigning their work world to bring out their best qualities and full potential by being their own ultimate leaders (Manz, 1991). Self-leadership moves beyond self-management strategies, which ultimately require reinforcement in order to be maintained, to emphasize the intrinsic value of tasks; intrinsic motivation in self-leadership stems from feeling competent, self-controlled, and having a sense of purpose (Manz, 1986). Therefore, creating an environment within healthcare organizations that fosters intrinsic motivation and self-leadership is critical to engagement, innovation, and long-term success.

Creating an Environment to Support Intrinsic Motivation

Since it is impossible to create motivation in others, the best way to foster intrinsic motivation is to create an environment that allows for intrinsic qualities to emerge. Intrinsic motivation can be viewed as empowerment, which is releasing the power from within people; this requires creating a culture of empowerment (Randolph, 2000). A culture of empowerment and intrinsic motivation can be created by:

- Having goals and rewards that are meaningful to people
- Having learning opportunities and activities that are important to people

- Having learning opportunities and activities that allow people to integrate themselves with others and the organizations so that they see a connection between what they want and what they have at work
- Promoting self-awareness and opportunities for having new thinking and new insights

The way organizations approach each of these to create an environment that supports a culture of empowerment is critical to how successful they will be. Ultimately, shifting people's thinking patterns is imperative for a healthcare organization in terms of sustaining a culture of empowerment and intrinsic motivation.

THE ROLE OF THINKING BEHIND MOTIVATION AND WHY INTRINSIC MATTERS

Motivation stems from how individuals think about themselves and the world around them; therefore, fostering intrinsic motivation requires first shifting thinking patterns. Neuroscience research indicates that expectations (whether conscious or unconscious) play a large role in perceptions. For example, two people working in the same customer service role in an organization could have different mental maps of the same customers. The first might only see the customers as unappreciative, immature whiners and subsequently only hear complaints; the second might see the customers as mature, concerned professionals and subsequently hear valuable suggestions for improvement. The *thinking*, or mental maps, is what makes the difference.

Consequently, one way to start facilitating change is to cultivate moments of insight; a complex set of new connections is created in the brain at a moment of insight that have the potential to overcome the natural resistance to change (Rock & Schwartz, 2006). As a result, it is argued that healthcare workers need to be clear about *why* they think and act as they do, and they need to perceive themselves as being empowered, in order to effectively meet the challenges of their profession (Bégat et al., 2005). Therefore, leaders who want to change the way people think or behave need to learn how to recognize, encourage, and deepen their team's insights because employees need to "own" any kind of change initiative in order for it to be successful (Rock & Schwartz, 2006). In order for leaders to shift how their employees think, they need to first understand how they themselves think and change their own thinking patterns. Understanding the core values that underlie people's thoughts and emotions can help establish a greater understanding of how people think and why the intrinsic dimension of thinking plays such an important role.

Values Thinking

Values drive thoughts and emotions. Axiological science, or value science, views core, habitual, and evaluative values as building blocks of an individual's personality, thinking, and understanding of others. It measures, assesses, and predicts likely emotional, motivational, and behavioral outcomes based on one's organization of three core dimensions of valuation that are common to everyone (Pomeroy, 2005). Dr. Robert Hartman (1967) developed a precise and operational definition of "good" and then constructed a profiling methodology derived from this mathematical model. The Hartman Value Profile (HVP) measures the sensitivity, balance, and order of influence of three core dimensions of valuation known as the Intrinsic (I), Extrinsic (E) and Systemic (S) dimensions of goodness. Hartman's hierarchy of values posits that intrinsic values have more worth than extrinsic values, and extrinsic values have more worth than systemic values. In simple terms, this means that people are valued more than things, and things are valued more than mere ideas of things or people; this is reflected with a simple equation: $I > E > S$ (Pomeroy, 2005). Table 8.1 describes each dimension in greater detail.

Examining I, E, and S within the context of a healthcare organization can help to better understand each dimension. The systemic dimension (S) is the organization itself; it is made up of a physical structure (i.e., buildings) and also has policies, procedures, and most likely a mission. Within the organization are many roles that make up the extrinsic dimension (E); this includes physicians, nurses, administration, specialists, patients, and others.

TABLE 8.1 Dimensions and Examples of Valuation

Valuation Dimension	Description	Example
I (Intrinsic)	The general capacity to distinguish the individuality, uniqueness, and intrinsic worth of self and others.	Unique, individual aspect of people; being in the moment and recognizing that things change from moment to moment; infinite possibilities; thinking includes that which is unknown and cannot be seen.
E (Extrinsic)	The general capacity to "see" and "do" with one's values.	Labels and categories; very practical; thinking is limited to what one knows or can see.
S (Systemic)	The general ability to think abstractly regarding rules, regulations, beliefs, and authorities.	Concepts and ideas; very either/or type of thinking (e.g., rules and regulations); available choices very limited based on this thinking.

Note: The descriptions in column 2 are from *The New Science of Axiological Psychology* by L. Pomeroy, 2005, New York: Rodopi.

There are also many labels that guide practices (i.e., diagnoses, procedures, past performance). The intrinsic dimension (I) includes the individual uniqueness of the people who fill each role and label. All three dimensions are needed, but they need to be in the proper order: I > E > S. Healthcare is designed around improving the health and wellbeing of people, yet too often the individual human (I) is ignored. As a result, healthcare organizations operate mostly within the E and S dimensions, thus leading to inefficiencies and challenges. However, if intrinsic capacity could be increased even just a small amount, the benefits would be profound.

What Happens When Intrinsic Thinking is Weak or Missing

When people lead with their E and S domains of thinking about others, they are limited in terms of what is possible because they are only working with what they can see, and they are working with their limited view. How often do people see others in terms of a label they have created for them? When people see someone and automatically think, "He/she is lazy and will never make a lifestyle change," or view a person as if he/she is a disease or condition, they minimize the contributions that that person can contribute to the outcome. Similarly, if leaders have labels for their employees, they will interact with them based on those labels (whether positive or negative). When people only work with what is apparent to them and their ideas about a person (E and S thinking), that person can never be anything other than those ideas about him or her. The result is judgment, impatience, frustration, and jumping to conclusions.

In our society, the intrinsic domain of thinking is inherently weak or missing; this means that our limited E and S thinking takes over, resulting in a great deal of judgment about people and the world. However, research shows that it is possible to increase and strengthen the intrinsic domain of thinking, also called *intrinsic capacity*. Intrinsic capacity refers to the general capacity one has to distinguish the individuality, uniqueness, and intrinsic worth of his or her self and others (Pomeroy, 2005). Because intrinsic capacity is so weak, increasing it even a little can have profound results and move a person to the optimum hierarchy of thinking: I > E > S. Leading with the intrinsic domain of thinking is recognizing that there is far more going on than anyone could possibly see and choosing to work with what is not merely apparent and honoring the uniqueness of others.

We know from neuroscience research that it takes time for new thoughts to become habits. Therefore, changing long-standing thinking patterns takes time and practice. Simply reading a book chapter or attending a seminar is not enough to spark a sustainable shift in thinking. However, recent research indicates it is possible to shift the hierarchy and build the skills necessary to be able to choose I > E > S as a habitual pattern of thinking. This shift takes time and dedication but appears to have profound benefits, and it offers great insight and practical application for healthcare organizations.

INCREASING INTRINSIC CAPACITY: A KEY TO FOSTERING INTRINSIC MOTIVATION

To date, the literature only substantiates one methodology that appears to be consistently effective in increasing intrinsic capacity and shifting thinking patterns to better reflect I > E > S. That methodology is Intrinsic Coaching®. It was developed by Christina Marshall of Totally Coached, Inc. and focuses on the thought styles and belief systems concerning good health choices and productivity within in individual's life and a corporate culture (Totally Coached, 2007). It is grounded in axiological science and is systematically validated by psychologist and biologist Leon Pomeroy, Ph.D. (Pomeroy, 2005). The core methodology is taught via a twelve-week phone-based course, the Intrinsic Coach® Development Series (ICDS). However, it appears that this methodology benefits people coached by someone trained as an Intrinsic Coach® as well as those who complete the ICDS. Current studies indicate that learning and using Intrinsic Coaching® measurably increases intrinsic capacity (Ward, 2006; Ward, 2008); improves life balance and life satisfaction (Ward, 2006; Ward, 2008); reduces health risk factors (Downs, 2007); and improves communication skills, work relationships, customer and client interactions, and personal relationships (Ward, 2008).

It is quite possible that other methodologies exist in addition to Intrinsic Coaching® that would also be effective in increasing intrinsic capacity; however, the research has yet to identify other approaches. What is more important is what the literature shows results from increased intrinsic capacity, which is a shift in how people view themselves and others. When people increased their intrinsic capacity, their thinking patterns shifted from focusing on the negative, being judgmental, and trying to fix things to focusing on the positive and true goal and recognizing that others have the solutions inside of them. People also found more meaning in their work. Finally, they reported shifting from acting based on habits and feeling like a victim of circumstances to acting based on what is important and recognizing that they can make a difference in their own lives (Ward, 2008).

Examples of the Benefits of Increased Intrinsic Capacity for Healthcare Workers

The best way to understand the importance and impact of increased intrinsic capacity for healthcare organizations is through real-life examples. Countless healthcare workers and leaders have shared impactful examples of how their approach to patient care shifted as their thinking shifted and their intrinsic capacity increased. One example involves a nurse who was brought into a situation involving a man who was "stubbornly refusing" to put his mother into hospice care. By doing so, he was prolonging his mother's suffering and depriving someone else of the bed. The other nurses had already labeled him as "difficult" because they could not change his mind; now it was this nurse's turn to work with him.

As she started talking to him, she began to put into practice the fundamental skill she had learned of seeing more than what is merely apparent, intentionally choosing to regard this man as capable, creative, and complete. Making this intentional choice disables the dominance of extrinsic and systemic thinking and allows for seeing beyond what is merely apparent and recognizing the uniqueness of others (i.e., working with the intrinsic domain of thinking about others). The nurse then asked him, "What are you wanting that is important to you regarding your mother's care?" That question (and her ability to listen more fully and not interrupt him) brought out a story no one previously knew because no one had asked the question. His mother had adopted him from an orphanage when he was little, and he felt she saved him and owed her his life. Now a team of healthcare professionals were asking him to give up on the woman who had never given up on him; he just could not do it.

The nurse's internal dialogue (her systemic thinking) gave her the impulse to start trying to convince him that he would not be giving up on her. However, she recognized it as just that—her trying to get him to replace his thoughts with hers, which is what everyone else had already been trying to do and judging him for refusing. With that recognition, she was able to stay quiet and listen some more to the man. Then she told him she was going to change his mother's dressings and asked him if he wanted to stay and see the extent of her condition; he said he did. Before, he had always been asked to leave, and now he had been asked to be a part of it (providing him with more extrinsic information than he previously had). As they talked, the man asked the nurse questions, and she answered them and also asked him what he was wanting for his mother's care based on what he was learning.

The nurse realized how limited she would have been by not leading with her intrinsic thinking with this man. By virtue of who she was being with him, he was also able to have new thinking and clarity about what he wanted for himself and his mother. His mother had dedicated everything she had to protect him from pain and surround him with all the comfort that she, as a loving mother, could provide. Now it was his turn to do the same for her, to protect her from pain and surround her with comfort, as only her loving son could do; it would be a hospice environment that would best support him in giving his mother all that he wanted for her. By being able to tap into her intrinsic domain of thinking (as a result of having increased intrinsic capacity), this nurse was able to provide a completely different experience for herself as well as for her patient and her patient's son. The other nurses were amazed that she was able to "get through" to this man, but this nurse knew that her shift in thinking was what made all the difference.

This story is not unlike hundreds of other stories of healthcare workers describing being able to suspend their judgments about patients to listen more fully, thus allowing them to provide better care. Others describe having less frustration because instead of "dumping their expertise" on patients, they are able to provide information but then engage the patients' *thinking* about the information; this way, they are making the patient more important than the information (i.e., making the intrinsic [I] more important than the extrinsic [E]). Healthcare workers have also described having less job-related stress when approaching people from an I > E > S paradigm as well as higher levels of job satisfaction (Ward, 2008). One physician described having a lower level of anxiety:

> Its' not my job to fix people; it's my job to tap into their good thinking.... I can help them; I can give them expertise when it's needed. I can be the expert at the time that I need to be. But the majority of what I do when people come in and say "I'm tired; I'm depressed and I can't get my diabetes and hypertension, obesity under control"—all that kind of stuff; that's all intrinsic stuff. I used to feel so frustrated that I couldn't fix them. Well it's not my job to fix them. It's my job to help them to fix themselves. I'm sort of the translator from medicine science to their health and how it applies, but I'm not the one who's going to be there telling them to take a pill and shoving a pill down their throat every day.

Too often, the communication between healthcare workers and clients is one-sided, with the healthcare worker holding most of the power in the relationship (Thomason & Lagowski, 2008). However, research has shown that clients are more empowered to take a larger role in decisions affecting their health when the decision-making power is shifted from nurses to clients (Hickey & Kipping, 1998). Furthermore, treatment adherence increases when nurses and clients collaborate in planning their care, which results in improved health for the client (Huffman, 2005). Therefore, it would seem that increasing intrinsic capacity and building skills surrounding using an I > E > S approach would provide great benefit for patient care outcomes. Consequently, the key is to find the best way to increase intrinsic capacity among healthcare leaders and healthcare workers.

HOW TO INCREASE INTRINSIC CAPACITY

Increasing intrinsic capacity takes time and starts with intentional focus on shifting thinking patterns. Using an extrinsic, strategic approach to increase intrinsic capacity is counterproductive to how the intrinsic domain of thinking functions. That being said, it is quite possible that multiple methodologies exist that may increase intrinsic capacity; however, Intrinsic Coaching® is the only methodology currently proven in the research to do so. Many coaching approaches look similar; the fundamental difference is the *thinking* behind the questions being asked and who is guiding the conversation. As long as the coach is asking questions based on his/her thinking about the coachee and the coachee's situation (i.e., what is merely apparent), the coach will ask questions based on his/her expertise (E) rather than the uniqueness of the coachee in that moment (I). This approach keeps the coachee's thinking in the E and S dimensions. The intrinsic dimension can only be elicited when the coach leads the conversation from a different pattern of thinking (I > E > S). Therefore, until more data is available to definitively show which approaches are the best for increasing intrinsic capacity, much can still be learned from existing research.

Based on what is known today, if leaders and organizations want to have increased intrinsic capacity and operate under a paradigm of I > E > S, developmental opportunities should be provided to increase intrinsic capacity. Knowing it will take time for the brain to overcome its natural resistance to change and make the new thinking patterns habitual, organizations would benefit from having leaders participate in training and development first (since they set the tone for the organization) and then expand to employees. One possible way to do this could include having leaders complete formal training in Intrinsic Coaching® or work with an executive coach trained in Intrinsic Coaching®. In the meantime, some of the fundamental skills that leaders can put into practice right away include:

- *Really listen to people without judgment;* choose to see more than your labels (E), ideas, and judgments (S) about another person and recognize there is far more going on than you can see (I). Approach each person and each situation with a beginner's mind and create a space for what is not merely apparent. When you find yourself wanting to jump in and offer your ideas, hold back and instead listen and tell yourself, "It's not about me; it's about *them.*" This allows you to lead with your intrinsic domain of thinking, putting the person

before the information or your labels and ideas about that person
(I > E > S).

- *Ask forward-moving questions that get to the core of what is important to the other person and what that person wants.* For example, ask, "What are you wanting for yourself in this situation?" or "When you think about X, what comes to mind that is important for you?" These questions elicit a person's intrinsic domain of thinking and allow for moving beyond strategies to find clarity. Another way to think about I > E > S is that gaining clarity (I) will better inform the next steps (E and S) and help people select the strategies that will be most effective in bringing them closer to what they want.

- *Stay focused on the goal rather than focusing on the problem.* Too often, people focus on problems or barriers when approaching change (partially due to the brain resisting change). This is not productive and keeps people stuck. Consider when someone is complaining: There is a goal inside of that complaint; there is something that person wants that he or she is not getting. By focusing on what the person wants (I), you are able to stay solution-focused and gain clarity to help better move forward beyond the excuses and being stuck. Therefore, leaders can effectively change their own or other people's behaviors by first shifting thinking—choosing to leave problem behaviors in the past and instead focusing on solutions. Using solution-focused questioning facilitates self-insight and starts the connection process so that the brain is less likely to resist change; advice giving does not allow for self-insight (Rock & Schwartz, 2006).

Being able to put simple skills into practice to better work with more than what is merely apparent is important in fostering a shift in thinking and creating a space for more intrinsic to emerge. This becomes especially important in healthcare organizations during times of goal setting since goals are frequently used as a method for increasing motivation. The use of goals and goal setting can become much more effective when created with a paradigm of I > E > S.

FOSTERING ENGAGEMENT AND INTRINSIC THINKING THROUGH EFFECTIVE GOAL SETTING

Organizations regularly use goal setting as a method for improving performance and increasing motivation. However, organizational goals are too often set without including input from the people expected to achieve them. A sense of belonging to something beyond oneself is an important component of employee engagement (Baumeister & Leary, 1995). Therefore, when decisions are made in organizations that affect employees, it is important that their opinions be heard and that employees be involved in the decisions. If an organization sets goals that involve employees but does not include the employees in the process of creating the goals, it is setting itself up for failure and is only working with the extrinsic and systemic domains of thinking. A recent article examined the side effects of over-prescribed goal setting, including sacrificing quality for quantity, increased risky behaviors, inhibited learning, and decreased intrinsic motivation (Ordonez, Schweitzer, Galinsky, & Bazerman, 2009). Therefore, understanding goals under the I > E > S framework is important.

Distinguishing Between Goals and Strategies

When operating from a framework of I > E > S, goals provide an opportunity for learning, allow for considering long-term and short-term needs, and provide opportunities for everyone to have a personal, meaningful connection to the goals. In order for this to occur, it is important to distinguish between *goals* and *strategies*. Consider that a *goal* is really the intrinsic dimension (I) and provides the clarity and vision for what people want for themselves and the organization. It is like the vision or North Star guiding next steps. Therefore, a goal is framed more as a state of being. What is typically called a *goal* is really an extrinsic strategy designed to get to something; that "something" is the true goal.

True goals align with individuals' values and describe what is important to them or the organization and what they ultimately want (e.g., excellence in patient care; a culture where employees thrive). Once that clarity (I) is determined, it can inform the strategies (E) and structures (S) put in place to meet the goal (e.g., to shorten patient wait times by 10%, to create learning opportunities for employees, etc.). Those strategies might follow the S.M.A.R.T. format (*specific, measurable, actionable, realistic,* and *timely*). Taking time to gain clarity first allows the next steps to emerge; it allows for more effectively selecting the best way to meet the goal. In other words, use I > E > S to clarify true goals first, then build strategies to met the goals.

The following example illustrates how this might be used within an organization. An organization has felt the impact of the challenges of today's economy and decided to do a small number of layoffs a few months ago and implemented a wage freeze. Research reports have indicated that the real impact felt on employees left behind occurs 4 to 6 months later, in terms of increased stress, anxiety, and feeling overwhelmed. The energy in the organization has dropped and employees seem to be less engaged—at a time when innovation and outstanding patient care are critical. In addition, the leaders are concerned about what the impact will be long-term with healthcare costs, worker compensation costs, and productivity, but they are hesitant to investing in anything that does not seem to provide some immediate results. They are concerned about the business surviving without more layoffs, but they also recognize that there may be long-term issues if employee engagement is not addressed. *As a leader of this organization, how would you start to address the challenges facing your organization?*

One common approach would be to start strategizing and trying to figure out the pros and cons of multiple options. Another, more effective approach is to take a step back and approach this with I > E > S thinking. The first step is to acknowledge the systemic realities of what is happening with the economy and the organization and then start asking questions to get clear about what the true goal is in this situation. Some questions that could be asked to gain clarity are:

- Given what has transpired, what are we wanting that is important to our business? (A)
- What does (answer to A) look like?
- What does success in accomplishing (A) look like?
- What does having (A) provide to our business? To our employees?

These are some questions that reflect the thinking process of staying in the intrinsic dimension of thinking and spending the time necessary to get completely clear about the goal (I), or what people want from this situation. Once they have clarity, they can start exploring the strategies (E and S) that will help them to achieve their goal. Some questions to consider asking to determine which next steps make the most sense are:

- How will we know we have achieved (A)?)
- How will we determine our progress along the way to having (A)?
- What support/structure do we need to have in place in order for (A) to be a reality?
- What approach(es) seem to fit best, given (A)?
- What do we need to keep in mind as we work toward (A)?
- How will our solutions integrate to create a culture that supports health, safety, and employee engagement?

In addition to approaching goal setting using I > E > S, it is important to also use this approach to ask employees what is important to them and what they are wanting for themselves and for the organization. Including them in the goal setting process using I > E > S will increase the chances of them being engaged in the change process and, therefore, being more engaged in their work. Shifting thinking throughout the organization to a pattern of I > E > S can not only improve goal setting and engagement, but it can also provide a solid foundation to provide a sustainable culture of engagement, performance, and wellbeing.

SHIFTING TO A CULTURE OF WELLBEING AND ENGAGEMENT THROUGH I > E > S

Although some organizational transformation may involve changing the culture, Scheimann (1992) states that "the worst way to change culture is by 'changing culture'" (p. 37). Furthermore, Schein (2009) argues that a new culture cannot actually be created. Leaders can merely support a change in behaviors and attitudes that, if successful, will become part of a new culture. Unless underlying assumptions are addressed, successful change will not be possible because the organization will eventually revert to how it originally operated (Schein, 1985). Therefore, it would seem that changing thinking patterns of people within an organization would be an effective way to change attitudes (which leads to a change in behavior) and ultimately shift a culture.

Based on what is known about culture, engagement, neuroscience, and motivation, one could argue that creating a culture of I > E > S would benefit healthcare organizations on multiple levels. The question then becomes, *How is a culture of I > E > S created?* Because leaders go hand-in-hand with culture, providing learning and development opportunities for leaders to increase intrinsic capacity so that they think and lead using an I > E > S framework would likely be quite impactful for internal operations. Additionally, providing healthcare workers with training and skill development to shift their thinking to I > E > S would also provide great benefit to patient care. One hospital system is doing just that—working to become an intrinsic organization.

Beaumont Hospital: An Example of I > E > S in Action

Beaumont Hospital is an example of a healthcare organization putting I > E > S into practice at multiple levels of the organization; they are working to become an "intrinsic organization." In 2008, staff from Beaumont Hospital's corporate university began learning Intrinsic Coaching®. They found that they were able to apply their newfound thinking skills in most of their professional practice areas as well as in their personal relationships. In addition to using I > E > S in one-on-one encounters, they began using it as they taught courses, facilitated workshops, and provided consulting services. By leading with I > E > S thinking in their roles, the corporate university staff members were better able to put people and their thinking about the information provided ahead of the information itself. The result is greater learning within the hospital university and a more profound impact.

For example, the corporate university staff members found that their services were enhanced as they weaved I > E > S into how they presented materials and facilitated sessions. At the beginning of the class sessions, they now do two things: (1) They assume that all of their learners are capable, creative, and complete; and (2) they start by asking each individual what they are wanting, which allows the intrinsic to emerge. Although there are always published course objectives (S), the university team is not ignoring them; they are enhancing them by simply bringing more intrinsic into the sessions. By asking participants what they want out of the session, the intent is to create a space where they can focus more on goals instead of strategies. The corporate university staff also challenges participants to explore what they are wanting (i.e., their goal) rather than a strategy. Then by listening and truly trying to learn their perspectives, the corporate university staff is better able to direct the session to best address what the participants want.

Jean Ann Larson, Chief Learning Officer, states,

> At Beaumont University, we say we are building capacity, one individual and one team at a time. Organizations can only learn if teams are learning and are willing to learn from each other. The first step is being able to help people self-manage and get out of the way of the process so that everyone can find their best thinking around what is most important. Development is an emerging process that is continuously unfolding.

I > E > S provides Beaumont Hospital and Beaumont University a framework with which to engage employees and help them bring their best thinking to work with their patients.

Beaumont Hospital recognizes that it cannot succeed as an organization if its people do not succeed. One of the key metrics it watches closely is employee engagement, using the Gallup Q12® engagement survey tool. Based on what they learn, managers initiate impact training plans. Being able to tap into best thinking (I > E > S) allows the corporate university staff to partner with managers to ask their teams what they are wanting before jumping into solutions and training programs. By involving the teams and engaging them through using I > E > S, they are able to allow everyone to contribute to the solution and design what they want for their teams and how they deliver patient care.

As OD practitioners, the staff of Beaumont University recognized that their thinking and approach had to change. This included listening more deeply and supporting their clients in finding their best thinking; the conversation then became less about their expertise and more about their client. They recognized that one-size solutions do not fit everyone. Shifting their approach by using I > E > S thinking has increased their effectiveness while also providing personal benefits. Beaumont is one example of the momentum that can build from having increased intrinsic capacity within an organization. Being able to use I > E > S in their daily interactions is allowing them to be more effective with strategic planning, corporate learning objectives, and problem solving. A great deal can be learned from what Beaumont is doing and can be applied in other healthcare organizations.

PUTTING I > E > S INTO PRACTICE IN YOUR ORGANIZATION

Hopefully it is evident that I, E, and S are dimensions of thinking that are all necessary; they just need to be in the proper order (I > E > S) for people and organizations to be effective. Furthermore, because intrinsic capacity is so weak in our society, increasing it just a little can have profound results. Therefore, the best thing leaders can do to increase engagement is to put the person first, before their role or any information. This requires a shift in thinking, promoting a constant learning environment, and engaging employees in any change process by building on their strengths and asking forward-moving questions to elicit their best thinking (I > E > S) and new insights.

Using a framework of I > E > S is not ignoring the very real systemic aspects of organizations; it is simply allowing more of the intrinsic to emerge. For example, suppose that you are the manager of Sue. She has had an attendance issue lately and has now missed the maximum number of non-pre-approved days off. If she misses one more day, disciplinary action will need to be taken. Therefore, you need to address this with Sue. If you were to approach Sue leading with your systemic thinking, you might simply say, "The policy is that you can't miss more than 5 days that aren't pre-approved; if you miss one more day, I'll have to write you up." Although this is true, and the systemic reality of Sue's attendance needs to be addressed, this leaves very few options for her to find her best thinking or be successful. If you were to bring in more of your extrinsic thinking, you might also start strategizing with Sue for how she could make sure to not miss any more days; again, this is limiting. However, you could bring more intrinsic into this situation by acknowledging the systemic (i.e., her attendance and the policy). Then, building on that, you might say, "I'd really like to support you in being successful in this organization. What might you want or need in order to be successful, given what is going on?" With that, a door is opened for Sue to talk about what she wants; now you both can work with more than what is merely apparent; you are now able to work by including the intrinsic.

Numerous opportunities exist for bringing I > E > S into healthcare organizations to create a culture that fosters learning, values employees, and increases engagement. Once leaders understand what employees value and want, they are better able to partner with them to build on their strengths and let them find their own way to be successful within the organization. This requires encouraging their team to deepen their insights (these insights and new thinking are critical in developing new mental maps to overcome the brain's resistance to change), recognizing that culture is essential to engagement, and understanding the missing link in engagement is intrinsic thinking (however, extrinsic and systemic are needed to support intrinsic thinking). Therefore, when using tools and resources (e.g., performance reviews, Strengths Finder®, surveys, focus groups, etc.), make the information *second* to the person. If there were such a thing as a magic formula that promotes engagement, it would be I > E > S.

REFERENCES

Accident Compensation Corporation. (2004). *New Zealand acute low back pain guide.* Retrieved from http://www.nzgg.org.nz/guidelines/0072/acc1038_col.pdf

Amabile, T. M. (1997). Motivating creativity in organizations: On doing what you love and loving what you do. *California Management Review, 40*(1), 39–58.

Anderson, D. R. (2002). Participation builders to increase ROI. *Absolute Advantage, 1*(8), 64–67.

Baumeister, R. F., & Leary, M. F. (1995). The need to belong: Desire for interpersonal attachments as a fundamental human motivation. *Psychological Bulletin, 117*(3), 497.

Bégat, I., Ellefsen, B., & Severinsson, E. (2005). Nurses' satisfaction with their work environment and the outcomes of clinical nursing supervision on nurses' experiences of wellbeing: A Norwegian study. *Journal of Nursing Management, 13* (3), 221–230.

Butterworth, T., Carson, J., Jeacock, J., & White, E. (1999). Stress, coping, burnout and job satisfaction in British nurses: Findings from the clinical supervision evaluation project. *Stress Medicine, 15,* 27–33.

Casida, J., & Pinto-Zipp, G. (2008). Leadership-organizational culture relationship in nursing units of acute care hospitals. *Nursing Economic$, 26*(1), 7–15.

Crabtree, S. (2005). Engagement keeps the doctor away. *Gallup Management Journal Online,* 1–5. Retrieved from http://gmj.gallup.com/content/14500/Engagement-Keeps-Doctor-Away.aspx

Deci, E. L., & Flaste, R. (1995). *Why we do what we do: Understanding self-motivation.* London: Penguin Books.

Downs, S. (2007, August). *Healthy employee 2010 pilot program: First year evaluation report.* Unpublished manuscript.

Edmondson, A. (2003). Speaking up in the operating room: How team leaders promote learning in interdisciplinary action teams. *Journal of Management Studies, 40,* 1419–1452.

Gagne, M. & Deci, E. L. (2005). Self-determination theory and work motivation. *Journal of Organizational Behavior, 26,* 331–362.

Harter, J. K., Schmidt, F. L., & Keys, C. L. M. (2003). Wellbeing in the workplace and its relationship to business outcomes: A review of the Gallup studies. In C. L. M. Keys & H. Haidt (Eds.), *Flourishing: The positive person and the good life* (pp. 205–224). Washington, D.C.: American Psychological Association.

Hartman, R. S. (1967). *The structure of value.* Carbondale, IL: Southern Illinois University Press.

Hickey, G., & Kipping, C. (1998). Exploring the concept of user involvement in mental health through a participation continuum. *Journal of Clinical Nursing, 7*(1), 83–88.

Huffman, M. H. (2005). Compliance, health outcomes, and partnering in PPS: Acknowledging the patient's agenda. *Home Healthcare Nurse, 23*(1), 23–28.

Kohn, A. (1999). *Punished by rewards.* New York: Houghton Mifflin.

Kruger, J., & Killham, E. (2006, March). Why Dilbert is right. *Gallup Management Journal Online,* 1–8. Retrieved from http://gmj.gallup.com/content/21802/Why-Dilbert-Right.aspx

Lahiry, S. (1994). Building commitment through organizational culture. *Training & Development, 48*(4), 50–52.

Mastal, M. F., Joshi, M., & Schulke, K. (2007). Nursing leadership: Championing quality and patient safety in the boardroom. *Nursing Economic$, 25*(6), 323–330.

Manz, C. C. (1991). Self-leadership...the heart of empowerment. *The Journal for Quality and Participation, 15*(4), 80–85.

Manz, C. (1986). Self-leadership: Toward an expanded theory of self-influence processes in organizations. *Academy of Management Review, 11*(3), 585–600.

Manz, C. C. & Neck, C. P. (1991). Inner leadership: Creating productive thought patterns. *The Executive, 5*(3), 87–95.

Neck, C. P., & Manz, C. C. (1992). Thought self-leadership: The influence of self-talk and mental imagery on performance. *Journal of Organizational Behavior, 13*(7), 681–699.

O'Donnell, M. (2007, March). *Building health promotion into national health policy.* Session presented at the 2007 Art and Science of Health Promotion Conference, San Francisco, CA.

Ordonez, L. D., Schweitzer, M. E., Galinsky, A. D., & Bazerman, M. H. (2009). Goals gone wild: The systematic side-effects of over-prescribing goal-setting. *Academy of Management Perspectives, 23*(1), 6–16.

Ornish, D. (2005, March). Keynote presented at the 2005 Art and Science of Health Promotion Conference, San Francisco, CA.

Petri, H. (1991). *Motivation: Theory, research and application* (3rd ed.). Belmont, CA: Wadsworth.

Pink, D. H. (2009). *Drive: The surprising truth about what motivates us.* New York: Berkley.

Pomeroy, L. (2005). *The new science of axiological psychology.* New York: Rodopi.

Randolph, W.A. (2000). Re-thinking empowerment: Why is it so hard to achieve? *Organizational Dynamics, 20*(2), 94–107.

Rock, D., & Schwartz, J. (2006, Summer). The neuroscience of leadership. *Strategy+Business, 43,* 1–10.

Schiemann, W. A. (1992). Organizational change: Lessons from a turnaround. *Management Review, 81*(4), 34–37.

Schein, E. H. (2009). *The corporate culture survival guide.* San Francisco: Jossey-Bass.

Schein, E. H. (1985). *Organizational culture and leadership.* San Francisco: Jossey Bass.

Thomason, D. L., & Lagowski, L. R. (2008). Sustaining a healthy work force in the 21st century: A model for collaborating through reciprocation. *American Association of Occupational Health Nurses Journal, 56*(12), 503–513.

Totally Coached. (2007). *About us.* Retrieved from http://www.totallycoached.com

Towers Perrin. (2008, August). *Building a more engaged health care workforce.* Retrieved from http://www.towersperrin.com/tp/getwebcachedoc?country=global&webc=USA/2009/200908/HarvardForcesWhitePaper.pdf

Ward, R. (2006). *Lifestyle makeover program: Results from a 6-month pilot program utilizing weekly Intrinsic Coaching® sessions.* Unpublished manuscript, Northwestern Health Sciences University.

Ward, R. (2008). *The relationship of individual intrinsic capacity with job satisfaction, organizational commitment, and perceived life balance: An exploratory study of the Intrinsic Coaching®* (Doctoral dissertation, Capella University, 2008). Available from ProQuest Digital Dissertations. (UMI No. 3329852).

PART IV

NEW VIEWS

CHAPTER 9

LEADING IMPORTANT CONVERSATIONS

The Schwartz Center Rounds®

Kathryn Kaplan

ABSTRACT

Unlike most traditional rounds in healthcare, the Schwartz Center Rounds® focus on difficult cases that are particularly stressful or evoke strong emotional responses. Facilitated by the Chief Learning Officer at Maimonides Medical Center in Brooklyn, NY, the institution has a contract with The Schwartz Center in Boston, MA to implement their signature program. This chapter examines the further contribution of healthcare OD in shaping the Rounds as part of an integrated and robust program for organizational change and leadership development. A case example illustrates how the internal OD practitioner and physician partner lead these important conversations at Maimonides. Seven challenges are presented with strategies to address them. Evaluation data and survey results reveal the impact of the Rounds on communication, empathy, teamwork, and patient care. The synergy of the Schwartz Center Rounds with OD in healthcare creates a potent process for developing healthcare professionals and influencing culture change.

Organization Development in Health Care, pages 173–196
Copyright © 2011 by Information Age Publishing
All rights of reproduction in any form reserved.

THE SCHWARTZ CENTER ROUNDS®

The Schwartz Center Rounds® are the legacy of Kenneth B. Schwartz, who was diagnosed with terminal lung cancer at age 40. As a lawyer and health-care advocate, he knew a lot about the healthcare system and the pressures from managed care, budget cuts, and regulatory agencies, and their impact on staff morale. However, he was not prepared for the pain of leaving his wife, two-year-old son, and life that he loved. As he stated in his July 16, 1995 story published in *The Boston Globe Magazine,* he was surprised at how much the engagement and kindness of his caregivers "made the unbearable bearable" (p. 1). Right before he died, Ken amended his will to form a center dedicated to strengthening the patient–caregiver relationship. The Center's signature program is the Schwartz Center Rounds®. Unlike most traditional rounds that focus on diagnosis and treatment planning or ethical issues and problem solving, the Schwartz Center Rounds® concentrate on difficult cases that are particularly stressful or evoke strong emotional responses for caregivers. These multidisciplinary Rounds provide an avenue for staff to talk openly about their feelings and coping strategies.

The proliferation of the Rounds, originating at Massachusetts General Hospital in 1997 and now in over 182 sites across the country, demonstrates the growing community of practitioners committed to furthering Ken's vision for compassionate health care. The Schwartz Center Rounds®, as originally conceived and as described in the contract with each institution, are one-hour sessions held monthly or every other month. The Rounds are headed by a physician leader and facilitated by a neutral party skilled in facilitating, such as a psychologist or social worker who is typically external to the organization. An interdisciplinary committee plans and coordinates the selection of a case, preparation of the presenters, and the submitting of evaluations.

This chapter examines the contribution of healthcare OD in shaping the Rounds as part of an integrated and robust program for organizational change and leadership development. None of these functions require, nor does the Schwartz Center suggest, that an internal OD practitioner facilitate the Rounds or co-chair the committee. However, based on our experience, the Rounds offer a fertile ground for OD in health care to take the lead.

The components of the Rounds that make them a natural fit for OD in health care include:

- The facilitation of important conversations: Encouraging dialogue and respect for each other as professionals and for humanity common to all; and compassion for patients, providers, and oneself that leads to deeper connections across differences.

- The system-wide focus: Bringing in disciplines and departments from the entire institution—essentially a form of large-group intervention.
- The orientation to organizational learning: Changing the norms over time about what can be discussed and what the culture values, loosening the hierarchy so common in healthcare, and striving to create a more healthy organization.
- The focus on people and process: Capitalizing on OD's expertise with program development and buy-in, conditions for successful integration of initiatives, and factors that foster more effective teamwork.
- The emphasis on care for the caregivers: Aligning with OD's core mission in health care to help the staff and leaders care for themselves and each other so that they can provide better care for patients and their families, directly or indirectly.

MAIMONIDES MEDICAL CENTER

The Schwartz Center Rounds® illustrate a case example for OD in health care to influence the values and culture of a large, urban, 705-bed tertiary care community and teaching hospital located in Brooklyn, New York. With over 6,000 extremely diverse staff (more than 70 languages are spoken), the Rounds provide a unique forum for developing institution-wide, interdisciplinary communication and understanding. Facilitated by the Chief Learning Officer (CLO) in partnership with the physician leader, the forum gives participants a safe place to explore together the social and emotional dilemmas of being care providers. Aligned with the other leadership development initiatives of the medical center, the Rounds contribute to organizational learning and culture change. A brief description of some of the other initiatives at Maimonides Medical Center provide the context in which the Rounds exist and the reasons why it is important in our culture.

A leadership development steering committee, chaired by the CEO with close guidance and support from the Senior Vice President of Nursing and the Vice President of Human Resources, has set the direction and priorities for the creation of programs to enhance workforce development. When the CLO was hired five years ago, a strategic alliance already existed with structured processes to strengthen labor and management relations and worker participation in decisions impacting departmental outcomes (Maimonides Medical Center, 2007). In addition, a nursing leadership academy had begun. To further development, the executive team asked the CLO to design a physician leadership development program in partnership with a Vice President, a dynamic surgeon who completed an MBA. Over three years, a cadre of physician leaders was developed and demonstrates the value of the program (Kaplan & Feldman, 2008). The nurse and physician leadership programs eventually were merged to address nurse–physician relations, challenges, and projects. Once these programs met their objectives, they evolved over several years into a similar leadership development program for non-clinical managers. (See Figure 9.1 for a graphical representation of current core programs.)

The CLO was also asked to conduct an organizational needs assessment and identify other areas for future focus. Particularly important was the potential for making respect not only a core value on paper in the innovative Code of Mutual Respect, but more importantly the norm for professional behavior in practice (Brier, 2009). Through a top-down and grassroots approach focusing on one department at a time, a multifaceted program was designed. Over three years of data from a Respect Survey indicates statistically significant results in willingness to speak up when someone violates the Code and the ability of leaders to handle disrespectful behavior effectively (Kaplan, Mestel, & Feldman, 2010). In addition to institution-wide efforts, focused strategic team and leadership development initiatives in areas such as the Ambulatory Health Services Network and the new Cancer Center used a similar approach to change and achieved similar results (Kaplan & Patel, 2009). Due to the financial context of health care, Maimonides is creating programs to enhance patient satisfaction and cost containment. A number of publications provide additional background and outcomes of Maimonides' culture and strategies for change (e.g., Feldman & Kaplan, 2007; Johnson, 2008; Salamon, 2008; Whitney, 2007).

The Schwartz Center Rounds® represent another strategic program aligned with the leadership development initiatives to enhance respect and contribute to culture change. A physician who leads the Rounds at a hospital in Rhode Island approached Dr. Alan Astrow, Division Director

Figure 9.1 Core programs.

of Medical Oncology and Hematology at the Maimonides Cancer Center, and asked if he would be willing to sponsor the Schwartz Center Rounds at Maimonides. Dr. Astrow has a strong interest in the spiritual aspects of healing and is known throughout the medical community for his commitment to caring for the whole patient—mind and body (Astrow & Sulmasy, 2004). Dr. Astrow put together a committee to explore interest in such an endeavor. He asked the CLO to be the facilitator and to use her skills in OD to weave the Schwartz Center Rounds® into the medical center's agenda for an explicit culture of mutual respect and leadership development.

THE ROUNDS AT MAIMONIDES

Maimonides began the Rounds in January of 2008, meeting bimonthly, and has conducted 12 Rounds to date. (See Table 9.1 for titles and themes.) The Schwartz Center offers expertise, resources, and support to help hospitals start the Rounds. While each institution puts its own stamp on the Rounds, each is consistent in duration (one hour), format, and purpose. The Rounds begin with a brief presentation of a case that serves as a catalyst for discussion. The panel typically consists of three professionals from different disciplines who speak about their experience with and response to the patient situation. The physician leader and facilitator moderate the discussion,

TABLE 9.1 Titles and Themes

Date	Titles and Themes of Rounds at Maimonides
1/8/2008	Rescuing the Patient: Navigating the Treacherous Waters of the Large Family (Breast Cancer Program)
3/11/2008	When the Unthinkable Happens, Right Before Our Eyes (Labor and Delivery)
5/13/2008	Communicating Goals of Care: Disconnects and Discontinuity (Geriatrics)
7/8/2008	Witnessing a Patient Assault: The Emotional Impact on Treatment Planning (Psychiatry)
9/9/2008	Hope in the Face of Adversity: Being Inspired by Patients and Families (Pediatrics)
11/11/2008	Caring for the Young Adult with a Life Threatening Illness (Surgical Oncology)
1/13/2009	When Doctors Disagree: Do Sparks Have to Fly? (Cardiothoracic Surgery)
3/10/2009	The Longest Month: Caring for the Impossible Patient (Internal Medicine)
5/12/2009	When Doctors and Nurses Become Patients: Taking Care of Each Other (CTICU Step-down Unit)
7/14/2009	H1N1: Professional Responsibility/Personal Risk (Medical ICU)
9/8/2009	Life in the ER: Whom Do You Trust? (Pediatric ED)
11/10/2009	Knocking Your Head Against the Wall: Treating the "Non-Compliant" Patient (Ambulatory Network, Primary Care)

beginning with an introduction to set the stage, especially for first-time attendees. The discussion is designed to generalize from the specific situation
to the broader experiences of those in the audience based on their own patients, memories, and responses. Toward the end, the facilitator synthesizes
the themes and reminds the participants to fill out the evaluations.

The Rounds are publicized with a flyer attached to a mass email to all
the Maimonides users at least a week before the Rounds and a voice mail
reminder the day of the session. The dates are established for the year and
sent out in advance. Attendance consistently averages about 150 participants, representing a wide range of departments (e.g., Academic Affairs,
the Blood Bank, ED, Finance, Geriatrics, Internal Medicine) and disciplines
(e.g., clergy, librarians, OT and PT, social workers, psychologists, nurses,
doctors, case managers, patient representatives, students, and administrators). When participants sign in, they are provided with resources relevant
to the case, such as an article from the Schwartz Center or our institution-
specific guidelines on "Ways to Participate in the Rounds."

Various locations were utilized for the first few sessions; seating "in the
round" in a crowded standing-room-only auditorium evolved as the ideal
setting. The leaders, panelists, and participants learn from each Rounds
how to have important conversations without solving problems or making plans. Because this differs from the purpose of a formal grand rounds
presentation, root cause analysis, or performance improvement meeting,
it takes a while for healthcare providers to understand this low-tech, non-
traditional approach. Yet, based on the full attendance and passionate participation, there seems to be a hunger for this type of reflection and exploration of complex themes.

CASE EXAMPLE

Our tenth Rounds, titled *H1N1: Professional Responsibility/Personal Risk*, was
selected as a topic due to the recent onslaught of admissions to rule out
the diagnosis of Swine Flu. Not only were healthcare providers facing compassion fatigue (emotional exhaustion and lessening of empathy) from
the increased number of patients, but also they were concerned for their
own health. The panel consisted of an attending physician specializing in
infectious disease, a nurse manager from the Medical Intensive Care Unit,
and an infection control practitioner. The synopsis of the case, written by
the physician, was printed for each member of the audience prior to beginning the rounds:

A 27-year-old pregnant (32 weeks) South Asian woman was admitted to Labor
& Delivery for fetal monitoring after she sustained a fall. While being moni-

tored she was noted to have a fever accompanied by productive cough. The timing of her presentation coincided with the beginning of the Swine Flu epidemic in the United States. Hence, antimicrobial treatment for both viral and bacterial pneumonia was begun and the patient was placed in appropriate isolation. She was then transferred to the medical ICU as her clinical condition worsened. She required mechanical ventilation, had an emergent c-section, and ultimately had to be transferred to another hospital for further care.

The patient was admitted early in the epidemic, when the Center for Disease Control and the New York City Department of Health were changing their guidelines frequently to adapt to the most recent information and predictions. The physician stressed how hard it was to enter the room due to the severity of the illness in such a young woman who did not speak English, nor did she allow males to touch her (fortunately, the attending physician was a female). The nurse manager spoke about how responsible the nurses were who took care of the patient, but how unusual it was to have an emergency c-section in the ICU and how concerned the nurses were about exposure for themselves and their families. The infection control practitioner addressed the evolving nature of the situation and how difficult that was for healthcare providers who wanted certainty when in fact there was none.

The discussion then was opened to the participants at large with contributions from new residents and experienced physicians, nurses who worked with the patient and those from other units, other infection control providers, a psychologist, a social worker, and representatives from over 30 different departments. The themes included:

- A clinician's fear of contracting a serious disease from a patient (H1N1, AIDS, TB) often surfaces as anger. Interestingly, this anger is not directed at the patient in question but at the institution for "not keeping us safe."
- Caring for a patient with a "new" disease means working in uncharted territory and frequently raises the patient's or family's suspicion that we are not doing the right thing.
- A patient with whom the staff more closely identifies (young, first-time pregnancy) causes more anxiety and fear. "This one was personal."
- Conflicting instructions and information that change over time reduces everyone's confidence that those in charge really know what they are doing.
- For those in charge (Infection Control staff), the frustration of being "caught in the middle" is very difficult. Line staff is pressing for definitive instructions and the external sources of guidance disagree on the required precautions.

- Personal risk does not occur often for most caregivers. When it does, one has to balance professional responsibilities and personal safety. Rising above one's sense of personal danger to care for others is a professional commitment that brings a level of heroism to being a clinician.
- Within the hospital, everyone has a slightly different perspective on the situation depending on his or her role. In this case, everyone involved was doing his or her best, but the various viewpoints inevitably color perceptions of one another.

The session ended with the facilitators acknowledging how sadly the case ended (first the baby and then the mother died) and how much courage was needed to take risks. Yet the healthcare professional, like the firefighter or police officer, makes a noble choice to face life and death struggles every day. During the synthesis, the different points of view and why they are so necessary in the comprehensive care of patients was noted. Afterward, many participants stayed to talk with the panel, emphasizing how important it is to have these conversations, especially with the prediction of further flu outbreak in the fall. Without any attempt to solve issues, the Rounds alert the organization to concerns that should be addressed.

CHALLENGES AND STRATEGIES

Based on our experience, any healthcare facility that implements Schwartz Center Rounds® will face a series of seven challenges. Strategies to address these challenges will be familiar to the OD professional in health care. While a physician leader is particularly needed to understand and negotiate many aspects of the Rounds, the OD facilitator is especially important in navigating the organizational dynamics and tracking the program evolution. His or her partnership is critical in designing the Rounds and role modeling the type of respectful, effective, and compassionate behavior that the Rounds exemplify. (In order to best express the experience of coleading the Rounds, the remainder of this chapter will change voice from third person to first.)

1. Starting the Rounds

The Schwartz Center Web site contains comprehensive guidelines for starting the Rounds, including creating a planning committee and identifying roles for the physician leader and facilitator; it also features a 10-minute video showing the Rounds in process. As physician leader and facilitator partners at Maimonides, we met to get to know each other and to plan an implementation strategy. In order to create buy-in across the institution, we arranged to visit already scheduled meetings to introduce the Rounds to physicians, nurses, and senior managers. We took turns describing the Rounds based on material from the Schwartz Center and explaining our personal and professional commitment to the endeavor. We then showed the video, which would noticeably change the emotional climate of the meeting, and address questions. Finally, we demonstrated how a Schwartz Center Rounds® case presentation would be different from clinical rounds by using a specific example and facilitating multiple types of conversations.

While these meetings took several months to complete and delayed our original start date, it was worthwhile because each of the major groups felt that they had a stake in the new program and were eager for its launch. In addition, we achieved consensus on when to host the Rounds, as the Medicine Department offered one of their noon conferences that guaranteed resident participation and was accessible for most staff. Our partnership also established a collaborative working relationship in which we share presenting information, realize each other's strengths, and use humor to put minor obstacles in perspective. Therefore, we refer to ourselves as co-leaders and co-facilitators, optimizing our unique backgrounds and roles.

2. Finding a Case

The most challenging part of the Rounds is finding a case. We knew we needed to have a win with the first Rounds, so we asked a charismatic breast surgeon to be the lead presenter. However, due to the usual identification of cases for teaching residents about diagnosis and treatment, it took brainstorming a dozen potential cases until our physician leader felt that we hit a good one. It turned out to be very effective because the case was about dealing with a large family who did not want their mother, the patient, to know she had cancer. On the panel, the attending physician and physician oncologist elaborated on how they formed a bond with the patient yet had qualms about how to respect her needs after a mastectomy, and the demands of the family to guarantee she would be ok. The nurse spoke about how difficult it was to set limits as 15 family members would crowd into her room, insisting on pain meds or feeding her. The ensuing discussion was animated and opinionated. It was validation that we had selected a good case for the Schwartz Center Rounds®.

Dr. Astrow, as physician leader, first suggested that we should find cases by going to various departments and asking physicians he knew about potential cases. This approach turned out to be very time consuming. In addition, because the Rounds were new, there was not a clear understanding by physicians of what constituted a good case. Once we had several Rounds, we realized a few criteria. The case needed to have some drama to hold the attention of the large audience. Even though it is not a performance, there is an aspect of engagement that is helped by a panel that speaks with animation, expresses feelings that arouse passion, and poses dilemmas raised by the complexities in the case. We also observed that with our diverse organizational culture, cases with underlying anger or sadness and conflict work better than those of inspiration or exemplary collaboration.

By the end of the first year, we wrote up guidelines for selecting a good case (Appendix A) and created an internal Web site with resources about the Rounds and a simple form to submit a case for consideration. However, it still was difficult to find cases. One of the program directors for residents said that in his experience, the same thing happens during teaching rounds. Residents have over 50 cases each, but when the chief resident asks for a case, no one volunteers one. Only by working through case options one by one is the resident able to recognize an appropriate case for the Rounds. Perhaps the pressure of trying to organize everything before the deadline adds creative energy, even as we wish it could be less of a cliff-hanger. What we decided to do was to involve our committee differently.

3. Managing the Committee

Each committee functions in ways that fit the hospital; our structure is organic to Maimonides Medical Center. We currently have about eight or nine members who attend meetings regularly. The committee includes five physicians, a nurse manager, and two administrators, and when available, a psychologist. The role of the committee includes taking initiative to find good cases and also being invested in the continuous improvement of the Rounds.

At the November, 2008 annual meeting for Rounds leaders and facilitators in Boston, prior to the Center's annual dinner, we shared our challenges with others who had been leading the Rounds for a longer time. Two strategies emerged that we implemented to better manage the committee. First, we changed the membership on the committee. We realized that many of the Rounds in other facilities are more nurse-dominated and ours were more physician-led. Since we wanted Rounds to be more interdisciplinary, we added a senior nurse manager to the committee. She greatly helped with finding cases, engaging the nurse managers, and also with involving more front-line staff on various units to be on the panel and to attend the Rounds.

However, we did not want the default dynamic in the committee to represent a traditional and outdated pattern in which doctors delegate and nurses implement. Therefore, the second strategy was to shift more of the responsibility for finding cases from the co-chairs to the committee. We asked each committee member to be the liaison for at least one session per year. We expect that once the committee members do the initial harvesting of a potential case—speaking with colleagues that might have ideas and departments that have not been represented—then we will get further information from the physician on the case to fine tune the theme, identify the panel, and work with the panel to prepare for the case presentation.

We are still experimenting with this approach, but it has promise. The Schwartz Center has a list of topics that have been successful at other Rounds, such as: *How to tell a patient it may be time to stop treatment; Humor and healing; Delivering bad news; Sexuality and illness: conversation comfort zone; When issues of your own mortality come into play;* or *Caring for a colleague.* The committee uses a hybrid of having a list of potential topics and then trying to find cases that exemplify that theme, such as therapeutic non-disclosure or parents refusing (or insisting on) care for their child.

We do not recommend using current cases because the staff tends to get emotionally derailed about discharge planning or treatment issues that are still current. On the other hand, we want to find cases that resonate with real conflicts among caregivers and the pulse of the institution. While we are trying to gather an inventory of cases to make planning for the Rounds easier (wishing we could plan for the year by topic and department), we actually end up planning for no more than two Rounds in advance in order to keep the process fresh and cases relevant.

Once we got clear that we wanted more involvement from the committee, we scheduled meetings at the hospital two weeks after each Rounds and one week before the next one. During the debrief meeting, we review how the session went subjectively and based on the evaluation summary (described below), and think of ways to improve, such as how to deepen the discussion, broaden participation, and better prepare the panel. The prep meetings help us to think through the aspects of the upcoming case that merit exploration. While the Rounds do not have a defined curriculum, it helps to anticipate the directions the case could go and identify the themes that would be desirable to examine. These two processes for debriefing and preparation have greatly helped the facilitation because if there are silences or comments that are not furthering the discussion, we have ideas for how to move the discussion forward. They also enable the committee to feel engaged and necessary, doing real work and not just meeting for the sake of meeting, which is important because the Rounds take time and rely on personal commitment.

4. Dealing with Logistics

Implementing Schwartz Center Rounds® takes structure and support. The Assistant Vice President for the Cancer Center, also a committee member, provided the part-time assistance of one of her staff members. Using a project management approach, we identified who is responsible for the various tasks to be done prior to, during, and after each Rounds. By the end of the first year, we had a template that was predicable and seamless. Preparatory tasks include ordering box lunches, requesting tables and environmental services help for setting up the chairs, and having the sign-in sheets and evaluation forms labeled. Our philosophy is to *hope for the best and plan for the worst.*We want every detail to communicate the values of the Rounds—respectful, welcoming, organized, and conducive to having important conversations.

During the Rounds, we have hand-held microphones so that everyone can be heard—one for the panel and two for the aisles in the audience. We place copies of the evaluation form and case summary on the chairs. The box lunches are available 15 minutes before the Rounds and no crunchy or noisy foods are used.

After the Rounds, we send thank-you notes to the panel and the support services personnel. The assistant creates an attendance document of all the names by department (a big job because many participants have illegible handwriting). She also collates all the evaluation data and sends it to the Schwartz Center and to the committee. The assistant also keeps track of the budget and other communications from the Schwartz Center.

5. Preparing the Panel

Once the case is selected, the physician helps identify other professionals who were involved with the case. Often the nurse manager from the unit will suggest a specific nurse who would be available the day of the Rounds. Then, depending on the topic, the other person may be a patient representative, a psychologist, a nurse practitioner, or a resident. Usually the physician will review the chart to gather pertinent information about the case, both for the presentation and the written case summary.

Prior to the planning meeting for the next Rounds, we send guidelines for preparing for the case, a link to the Schwartz Center Web site, and encouragement to view the 10-minute video. When we meet, we explore the caregivers' experiences with the case and then help them focus on their emotional reactions. When there are disagreements and differences, we emphasize speaking about these during the Rounds. We explain that the most effective Rounds have some conflict and "narrative arc" that makes the story compelling.

We have found that many of the panel members are very nervous about public speaking and even reluctant to participate. We reassure them that they are only speaking initially for 2–3 minutes and remind them that they know their experience and that the purpose of their presentation is to be a catalyst for the ensuing conversation. Once we get into the actual Rounds, the opposite often happens: They cannot stop speaking and end up going into too much detail about the case. Although through our facilitation we try to interject and invite the audience to speak, sometimes the case is cathartic for others who were involved in the care. Other times, the department appears to use the opportunity to present for an undisclosed secondary agenda.

What we have learned from these situations is to be as clear as possible about the purpose of the Rounds, how to best prepare, and what is expected. If we had time, we would have a second panel meeting to actually rehearse. We also think the more we have "good" Rounds, the more the organization will know what is expected. Yet, the underlying challenge is that the panel is taking on extra work and, in a way, "doing us a favor." They also are used to being in control during other types of presentations. We do not want to seem too controlling and lose them, yet we want to have an experience that is aligned and useful for the panel, the audience, and the legacy of the Rounds. It is a work in progress and a study in diplomacy.

6. Engaging the Group

Every Rounds is a new group. While most have been there before, there are always new people. We take the first ten minutes to tell the story of Kenneth Schwartz and the purpose of the Rounds. We review the ground rules, such as confidentiality, beepers and phones on vibrate, and not using "diagnosis/fix-it speak." We set the stage for the underlying themes that we want to explore, using the case as the concrete catalyst from which to generalize by at least 30 minutes into the hour. In a hospital with a habit of starting meetings 10 minutes late, we begin and end precisely on time, using the ritual of a Tibetan bell to signal the special nature of the session. We frame the Rounds as a place to personally reflect, learn from colleagues, and enhance respect and compassion.

The facilitation challenge is how to keep the audience involved when they are not familiar with the case, tend to ask the panel more questions than are necessary about the specific case, and sometimes revert to behavior used in other kinds of meetings. Some respond to the subject at hand by pontificating, while others share extremely personal reactions. There are always the same people who tend to dominate discussions and those who prefer to be silent and listen. We want to create an inviting space to speak, which we have discovered entails that the facilitators listen with discernment—not too permissive and not overly directive or confrontational. At the same time, the group needs to gain confidence that the Rounds are a place to air disappointments without the fear of judgment and to receive support from others who have been there before; to see that a sense of team failure can be transformed to a feeling of connection and humility.

We received excellent guidance from the Schwartz Center physician who consults with organizations new to the Rounds. She came to our first Rounds and another a few months later, helping us conceptualize our role as guardrails that keep cars from going off the side of the road, hitting trees, or merging too quickly. In concrete terms, that means politely interrupting people by asking them to summarize their comments, asking directly for comments from voices that have not contributed or who may disagree, and naming emerging themes and suggesting possible unspoken issues. She encouraged us to be aware of comments that were problem-solving and prescriptive, rather than emotive and based on personal experience, and made suggestions for how to respond in the future. For instance, we could ask those speaking what makes them feel so strongly or inquire, in a non-defensive way, how they would feel if they were in the caregiver's position. She also validated our complementary styles and encouraged us to be spontaneous.

As a facilitator, Dr. Astrow has a warmly provocative approach, calling on specific people to speak and asking questions that delve deeper into what they were feeling at the time or really felt like doing. I have a more earnest and reflective demeanor, and usually take the initiative to set the context in the introduction, summarize group themes, and encourage participation. He is drawn to colleague interactions and surfacing team conflict; I resonate with caregiver grief, loss, and pain. During the discussions, he is sensitive to the physicians who may not be listening to nurses, and I listen for concerns from nurses and other providers to see if they are expressing their thoughts. Both of us try to loosen the hierarchy, assumptions, and taboos and discuss the previously undiscussable in a contained and sensitive environment. He is present and comfortable in the moment; I tend to do more research to prepare for the topic and group dynamics. We easily weave comments and build on what the other has said in a way that benefits the group as a whole.

Facilitating the Rounds has been a path for growth that has captured my curiosity and desire to help the institution. It led to formally interviewing experienced facilitators who have been leading the Rounds for many years and writing up the interviews for the Schwartz Center Web site. The experiences and differences among facilitators have helped me feel more comfortable with my anticipatory style and at the same time take more risks in the moment. It makes sense that, not being a clinician, I would read about the syndromes presented, feel empathy for the caregivers, and wonder how they cope with vulnerability and less than politically correct feelings. For instance, during the recent Rounds on H1N1, a nurse in the audience asked us why she was there, as if her manager had not told her (not true) and as if she was getting ready to defend herself from criticism. I looked her right in the eyes and authentically praised her courage and compassion with her work with this difficult patient situation. Then I told her that she and her fellow nurses were invited to share their experiences and learn from others. She sat back, as if the wind was unexpectedly taken out of her sails, and the ensuing conversation went in the direction we encouraged. Later, the committee gave me positive feedback on that intervention.

Experience builds confidence, and doing the Rounds over time and realizing that they are interesting, always different, and still go well has helped decrease my anxiety and increase trust in the group. In the beginning, I prepared notes with options for dealing with disruptive comments, statements for encouraging participation, and questions that would focus the discussion. Now they are internalized and I respond to observations of group dynamics and resistance more quickly and creatively. We are able to adjust our approaches intuitively, enjoying how often participants are able to express feelings, offer support, share insights, and look engaged.

7. Strengthening the Partnership

Without a department or staff to rely on, a key strategy in my role as CLO at Maimonides has been to partner with different leaders for various projects and programs. Therefore, I brought awareness of what is important for creating strong partnerships when Dr. Astrow and I first met. We explored our backgrounds, strengths, intentions, and commitments. We saw immediately our differences regarding time and spontaneity. We built in the norm of expecting and working through conflicts.

By the end of the first year, we needed to address some tension. Dr. Astrow ever so respectfully explained how busy he is and the limits to time he can spend preparing for the Rounds. I expressed the impact for me on planning and achieving desired outcomes. We came to an understanding, cleared the air, and were able to make the changes described above that benefited the committee, the Rounds, and our leadership styles. We enjoy working together and are the collaborative partners associated with this successful endeavor.

EVALUATION

At the end of each session, participants are asked to fill out the Schwartz Center evaluation form. Even though they are told at the beginning of the session why these are necessary and how the information is used, less than half fill out an evaluation and we have not yet figured out how to increase the number. The questions were developed by the Schwartz Center and we added questions consistent with Maimonides Continuing Medical Education requirements. It also includes qualitative statements about the session and suggestions for future Rounds.

An example of an evaluation form is in Appendix B. We found insignificant variation in the 12 sessions to date. Data from 2009 shows that 78–94% of the participants agreed or strongly agreed with the each of the eight questions asked (Appendix C). Overall, the Rounds have sustained an "excellent" rating, although sometimes with fewer "exceptional" and more "good" scores ("poor" and "fair" are neglible and deleted from Appendix D).

In terms of OD and linking the goals of the Rounds to leadership development, mutual respect, and organizational learning, we were particularly interested in three of the questions:

- #3: The Rounds will help me work better with my colleagues.
- #5: The open discussion was helpful to me.
- #8: I plan to attend the Rounds again.

For question #3, the data shows a slight downward trend with fluctuation (Appendix E). One possible explanation for this would be the large numbers of attendees, representing over 30 different departments whose personnel might have different topic interests. Since not every case is relevant to each participant's work, lack of direct applicability may impact their feeling that the Rounds topic will help them work better with their colleagues. They may need to attend more Rounds before they strongly agree with this statement.

For both questions #5 about the open discussion and #8 about planning to attend again, the trends are fairly stable and at a high level. One possible explanation for these results is that although a particular topic may not be relevant, the themes of mutual respect and compassion are sufficiently universal to not only allow participants feel that the discussion was helpful, but also that the themes inspire them to want to attend again. In fact, people are voting with their feet! Since the first Rounds with a packed room of people curious to see what the Rounds were all about, the Rounds have ranged from 125–170 attendees each time. Clearly, there is a palpable commitment to the learning derived from the Rounds at Maimonides. In addition, the planning committee has started to feel more comfortable presenting cases that raise sensitive organizational issues.

More than the quantitative data, the committee relies on qualitative factors to assess the effectiveness of the Rounds. If caregivers speak about their experiences as patients or family members, we think that enough safety has been achieved to expose a personal reaction. Sometimes there is a wide variety of comments, as if filling a basket, and although they tend not to build on each other, there is no need to end with consensus. Other times there is crying and obvious expressions of being touched by the discussion. Each Rounds is quite unique and valuable in its own way. If people stopped coming, became argumentative and disrespectful, or were not able to learn to go deeper and be more vulnerable over time, then we would be concerned that the Rounds were not effectively fulfilling their purpose at Maimonides.

In 2007, prior to Maimonides initiating the Rounds, the Schwartz Center hired Goodman Research Group, Inc. (an independent evaluation, research, and consulting firm in Cambridge, MA) to conduct a survey with 500 attendees at 16 hospitals. Six of the surveyed sites had been holding the Rounds for at least three years (Lown & Manning, 2010). The findings from the attendees included:

- 86% reported that Rounds made them more likely to consider the effects of illness on the personal lives of their patients.
- 84% reported that Rounds have helped them have more compassion for patients and their families.
- 84% reported that Rounds have helped them feel more energized about their work with patients.
- 93% reported that they have a greater appreciation for the roles and contributions of colleagues from other disciplines.
- 89% reported that their cooperation and coordination with colleagues on behalf of patients has improved.
- 88% reported a greater sense of belonging to a caregiving team.
- 87% said they have new ideas or strategies for patient situations.
- 76% said they feel less alone in their work with patients.

The investigation by the Goodman Group is grounded in the growing scientific evidence for addressing common issues in health care and the patient–caregiver relationship. The outcomes of the Rounds at Maimonides over the past year and a half also reveal the growing impact on communication, empathy, teamwork, and patient care. Examples of anecdotal comments include:

- "The Rounds bring visibility to staff that I never get to see. The medical center may not realize it yet, but it's healthy for us to engage with each other in such an institution-wide forum. It increases communication and makes it easier to contact people."
- "The Rounds raised a sensitive issue that I happened to be dealing with outside of work. I was able to feel more courage to reach out to my friend and his wife before he died. Thank you."
- "I never knew that doctor personally, but after hearing him present, I would go to him if I ever needed surgery. The Rounds lets us know people in a different way."
- "I had no idea other people struggled with speaking up. I learned how to better deal with a co-worker situation, and that ultimately impacts patient care."

Although the Rounds are not designed to solve problems or create new programs, at times needs of the institution are revealed and lead to specific changes in practice. The Goodman evaluation showed that more than 50% of the respondents said that Rounds discussions led to specific changes in practice or policy at their hospital. A few examples from Rounds discussions at Maimonides include ideas to

- design a consult service for staff after a code, violence, or death of a colleague;
- expand Palliative Care services and education;
- and use the Psychiatry Department to help interdisciplinary staff understand the emotional impact of diseases on patients or help colleagues approach disagreements with each other in a more professional manner.

CONCLUSION

The Schwartz Center Rounds® offer OD in health care a potent process for intervening in a medical center and influencing culture change. The experience at Maimonides demonstrates the relevance of the Rounds to an overall leadership development focus. The ongoing challenges, strategies for dealing with them, and lessons learned are well served by the training and expertise of OD practitioners. Having these important conversations deepens the capacity of caregivers to understand themselves and show their vulnerability, have compassion for their patients and families, and appreciate their differences and commonalities with their colleagues.

As a stand-alone offering, the Schwartz Center Rounds® bring an unusual and valuable perspective to caregivers, as demonstrated by the Goodman

Research Group report (Lown & Manning, 2010). In combination with a vigorous organization development program, the Rounds provide a unique opportunity to shape an organization's culture. The expertise of the OD professional creates a synergy between the Schwartz Center Rounds® and the hospital's larger goals for OD. The contribution of the OD framework makes the Rounds a significant tool in the development of healthcare professionals.

REFERENCES

Astrow, A., & Sulmasy, D. (2004). Spirituality and the patient–physician relationship. *JAMA,* 291, 2884.

Brier, P. S. (2009). Teaching respect at Maimonides Medical Center. *Frontiers of Health Services Management, 25*(4), 25–31.

Feldman, D. L., & Kaplan, K. (2007). Crucial Conversations improves patient safety at Brooklyn hospital by building a culture of respect. Retrieved from http://www.vitalsmarts.com/corporatecasestudies.aspx

Johnson, J. (2008, April). Connecting with compassion: How Schwartz Center Rounds are humanizing healthcare. *New York Nurse, 39*(4), 1–2.

Kaplan, K., & Feldman, D. L. (2008). Realizing the value of in-house physician leadership development. *The Physician Executive, 34*(5), 40–46.

Kaplan, K., Mestel, P., & Feldman, D. L. (2010). Creating a culture of mutual respect. *AORN Journal, 91*(4), 495–510.

Kaplan, K. & Patel, J. (2009, May). Developing a communication-focused leadership development programme for non-clinical managers. *Journal of Communication in Healthcare, 2*(2), 131–147.

Lown, B. A., & Manning, C. F. (2010). The Schwartz Center Rounds: Evaluation of an interdisciplinary approach to enhancing patient-centered communication, teamwork, and provider support. *Academic Medicine, 85*(6), 1073–1081.

Maimonides Medical Center. (2007). *Creating competitive advantage in a changing health care environment through worker participation.* Strategic Alliance Report. Brooklyn, NY. Retrieved November 19, 2009 from http://www.theschwartzcenter.org/about/casestatement.html

Salamon, J. (2008). *Hospital: Man, woman, birth, death, infinity, plus red tape, bad behavior, money, god, and diversity on steroids.* New York: The Penguin Press.

Schwartz, K. (2005, July 16). A patient's story. *The Boston Globe Magazine*, pp. 1, 15, 17, 18, 19.

Whitney, K. (2007, October). Maimonides Medical Center's Kathryn Kaplan: Weaving a culture for institutional leadership. CLO Profile. *Chief Learning Officer*, 30–35.

APPENDIX A
A Good Case for the Schwartz Center Rounds

- The case gets others to talk about their own experience: The purpose of the Rounds is not to stay on the ins and outs of the presented case, but to diverge to the audience's experiences with the overarching theme. A good case gets the audience to see the panelist's point of view and empathize with how difficult it was for the caregivers. The participants then feel prompted to share what they felt or did in similar situations on their unit or in their department.

- The case involves interdisciplinary conflict and cooperation: When the case focuses mostly on physicians, for instance, the rest of the staff is less engaged and may feel excluded. The actual care of patients is a complex, multifaceted, and unscripted scenario that has lots of challenges, choice points, and possible outcomes. A good case builds a dramatic arc that holds the large group's attention and draws in diverse opinions and enthusiastic responses.

- The case raises issues that usually are not discussed but provide value in hearing about others' perspectives and practices: What are the taboos that occur in your practice, the sticky issues that are judgment calls? What are the situations that people can take issue with and might handle quite differently? A good case does not duplicate a root cause, Grand Rounds, or treatment planning meeting. Instead, it gets to what is going on in the caregivers' minds and hearts that impacts how decisions are made and results achieved. There is no need to agree or reach consensus; a stimulating discussion and even some controversy is preferred, depending on the topic.

- The case draws on our humanity and compassion as providers: Maybe we made a human error, but we still feel guilty and it is hard to forgive ourselves. Or no mistake was made but the patient course was unfavorable and we feel remorse and loss. Or the patient's diagnosis or personality or cultural bias made it challenging for us to be professional—they just got under our skin. Or we were unprepared for the way in which administration, the community, or our colleagues in a different profession responded to our approach. The good case has a relevant theme from which it is easy to generalize. It is not a problem to solve or a policy issue, nor should it be too politically sensitive, complicated, or criminal. Instead, it is an unfinished lesson on a past event that has the potential for enduring value for learning.

APPENDIX B
Maimonides Medical Center Schwartz Center Rounds®
Evaluation

 Maimonides
Medical Center

Date: July 14, 2009
Title: H1N1: Professional Responsibility/Personal Risk

Schwartz Center Rounds® Evaluation

Please return the completed evaluation form at the conclusion of the program. Thank you.

Thank you for attending the Schwartz Center Rounds® today. The goal of the Schwartz Center Rounds® is to provide a multidisciplinary forum in which caregivers can comfortably discuss issues they face in providing compassionate care to patients. Please take a minute to answer these questions. The Planning Committee will use your responses and comments to develop future Schwartz Center Rounds®.

Please respond to the following statements by checking the box that most reflects your opinion of today's Schwartz Center Rounds®.

	Disagree completely	Disagree somewhat	Neither agree nor disagree	Agree somewhat	Agree completely
The case discussed today was relevant to my daily clinical work.					
I gained knowledge that will help me in caring for my patients.					
Today's Rounds will help me work better with my colleagues.					
The overview and presentation of the case today was helpful to me.					
The open discussion was helpful to me.					
The facilitator helped the discussion today.					
The program met the objectives.					
I plan to attend Schwartz Center Rounds® again.					

Please rate today's Schwartz Center Rounds®
☐ Poor   ☐ Fair   ☐ Good   ☐ Excellent   ☐ Exceptional

In your opinion, did you perceive any commercial bias in any of the presentations?
☐ YES   ☐ NO
If yes, please give specific example: _____

Do you plan on making any changes in your practice as a result of this activity?
☐ YES   ☐ NO
If yes, please explain: _____

(Optional) Comments and Feedback on Today's Schwartz Center Rounds®:

Professional affiliation (please check one box)
☐ Physician   ☐ Nurse   ☐ Psychologist Case Mgmt/Soc Worker   ☐ Admin
☐ NP, PA, CNM   ☐ Other (Please specify) _____

Suggestions for future topics (please give your contact information for follow-up):

**Maimonides Medical Center designates this educational activity for a maximum of 1 *AMA PRA Category 1 Credit*™. Physicians should only claim credit commensurate with the extent of their participation in the activity. Maimonides Medical Center is accredited by the Medical Society of the State of New York sponsor continuing medical education for physicians.

APPENDIX C
Summary Top 2 Responses (2009)

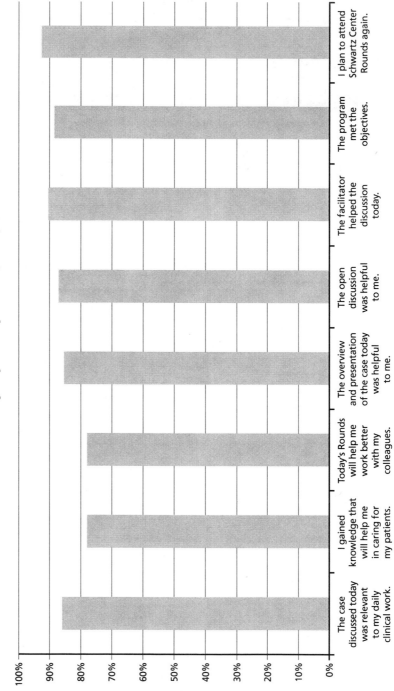

APPENDIX D
Overall Rating Question (2009)

APPENDIX E
Schwartz Center Rounds® Critical Questions:
Top 2 Responses (2009)

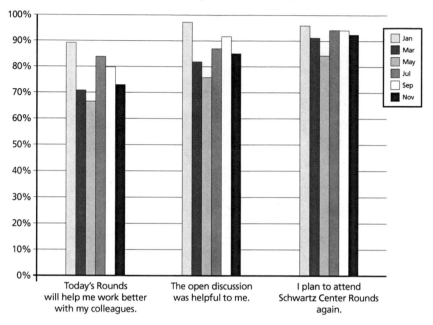

CHAPTER 10

THE VALUE OF APPRECIATIVE INTELLIGENCE IN THE CULTURE OF SENIOR LIVING

Diane Doumas

ABSTRACT

Appreciative intelligence is a skill that we all have to some extent and one that helps to create the kind of environment in senior living that is important to quality of life for the residents and team. The following chapter identifies what appreciative intelligence is and how leaders in senior living can apply the strategy in day-to-day operations. By sharing case studies and stories from my personal experiences, the successful application of appreciative intelligence is demonstrated in positive team development and enhanced resident care. One of the interesting discoveries is how often appreciative intelligence happens spontaneously in senior living because of the natural talents and skills of the team members that may be drawn to this type of work.

A TEAM APPROACH

After working in senior living operations for 25+ years, I adopted the saying that "senior living management is a team sport," because it takes a team approach to effectively manage a senior living community. The team includes

Organization Development in Health Care, pages 197–210

staff that work in the community, residents, their extended family, healthcare providers of the residents, and the support services in the community-at-large. It takes strong leaders with excellent coaching and interpersonal skills to manage this very diverse interdisciplinary team for excellent operational results.

WHAT IS APPRECIATIVE INTELLIGENCE?

Senior living professionals are faced with complex human interactions that include residents, staff members, extended family, healthcare professionals and business stakeholders. It takes leaders with a broad range of skills and intelligence to successfully navigate and manage all of these relationships. There have been several new forms of intelligence introduced over the past few years, including social (Albrecht, 2006) and emotional intelligence (Goleman, 1997). I find them all to have valuable aspects for application in the senior living setting. However, through my leadership experiences working with seniors, and as I get older myself, I have come to understand that asking the right questions, focusing on what is working, and embracing learning opportunities when faced with the challenges and losses of aging can dramatically affect a more positive outcome. That is why I have become such an advocate of applying appreciative intelligence (Thatchenkery & Metzker, 2006). Victor Frankl, a German concentration camp survivor, shared some thoughts that capture the essence of appreciative intelligence in situations of challenging loss. Mr. Frankl says, "Everything can be taken from a man but one thing: the last of the human freedoms—to choose one's attitude in any given set of circumstances, to choose one's own way" (Thatchenkery & Metzker, 2006, p. 12).

Having the ability to appreciate what works and to apply appreciative intelligence principles to achieve positive outcomes is a timely and necessary tool in the senior living field. I believe that appreciative intelligence is intuitively applied in the senior care setting on a regular basis by professional and family caregivers. By doing so, they naturally identify future possibilities in present circumstances, see and nurture the hidden potential in people, and recognize products that become breakthrough successes. Dr. Tojo Thatchenkery, who coined the phrase in his book *Appreciative Intelligence*, describes it as "the ability to see the mighty oak in the acorn" (Thatchenkery & Metzker, 2006, p. 4).

The three basic components of appreciative intelligence are

1. *reframing*, or seeing people, problems, or things in a new way so that something good or useful is visible;
2. appreciating what is positive or useful;
3. and seeing how the positive and useful attributes can be applied to a goal.

A good example of the intuitive application of appreciative intelligence in senior care is the recent program that Brookdale Senior Living has designed around capitalizing on frail residents' strengths in the area of dining services. Recognizing that about six hours out of the residents' day in a specialized dementia program is spent preparing for, engaging in, and cleaning up from mealtime, Brookdale staff members decided to find ways to create a more positive experience around mealtime. A team of gerontology and culinary experts designed menus with dementia in mind, thinking about things like not having finger food and fork food in the same meal. The results have been very positive, and include residents who were previously unable to feed themselves now utilizing a hand-over-hand technique to pick up their own glass and bring food to their own mouths. By recognizing abilities instead of disabilities, the specialists at Brookdale Senior Living created an opportunity for success for their residents with dementia (Martin, 2009).

WHY APPLY APPRECIATIVE INTELLIGENCE IN SENIOR LIVING NOW?

I think it would be useful to educate the senior living industry in the application of appreciative intelligence principles and processes because of the current and continuously increasing aging population. According to a report by the U.S. Department of Health and Human Services, Administration on Aging (U.S. DHHS, 2004), the population of seniors in the age group 85+ is expected to increase to 9.6 million from 4.6 million by the

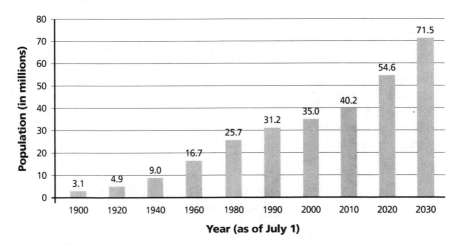

Figure 10.1 Number of persons 65+, 1900–2030. (*Source*: U.S. DHHS, 2004)

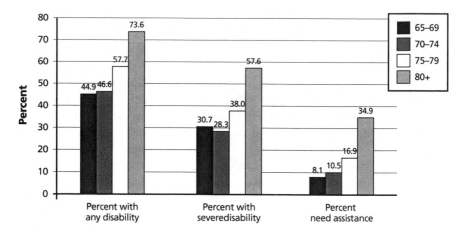

Figure 10.1 Percent with disabilities, by age: 1997. (*Source*: U.S. DHHS, 2004)

year 2030. At that time, it is estimated that there will be about 71.5 million Americans over the age of 65, more than doubling in number over a 30-year period (U.S. DHHS, 2004).

With increasing age comes the opportunity for multiple and more severe disabilities. The same study indicates that seniors reporting the most disabilities were 85+ years of age, the fastest growing segment of the aging population (U.S. DHHS, 2004).

Rather than taking the typical approach of focusing on problems and deficits, appreciative intelligence allows us to focus on what is working and capitalize on strengths to maximize potential. Particularly in senior living, where the work impacts quality of life for the elders in our society, I think creating an appreciative environment is critical to maintaining excellent quality care and high staff retention.

While doing his research, Dr. Thatchenkery studied many organizations where he noticed that the culture encouraged a high incidence of innovation and he examined the stories of hundreds of real-life leaders who supported positive outcomes within their teams. As he describes in his book, *Appreciative Intelligence* (Thatchenkery & Metzker, 2006), taking the positive approach is where innovation and creativity can flourish and is where team productivity and business development are at their best.

APPLYING APPRECIATIVE INTELLIGENCE IN DEMENTIA CARE

One of the most complex areas in senior care, from physical plant design and programming to staff training and family concerns, is dementia care.

It is a specialized area of care that requires a unique set of skills and talents to manage. Yet, even in this most challenging of circumstances, as Frankl (1984) says, we always have the ability to choose our approach and attitude. Through training and experience, both caregivers in senior living settings and family caregivers at home can be encouraged and taught to focus on the skills and abilities that are still available to the dementia sufferer instead of what is lacking. By capitalizing on strength and ability, the individual can function at her or his highest capacity and the caregiver will feel more accomplished.

Alzheimer's disease is a heartbreaking, fatal, dementia-causing illness that robs its victims of their dignity and independence. Statistically, as medical science is making it possible for Americans to live longer, at least 50% of those over the age of 85 will develop Alzheimer's disease. On the Alzheimer's Association Web site there are numerous personal stories shared by caregivers and victims recounting their pain and heartbreak dealing with the overwhelming task of managing the progression of the illness day after day. I believe that there is a huge opportunity to embrace the principles of appreciative intelligence in the work with Alzheimer's and dementia.

It takes the ability to see beyond the disabilities of dementia to embrace the positive that can be found. I found the dementia care area a refuge at times when I was feeling overwhelmed with the burdens and issues of being the administrator in an assisted living community. I could venture to the dementia care neighborhood to get just the therapy I needed, and in turn share some nurture and care with the residents as well. A resident with dementia would catch sight of me and smile as though I were her long-lost friend. Approaching with open arms, she would embrace me lovingly, and I would tell her how good it was to see her. I meant those words with all my heart. Her unconditional love was just what I needed to make it through the rest of the day. I could then enter the room of a resident in the final stages of Alzheimer's disease, arranged comfortably in bed where he now spends most of his day. I would speak gently and lean in slowly so as not to alarm him, taking his hand into mine. His eyes would slowly focus on me, and I would wait patiently for some level of awareness that I was there. Smiling and talking, rubbing some lotion on his hands, I would remind him that I love him and ask him for a smile, waiting patiently again until selfishly I got just what I came for. Then I could go back to my office remembering what was truly important about my work.

Don, a gentleman diagnosed with Alzheimer's in his early 70s, began chronicling his journey through an Alzheimer's Weblog as well as his own blog called "The Trip Over," some of which is being captured on the Alzheimer's Association Web site. Don has come to appreciate certain aspects of his illness, embracing his newly found focus on the here and now. He shared, It's strange, but being diagnosed with Alzheimer's has made a profound difference in me—for the better! When I was younger, I was always waiting for or reaching for another goal, instead of living in the moment. I'm comfortable with where I'm at. I'm not preoccupied with something you can't control. (Alzheimer's Association, *Don's Story*, 2009)

Marilee Adams, Ph.D., author of *Change Your Questions, Change Your Life* (2009), takes an appreciative approach by changing the questions that we ask to change the outcomes and results that we see. She recommends thinking in a "learner mindset," and in any given situation asking questions like "What works?"; "What's valuable here?"; "What can I learn?". I have found occasionally in senior care that caregivers assume and accept behaviors or conditions in seniors as simply inevitable and do not necessarily take proactive measures to remediate them. For example, if a senior living resident with dementia begins to display a troublesome behavior such as wandering throughout the day, it is common for caregivers to simply accept such behavior as unavoidable because people with dementia wander. They may try to still the resident or move the individual to a place where he or she will not be a bother to others. However, if caregivers are trained to take the appreciative approach with a learner mindset, they could utilize the tools available such as the resident's history, family, and health record, observing and learning from the resident's behavior to determine possible underlying causes. By acting in a creative and nurturing way there can be a successful calming of the behavior.

APPRECIATIVE INTELLIGENCE AND OVERCOMING AGEISM

I am using *ageism* in the sense of stereotyping or making assumptions about people simply because of their age. As I will demonstrate, ageism is a common issue in senior living that can have dangerous results for seniors. Despite the well-documented deficits that come with age, however, researchers are discovering that the adage "older and wiser" is true in some areas of cognitive functioning. For example, a study published in April, 2010 in the Proceedings of the National Academy of Sciences reports that older people are better able to navigate and reason through social dilemmas and interpersonal conflict than their younger counterparts (Grossmann et al., 2010). By applying the principles of appreciative intelligence, the researchers suggest that we might use this information to utilize capable seniors in "key social roles involving legal decisions, counseling, and intergroup negotiations. Furthermore, given the abundance of research on negative effects of aging, this study may help to encourage clinicians to emphasize the inherent strengths associated with aging" (Grossman et al., 2010, p. 7246).

I had a personal experience with a senior living resident that illustrates what can happen when judgments and assumptions are made about aging instead of using a process of intelligence and learning. The gentleman lived in an independent apartment on a senior living campus where I was the administrator. This gentleman, who had beautiful white hair and used a walker, was able to manage his own affairs, including his diabetes medications. On this particular day, he had arranged for a taxi to a local university hospital for blood work that required him to skip breakfast.

Unfortunately, the taxi driver misunderstood and drove the gentleman to the opposite side of town and the wrong university. With the effects of missing breakfast, blood sugar levels dropping, and lessening awareness, he did not realize that he was in the wrong location upon exiting the taxi.

The gentleman began wandering around campus with his walker, becoming increasingly disoriented as his blood sugar levels continued to drop. Thankfully, a campus security guard spotted him and came to help. But instead of calling for emergency medical assistance, the campus security guard assumed he was a confused senior who had wandered off from the local assisted living community. Unaware that he was wasting precious lifesaving time, the security guard called the local assisted living community, only to find that all of their residents were accounted for.

Thankfully, at this point, the security guard took the time to patiently inquire with the resident, still thinking he was simply confused. In his weakened and disoriented state the gentleman was finally able to convey the name of the community where he lived. Of course, when we heard what was happening we immediately instructed the security guard to please call 911 and get the gentleman emergency intervention. The emergency responders arrived in time to administer life-saving treatment, and the gentleman's thinking cleared. It became clear to the campus security guard that this elderly gentleman's temporary dementia was symptomatic of a serious medical condition.

I think this story illustrates the difference between taking the approach of judgment and assumption and taking the approach of learning and intelligence. The security guard's first reaction to the situation of the elderly gentleman was to make a judgment about the situation based upon his appearance and behavior. I do not think that is at all uncommon with seniors, even in senior living communities. However, once he realized that his initial assumptions were incorrect, the security guard was able to step back and reframe the situation, taking the time to ask what was really going on, and he made a much better determination about the situation. I imagine that this learning experience was invaluable for him and serves him well going forward.

In the preceding illustration, the senior was fortunate that his dementia was an acute condition due to his low blood sugar. However, for seniors who suffer with Alzheimer's disease and other chronic dementia-causing illnesses, appreciative intelligence can be used to find what is still valuable and viable in the dementia sufferers' memories and abilities. Because dementia is the loss of short-term memory while retaining long-term memory, the idea of reminiscing has become very popular in dementia care. While the individual may not recall what they just ate for breakfast, or who just visited an hour ago, they will recall in vivid detail events from 20 or 40 years ago. Knowing this, the caregiver can take advantage of the long-term memories and in doing so design activities and provide opportunities for success for the resident.

For example, some dementia programs attempt to orient residents to current events daily even though they will not retain the information. Sometimes residents can find this frustrating because they do not recognize the names, do not remember the important figures (such as the President), and are not oriented to the date. By changing the paradigm and using the principles of appreciative intelligence, the caregiver can capitalize on the memories the resident does have. Events on the current date but perhaps years ago can be discussed, and residents will quite often successfully recount vivid stories from a former era. By reframing the idea of "current events," the caregiver can actually help the resident to feel validated by successfully remembering important details, and create positive feelings that will enhance the resident's experience of the day.

A gentleman named David shares his story on the Alzheimer's Association Web site about his grandmother who, he recalls, enjoyed knitting beautiful afghans before dementia robbed her of the ability to participate in her favorite pastime. Her confusion caused her to wander away, attempting to "go home" to a place she had not lived for a long time. Following is the story in David's own words:

> She was confused and looking to go home to "Harrison Avenue," which is the home where she raised her children in Scranton, Pennsylvania. I assume she refers back to that time of her life because it is where most of her good memories took place. At least I like to think of it that way. She continually asks to be taken home to "Harrison Avenue." The not-so-funny thing is [she] has not lived on Harrison Avenue for over 30 years. It's like the last 30 years have disappeared and there are very few signs of the rest of her past. (Alzheimer's Association, *David's Story*, 2009)

A dementia care program can be designed in collaboration with family members like David who can help reframe a resident's wandering and desire to "go home" into precious memories that can be turned into photo albums, pleasant discussions, and other tangible activities that create a nurturing reality for the dementia sufferer.

EFFECTIVE TEAM DEVELOPMENT USING APPRECIATIVE INTELLIGENCE

The work in senior living revolves around taking care of the residents. But the staff needs to be taken care of as well. Because the work, particularly in dementia care, is intellectually, physically, and emotionally challenging, it is of critical importance that leaders use appreciative intelligence principles to create a supportive work environment that nurtures and enables success for the team. Benjamin W. Pearce (1998) intuitively discusses an appreciative approach to management in his book about senior living management. He recognizes that most people want to perform well in their work, but the leader can motivate the team by communicating expectations clearly and collaboratively. He also stresses "hands-on" management, which includes modeling the appropriate behavior for the team. Pearce quotes Walt Disney's famous line, "You can dream, create, design and build the number one place in the world, but it takes people to make it happen" (quoted in Pearce, 1998, p. 56).

One challenge that has consistently faced the senior living industry is a high turnover rate for front-line team members, specifically the ones providing direct care to the senior residents. Pearce discusses the high turnover rate this way:

> CNAs [Certified Nursing Assistants or caregivers] cannot be motivated simply by the pay they earn, but they will stay if they are given supportive management and recognition. Over time, a symbiotic and even loving relationship may develop between residents and their CNAs. Residents will tell the CNAs how much they appreciate them, comment on their appearance, and help them through personal problems. For many employees, this recognition and encouragement is a valuable source of support and job satisfaction, and they reciprocate by giving residents the best care they are capable of.... Managers who value and nurture this bonding can enjoy lower turnover and a higher employee commitment to quality care. (1998, p. 36)

The application of appreciative intelligence (AI) has proven to have long-term positive effects in many organizations. AI uses a process that involves all stakeholders mining for what is working well in an organization and builds on that data to leverage ongoing success. More than a training program, it is a strategic approach to organizational change. The approach has proven to, among other successes, reduce employee turnover and improve morale. As opposed to the problem-solving paradigm of organizational change, my understanding of AI is to approach a challenge or improve an organization by spotlighting the best of what actually exists, envisioning what might be possible, dialoguing and building on those possibilities to design the ideal condition, and finally implementing an appreciative environment that promotes learning and engagement.

Carol Metzker, coauthor of *Appreciative Intelligence: Seeing the Mighty Oak in the Acorn* (2006), points out that good managers realize that the best employees are not waiting to be found. The top employees are already working for them, and it is the manager's job to create a work environment that brings out the best in the team. She created a top-five list of ways for managers to bring out the best in their employees (Metzger, 2007, pp. 1–6):

1. Know each individual on the team and his or her talents, the ones that are needed for his or her specific role and the talents that are outside the scope of his or her job. Do not keep people in a box or limit them according to a job description. Senior living offers a multitude of opportunities for this. For example, a caregiver who has musical or artistic talent can help the activities director from time to time with a stimulating activity for the residents. A caregiver's relationship with the rest of the team and the seniors in their care is reframed as he or she lets his or her talent shine. Allowing your team members to play to their strengths will improve morale and create a positive work environment for the team and the senior living residents.

2. Avoid asking "why," but instead begin questions with "what." This will cause you to take a stance of intelligence and not put your employees on the defensive. Balance the negative with the positive, still following up on complaints but also remembering to pat people on the back for the compliments that are received. Family members of senior living residents will have concerns from time to time, and the way questions are framed when following up on those concerns makes a big difference. When approaching a caregiver, a question such as "Why didn't you do Mrs. Smith's laundry last night?" sounds like an accusation and immediately puts the caregiver on the defensive. Rephrased as "What kept Mrs. Smith's laundry from getting done last night?" creates an opportunity for discussion and allows for the possibility that there is a valid explanation, which there very likely might be.

3. Select your words carefully, avoiding negativity. Words paint a picture that is powerful to you and others. A "big problem" may feel insurmountable. Reframed as "an opportunity for improvement," it might be seen as something the team can overcome and learn from by working together. I was asked to "turn around" several senior living communities, which usually included increasing the occupancy.

Some of our greatest successes came when we made it a goal that everyone participated in. We would set interim occupancy goals and reward the entire team when they were reached. We recognized and rewarded team members that helped with a new resident tour and move-in. By making it an opportunity for all to participate in and benefit from, the outcome was much more successful.

4. Managers are on stage most of the time. What you wear, what you say, and how you act just seems bigger and louder than what anyone else does. James B. Anderson, author of *Speaking to Groups: Eyeball to Eyeball* (1991), calls this the "megaphone effect." So make sure that if you say or do something you want it to be noticed. I made the mistake several times of telling a front-line team member that I needed to talk with him/her, and would s/he please stop by my office when s/he had a minute. Usually it was because I had a nice thank-you note to show him or her or a generic question to ask. But because of my position as administrator, s/he would worry about it all day and show up in my office worried and shaking, and I would be so sorry because I had completely forgotten to assure him or her that s/he was not in trouble.

5. When presented with an idea that does not seem viable, take a moment and ask some questions. Perhaps the idea's originator is thinking with appreciative intelligence and has something innovative that on the surface does not make sense. Inquire further how they are seeing the solution, what they think makes the idea viable, and what resources already exist in the organization that could make it work. Whether or not they can answer these questions will provide insight into the viability of the idea. We held a manager meeting everyday in the senior living communities where I worked to make sure everyone was on the same page. But I tried to always talk to the front line team as well, and get their ideas about how things could be improved. The frontline team really knows what is going on in a senior living community, and if the managers are not talking with them, they are missing out on a lot of valuable information and ideas.

We all have some level of appreciative intelligence, and the good news is that we can learn and develop the processes in ourselves and encourage our teams as well to become more effective at putting them into practice in our work in senior living. Pearce (1998) says, "The professional manager is 'hands-on' and looks for opportunities to develop the strengths of employees, rather than assign blame when things go wrong. The professional manager defines excellence specifically for employees and charts their successes rather than documents their failures." (pp. 52–53). By utilizing "what" rather than "why" questions when clarifying situations with staff such as tardiness to work or resident care challenges, relationships can be preserved by demonstrating concern and trust.

Following are some simple recommendations for applying appreciative intelligence in senior living.

- Try to develop a new appreciative habit in the workplace. Call a family member each week to tell them something positive (e.g., express appreciation for coming by to volunteer or share how much their resident enjoyed an activity). Send a personal note each week to a staff member describing some action he or she took that exemplified the organization's mission and principles. Develop a positive behavior and stick to it until it becomes a habit. Carol Metzker (2007) uses the example of a senior living community that developed a complaint management process as a response to regulations. Because so much attention was being paid to the negative comments and complaints, morale began to suffer, even though some of the complaints were unjustified. The administrator developed a concurrent program that highlighted compliments, which included recognition for staff members at group meetings, in newsletters, and with family members. This counterbalanced the negative effects of the complaint management program, improved morale, and reframed the entire process for the team (Metzker, 2007).

According to the Alzheimer's Association (2009, *Brain Health*), research indicates the following:

- "Keeping the brain active seems to increase its vitality and may build its reserves of brain cells and connections. You could even generate new brain cells. Low levels of education have been found to be related to a higher risk of Alzheimer's later in life. This may be due to a lower level of life-long mental stimulation. Put another way, higher levels of education appear to be somewhat protective against Alzheimer's, possibly because brain cells and their connections are stronger. Well-educated individuals can still get Alzheimer's, but symptoms may appear later because of this protective effect" (Alzheimer's Association, 2009, *Brain Health*, n.p.n.). Choosing to keep the mind active may ward off the potential for developing dementia.
- Smile. Evidently the brain cannot tell the difference between a smile brought on by external stimuli or simply by muscle movement. Holding that smile as long as possible may actually influence happier and more relaxed feelings, and a new perspective. It may also influence a positive response and environment among others. An important part of working in senior living is influencing

the environment, and simply smiling can make a difference in the atmosphere of the senior living community. By keeping a positive attitude, it may help to keep one from losing sight of the reason for the work regardless of the challenges. And the smile will mean so much to those on the receiving end.

CONCLUSION

Providing excellent quality services is the priority in senior living. Applying the principles of appreciative intelligence to all the complex relationships in senior living may enhance the opportunity for success in a variety of ways. Using appreciative intelligence in team member development may help to reduce the traditionally high turnover and improve team member engagement and opportunities for advancement. By modeling appreciative intelligence approaches in their day-to-day interactions, senior living leaders might influence other members of the interdisciplinary team to practice more positive approaches as well. By applying appreciative intelligence in senior living, the opportunity for appropriate responses to resident and team situations can be increased, resulting in better quality care provided in a positive, appreciative environment.

REFERENCES

Adams, M. (2009). *Change your questions, change your life.* San Francisco: Berrett-Koehler Publishers, Inc.

Albrecht, K. (2006). *Social intelligence: The new science of success.* San Francisco: Jossey-Bass.

Alzheimer's Association (2009). *David's story.* Retrieved from http://www.alz.org/living_with_alzheimers_10926.asp

Alzheimer's Association. (2009, September 24). Brain health: Stay mentally active. *Alz.org.* Retrieved from http://www.alz.org/we_can_help_stay_mentally_active.asp

Alzheimer's Association. (2009). *Don's story.* Retrieved from http://www.alz.org/living_with_alzheimers_8707.asp

Anderson, J. B. (1991). *Speaking to groups: Eyeball to eyeball.* Vienna, VA: Wyndmoor Press.

Cooperrider, D., Whitney, D., & Stavros, J. (2003). *Appreciative intelligence handbook: The first in a series of AI workbooks for leaders of change.* San Francisco: Berrett-Koehler Publishers, Inc.

Frankl, V. E. (1984). *Man's search for meaning.* New York: Washington Square Press.

Goleman, D. (1997). *Emotional intelligence: Why it can matter more than IQ.* New York: Bantam Books.

Grossmann, I., Na, J., Varnum, M. E. W., Park, D. C., Kitayama, S., & Nisbett, R. E. (2010). Reasoning about social conflicts improves into old age. *PNAS, 107*(16), 7246–7250. doi:10.1073/pnas.1001715107

Martin, A. (2009, July/August). New reality for residents with Alzheimer's. *Assisted Living Executive.* Retrieved from http://www.alfa.org/assnfe/Article.asp?clArticleID=221&SnID=515445119

Metzker, C. (2007). The best employees are right under your nose: Because you create them. *A-ideas.com.* Retrieved from http://www.a-ideas.com/BestEmployeesbyCMetzker.pdf

Pearce, B. W. (1998) *Senior living communities: Operations management and marketing for assisted living, congregate, and continuing care retirement communities.* Baltimore: The Johns Hopkins University Press.

Thatchenkery, T., & Metzker, C. (2006). *Appreciative intelligence: Seeing the mighty oak in the acorn.* San Francisco: Berrett-Koehler Publishers, Inc.

U.S. Department of Health and Human Services, Administration on Aging. (2004). *A profile of older Americans: 2004.* Washington, D.C.: Author. Retrieved from http://assets.aarp.org/rgcenter/general/profile_2004.pdf

CHAPTER 11

SPAN OF CONTROL

Designing Organizations for Effectiveness

Kelly Topp and Jon H. Desjardins

ABSTRACT

As organizations strive to be more effective, one of the variables they consider is how many direct reports their leaders can effectively manage; this is referred to as *span of control* (SOC). Although much research has been conducted on this topic, the literature does not identify an optimal SOC for leaders; appropriate SOCs reported in the literature range from 5 to 30. This is due to the significant number of factors that need to be taken into consideration when determining the optimal number of direct reports for a manager. These factors fall into four categories: employee characteristics, manager characteristics, work characteristics, and organization characteristics. Central questions explored in this chapter are whether or not it is appropriate, given the complexity of health care, to have SOCs that are more than double what they are in less complex industries and what can be done to optimize the number of direct reports a manager might have. This chapter concludes with a case study that explains a systematic approach for exploring, analyzing, and optimizing an organization's SOC, while highlighting the role of the OD practitioner in this process.

Organization Development in Health Care, pages 211–230
Copyright © 2011 by Information Age Publishing
211

INTRODUCTION

In a down economy, nearly all companies cut expenses. Even when times are good, organizations are trending toward leaner, flatter organizational structures. Removing layers in the organization, most commonly middle management, often results in increased SOCs for many managers. SOC commonly refers to the number of direct reports that people have and does not typically refer to the number of FTEs (full time equivalent) assigned to that manager (Cathcart, Miller, Jeska, Pechacek, Karnas, & Rheault, 2004).

It is difficult to determine the optimal SOC for organizations. This is due in part to the many variables that must be factored in to determine optimal SOC and the fact that much of the research on this topic is contradictory. Coupled with such a complex environment as health care, the challenge of determining the optimal SOC increases greatly. Thus, many articles on the topic focus not on what the optimal SOC should be, but rather how large it can be while still allowing healthcare managers to be effective.

The question central to this chapter is whether it is appropriate to have SOCs in health care that are more than double what they are in less complex industries. If it is not appropriate, what can be done to optimize the number of direct reports a manager might have? To explore this topic, this chapter will briefly review the history and background of SOC research, relate the current research on the topic to health care, and offer recommendations for analysis using data from a large healthcare system.

HISTORY OF SPAN OF CONTROL RESEARCH

SOC has long been a topic of discussion, going back thousands of years. In Roman times, it was widely believed that an SOC of 10 was effective, but nearly two millennia later, Napoleon felt that an SOC of only 5 was more appropriate (Hopej & Martan, 2006). When research began in earnest on this topic in the 1950s, Fayol, a management theorist, wrote that between 5 and 15 was appropriate (Hopej & Martan, 2006; McManus, 2007; Pabst, 1993). Other researchers and theorists in the '50s specified that executives should limit their SOC to four or five, but that other organizational layers could manage between 8 and 12 (Pabst, 1993; Hattrup & Kleiner, 1993). Classic studies on SOC typically find that smaller SOCs are optimal, with most stating that between 8 and 12 is ideal. When the work is quite simple, the optimal SOC can possibly be increased to 20–30 direct reports (Cathcart et al., 2004). From these numbers alone, one can see how difficult it might be to determine what is effective and appropriate for one's organization.

Much of the research initially conducted on SOC was done with manufacturing companies, military organizations, or organizations that have been around a long time, such as the Catholic Church. Because of the specific nature of these types of organizations, the findings cannot necessarily be applied to other types of organizations or industries (Hattrup & Kleiner, 1993; Altaffer, 1998). In particular, the findings may not translate well to healthcare settings because demands on front-line nursing managers are greater due to complex hospital environments. In the 1990s, research on SOCs in health care increased, but this only focused on a few variables, most notably relationship between manager and staff, complexity of work, and the capabilities of the manager and the staff (Cathcart et al., 2004).

The research was consistently flawed because it did not effectively consider all variables when trying to determine optimal SOC (Hattrup & Kleiner, 1993). Variables related to the organization, manager, employee, or work being conducted need to be considered when examining SOC, but including all of the variables necessary for an accurate picture would have made the research overly complex. Had the previous research taken into account all of these factors, despite the complexity, the research would have been viewed as more valid (Pabst, 1993).

DEVELOPMENT OF SOC

Given the documented drawbacks to large SOCs, which will be discussed later in this chapter, what accounts for the ever-increasing SOCs? Several reasons are cited: the desire that people have to report to the boss directly; empire-building; cost reduction and overhead cutting; gains associated with shorter chains of command, such as faster response time and quicker decision making; and the desire to push authority and responsibility down the chain (Davison, 2003). Primarily, the key reason is budget. SOC decisions are often brought about because of the need to cut costs, with little regard for the effectiveness of the organizational structure. One author illustrates this dramatically: "[D]ecreasing the SOC from eight to four in a company of 4,000 nonmanagerial employees can make a difference of nearly 800 managers" (Bell & McLaughlin, 1977, p. 23). Not only are managers within an organizational level eliminated, sometimes entire levels of management are eliminated, which can dramatically increase SOC. This is often referred to as "delayering" and is often done without fully thinking through the implications.

Building the organizational hierarchy and structure this way results in an organization that is built reactively, not proactively and according to a plan. These decisions are often made in a time of crisis, financial or otherwise. In these instances, leaders have no good method for assessing which parts of the management structure are needed and which are superfluous. These changes are often made with no assessment of the current structure's effectiveness (Dive, 2003). The lack of a well thought out process, methodology, or formula for how SOCs are determined is especially common for health-care systems. Organizational structures generally come to be without much deliberate thought (Cathcart et al., 2004).

APPLICATIONS OF SOC RESEARCH TO HEALTH CARE

Examining the effectiveness of SOCs in health care is important for several reasons, the first being that health care as an industry has a significant presence in our country. In fact, health care as an "organized endeavor is the 3rd largest employer in the United States" (McConnell, 2000, p. 2) and ranks as the 2nd largest service industry in the States, outranked only by government (local, state, and federal combined). Secondly, health care is a diverse, complex industry. Health care is subject to frequent, significant technological changes. Historically, many proven and reliable management practices were not applied to health care because those in health care believed them to be inapplicable due to the unique nature of healthcare industry. Health care is characterized by very close customer contact, possibly more so than any other industry, so there is some validity to the belief that health care is unique. The third factor that makes health care unique is the inability to predict outputs. In manufacturing, both inputs and outputs are consistent and predictable. Not so in health care. This lack of predictability is also reflected in job structure. One thing that nurses often cite as a desirable aspect of their job is that every day presents a different set of challenges; it is not repetitive work (McConnell, 2000).

Taking all of these factors into consideration forces one to question whether the SOC research conducted in manufacturing is applicable to health care. There is also a significant difference in SOCs of healthcare organizations compared to other organizations. Referring back to the classical studies done on SOC, we can see that most recommendations for SOC fall into the 8–12 range, with only the simplest jobs allowing for larger numbers of direct reports. In health care, however, it is not uncommon to see the number of direct reports upwards of 20 to 30 in some clinical units. Similarly, a 2001 benchmarking report (as cited in Davison, 2003) found that the median SOC in health care is 16, but for all other organizations it was only 7. With a more complex, unique environment, one must ask if it is appropriate to have a SOC in health care more than double that of other industries (Davison, 2003).

THE IMPORTANCE OF SOC

Studying SOC and reaching some recommendation on what is appropriate and effective is important, as it impacts many organizational variables, including:

- *Organizational effectiveness*: Effective organizations have significantly different SOCs than ineffective organizations (Pabst 1993).
- *Decision making*: A specific study on Sears and Roebuck in the 1950s found that SOC was related to the quality of decisions made (Bell & McLaughlin, 1977).
- *Revenue growth*: Companies with the narrowest SOCs had the highest rate of revenue growth (over 20%), but companies with the largest SOCs had low to medium growth rates (Davison, 2003).
- *Agility*: Organizations with large SOCs tend to have decreased agility and flexibility in responding to external factors (Davison, 2003; Morash, Brintnell, & Lemire-Rodger, 2005). *Communication*: A flatter organization can be more effective and accurate in getting information from the top layers of the organization to the bottom (Hattrup & Kleiner, 1993; Doran et al., 2004; Morash et al., 2005).
- *Employee satisfaction and engagement*: Gallup Q12 scores that measure employee engagement decrease as SOC increases (Cathcart et al., 2004).
- *Job satisfaction*: Narrower SOCs contribute to higher levels of job satisfaction (Davison, 2003; Morash et al., 2005; Hechanova-Alampay & Beehr, 2001).
- *Patient satisfaction*: Patient satisfaction is lower on units where managers have a large number of direct reports (Doran et al., 2004).
- *Turnover*: Turnover tends to increase as SOCs get larger (Morash et al., 2005). *Relationships*: Relationships between managers and subordinates become less positive as the SOC increases (Doran et al., 2004).
- *Safety*: Increased SOCs are often coupled with greater responsibilities, increased work load, longer hours on the job, and decreased monitoring of employees, all of which are linked to an increase in unsafe work behaviors and accidents (Hechanova-Alampay & Beehr, 2001).
- *Promotional opportunities*: Because traditional career paths may not be present in flatter organizations, there are fewer promotional opportunities for employees (McConnell, 2000).

Despite the many reasons to achieve optimal SOC, the need to review SOCs in the organization can also arise for operational reasons. The healthcare organization highlighted in this chapter became interested in SOC because of a need to improve its performance management system. One recommendation that resulted from this work was to have all individuals in the organization on a common review period that aligns with the strategic planning and budgeting cycles. The strain that a common review period can place on leaders with large SOCs can be overwhelming and can make the performance review process ineffective. Before making a final decision to move to a common review period, the organization needed to assess the SOCs and look for the optimal leader-to-employee ratio that would improve their effectiveness and allow for a common review period.

FACTORS THAT IMPACT OPTIMAL SOC

There are four categories that must be analyzed to determine the appropriate SOC for an organization. Those include employee characteristics, manager characteristics, work characteristics, and organizational characteristics. How those characteristics drive SOC will change depending on the level of the organization. Factors that may be important in determining SOC at one level of the organization may be irrelevant at another (Meier & Bohte, 2003). This chapter will examine the factors that determine optimal SOC as they relate to a healthcare setting to see if a recommendation on SOC can be determined. Because no optimal or recommended SOC can be found in current literature that relates to health care, each organization must weigh the variables to determine what is most appropriate.

Employee Characteristics

The employees themselves can impact how large an SOC a manager can effectively handle. Experience level is one variable that must be taken into account when determining a manager's SOC. The more experienced employees are, the larger the SOC that manger can tolerate. This is because these are highly developed employees who tend to function effectively with less supervision and who can monitor their own performance (Texas State Classification Office, 2003; Meier & Bohte, 2003). If your unit has a great deal of new-grad nurses, the SOC must be more narrow for managers as they mentor, on-board, and proctor new nurses. According to a survey done in 2004 by the American Association of Critical-Care Nurses (AACN), 81% of all critical care nurses are over the age of 40 (Siela, Twibell, & Keller, n.d.), which implies that they are generally a very experienced group; this indicates that a manager might be able to function effectively with more direct reports because employees require less guidance and can self-monitor their performance. As these nurses grow older and approach retirement, though, younger (and, thus, less experienced) nurses will replace them, which will require a narrowing of SOC for managers to remain effective. The point to note here is that what is an optimal SOC one year may change as the organization and the staff evolve. Nursing units that perform less routine work also generally require smaller SOCs because of the increased need and complex nature of the information required to make decisions.

Thus, a nursing unit such as the emergency department would require a more narrow SOC than a pre-op nursing unit, which can tolerate a larger SOC. Similarly, employees who need more hands-on coaching and development require more time from their manager, so a more narrow SOC is more effective (Davison, 2003).

The competence and level of education of the staff has a similar impact as experience. Nurses who are highly educated and competent tend to work autonomously and need less supervision, which means that the manager can handle a larger staff (Bell & McLaughlin, 1977). Collectively looking at all nurses, almost 31% hold a bachelor's degree, while only 13% hold an advanced degree (Siela, Twibell, & Keller, n.d). Managers will need to examine the mix of degrees in their unit and weigh this when determining an appropriate SOC.

Employee characteristics such as self-control and trustworthiness also need to be taken into account when determining SOC. Nurses who are disciplined and have a high degree of self-control tend to need less supervision than other nurses who may not be as skilled at self-control. Similarly, those who are trusted and empowered to make decisions need less supervision than others (Texas State Classification Office, 2003; Hattrup & Kleiner, 1993).

Interdependence between employees and the geographical dispersion can also impact what an appropriate SOC would be. Greater and more complex interdependence between employees and geographical dispersion of employees work best with narrower SOCs (Hopej & Martan, 2006; Davison, 2003). Units that tend to require more collaboration and interdependence are units such as labor and delivery or medical imaging because of patient flow between units. Thus, managers in these types of units will not be as effective with large numbers of direct reports.

Manager Characteristics

The characteristics of the manager can impact the size of the SOC that he or she can effectively manage. Some of these characteristics are related to the nurse manager, but others are related to his or her position in the organization. One characteristic related to the manager is that of leadership style. Managers who are well liked and who lead by encouragement and inspiration can effectively manage larger SOCs because they inspire better performance in their employees. Yet, the AACN reports that less than half of nurses report that their relationship with their manager is positive (AACN, 2005). This would imply that nearly half of all nursing managers would function better with smaller SOCs. This could potentially be mitigated by nurse mangers who are effective at delegation and have a participatory leadership style, characteristics that can allow them to manage a larger staff effectively (Hattrup & Kleiner, 1993). The competence and experience of the manager needs to be factored in when determining SOC. As with employees, the greater the competence and experience, the larger SOC that manager can tolerate (Texas State Classification Office, 2003; Hattrup & Kleiner, 1993).

Middle managers tend to have more diverse functions reporting up to them than front-line managers do, and they tend to deal with more complexity, which would indicate that SOCs should be narrower. The middle-level nurse manager is often a Senior Clinical Manager or Director, and these roles tend to have smaller SOCs in our data sample. Conversely, managers at this level tend to have more experience, which would indicate that a larger SOC could be tolerated for these types of roles (Hopej & Martan, 2006). It is common for the largest SOCs to occur with the front-line nurse leaders, who also tend to be the least experienced. This is an issue that needs to be corrected, based on the research.

Pressure put on the manager can also influence appropriate SOC. Managers who feel a great deal of performance pressure tend to be less likely to delegate decisions, which would cause them to need a more narrow SOC (Simet & Dewar, 1981). With budget cuts, publicly reported CMS measures, and increased transparency of patient satisfaction scores, performance pressure is increasing for nursing managers. This makes delegation riskier. Shared leadership, which is becoming increasingly popular, could be one avenue that would allow managers to effectively delegate, allowing them to operate more effectively with a larger SOC, despite the increasing performance pressures. Also related to the manager's role is the significant amount of administrative work many nursing managers have as part of their role. Those with a large administrative burden need a narrower SOC (Hopej & Martan, 2006). We often see that frontline nursing managers still have to remain "in the count" and deliver nursing care. They are required to do this while juggling the significant administrative duties that accompany a front-line manager's role. This cuts down on the amount of time they have to dedicate to leadership activities, which would necessitate fewer direct reports.

Work Characteristics

Not only are characteristics related to the employee and the manager relevant when examining SOC, the variables related to the work itself must be factored in. Work complexity is a key factor. Greater complexity and diversity of work requires a narrower SOC for managers to be effective (Davison, 2003). In one study, complexity of work was identified by the following variables: hours of operation, unpredictability, high patient turnover, risk of litigation, and number of adverse incidents (Morash et al., 2005). An example of such a unit would be a neonatal intensive care unit or an emergency department. If work is standardized by procedures and clear policies are present, a larger SOC can be tolerated (Bell & McLaughlin, 1977; Hattrup & Kleiner, 1993). This is difficult to achieve for all but the most basic, routine nursing procedures. Organizations or units that have more routine, more homogenous, and less specialized work (both in task and personnel) can tolerate larger SOCs. This is the case in part because of the need for information. Subordinates who work in a department that is routine and consistent require less information from their supervisors. Few of these types of units exist in health care, but one example might be physical therapy. Supervisors of highly-specialized functions, such as a bone-marrow transplant unit, are a primary source of information and will need to spend more time communicating, which necessitates smaller SOCs. Highly specialized functions also tend to demand leaders with the same specialization, thus increasing the need for more managers with narrow SOCs (Simet & Dewar, 1981).

The responsibilities of front-line staff impact how many layers are needed to support them. Further, treating all departments the same and giving them an identical number of layers will introduce unnecessary hierarchy into some departments. Because the responsibilities of a function such as central scheduling are different than, for example, the responsibilities of front-line nursing, the organizational structure needs to be flexible to support them accordingly (Dive, 2003). In other words, different functions in the organization will need different numbers of layers to effectively support them because highly professional staff (e.g., engineers, doctors, and lawyers) can function more effectively with larger SOCs (Hattrup & Kleiner, 1993).

One of the key responsibilities of a manager is to provide an employee with feedback. Thus, an organization with tools and jobs designed to provide employees with direct feedback can support a larger SOC, as can organizations that successfully employ self-managed work teams (Davison, 2003; Texas State Classification Office, 2003). As healthcare organizations evolve and catch up with other industries in terms of systems and formal structures, they are improving their performance management systems. A mature, well-developed performance management system will allow nursing managers to have larger numbers of direct reports because the process of providing feedback will be more meaningful and less arduous. Jobs that have built-in feedback mechanisms, such as monitoring equipment, allow for larger SOCs because nurses receive immediate feedback on their actions and performance and do not need a manager to continually provide that for them. Goal alignment can also increase the ability for a manager to deal with a larger SOC. This relates to performance management because many well-developed performance management systems promote goal alignment and cascading. Congruence among direct reports' goals as well as cascaded goals from the manager and the organization can allow for greater SOCs (Hattrup & Kleiner, 1993) because everyone will be on the same page and striving for the same results and outcomes. Nursing managers who have strong goal alignment with their direct reports will need to spend less time focusing everyone's work.

The equipment or materials needed to support the work are also a factor. Groups with equipment that is highly specialized and that requires regular monitoring and maintenance, vendor interactions, and quality checks will necessitate a smaller SOC (Morash et al., 2005). Such examples can be found with the high-frequency oscillatory vent in the neonatal intensive care unit.

Organizational Characteristics

Organizational characteristics are often overlooked when determining what the optimal SOC is, but they are just as relevant as employee, manager, or work characteristics. Three related organizational factors that help determine SOC are: change, stability, and diversity. An organization that has significant amounts of change in the work environment and high levels of diversity would be better suited with a more narrow SOC (Davison, 2003; Texas State Classification Office, 2003). Similarly, when the organization and its environment is more stable, managers can handle a greater SOC than when the organizational and environment is more dynamic (Hattrup & Kleiner, 1993). Much has been documented on the state of change in health care and the rapid advances in medicine; all of these advancements point to the need for smaller SOCs because of the necessity to disseminate information as well as help employees deal with the stress of constant, never-ending change.

One type of stability is related to turnover. As stated earlier, stable organizations with less turnover can also tolerate larger SOCs because managers will be involved in less training, development of new staff, and on-boarding (Davison, 2003; Meier & Bohte, 2003). In addition to turnover, significant hiring can decrease the stability of an organization. The Department of Labor recently stated that more than 1 million new and replacement nursing positions will be needed by 2016, which will make nursing the fastest growing profession in the country (Dohm & Shniper, 2007). A significant number of new, less experienced nurses and this decreased stability will require smaller SOCs in nursing.

Organizational size and growth can also dictate what is an appropriate SOC. Larger organizations tend to have both larger SOCs and more layers of management, but smaller organizations tend to have narrower SOCs and fewer layers (Davison, 2003). The size of the healthcare facility often dictates how many functions report to one nursing manager. Nursing Directors in smaller healthcare facilities often have multiple functions reporting up to them, which necessitates a smaller SOC, but Directors in larger facilities tend to be more specialized and have fewer functions reporting up to them, factors which also need to be taken into consideration when looking at the number of direct reports that is optimal.

Organizations that are geographically spread out or housed in multiple buildings require smaller SOCs because of the coordination required by managers. This is related to organizational size in the sense that larger organizations are often more spread out and geographically dispersed (Davison, 2003; Meier & Bohte, 2003; Texas State Classification Office, 2003). The case study in this chapter highlights an organization that has 22 locations across 7 states in the western U.S. Such a geographically dispersed organization would require smaller SOCs according to such theories. If each facility is allowed to operate autonomously, though, this variable is less of a factor when determining optimal SOC.

OPTIMAL SOC

Despite the significant need for best practice data around SOC, no recommendation of optimal SOC in health care can be found in the literature. This is because of the great variability in different units within health care and the factors that must be taken into consideration when examining appropriate SOC. A recent survey of 22 magnet hospitals revealed that not one hospital surveyed had a standardized SOC for front-line nursing managers (Morash et al., 2005). Based on the overwhelming evidence that points to the importance of achieving optimal SOC, it is worthy of concentrated organizational effort to improve SOC for managers in healthcare.

There are some methods or tools available to help determine the appropriate SOC. All of these methods are useful to some degree, but research highlights potential flaws in each method. Methods that assign values to factors related to the job or organization are criticized for not taking all factors into consideration or because the rating scale and values are too arbitrary (Hopej & Martan, 2006). Thus, it is our recommendation that healthcare leaders begin with the healthcare industry median and add or subtract based on the variables above to achieve their organization's (or unit's) optimal SOC. This will allow organizations to take the variability of each unit and organization into consideration.

Determining SOC is an iterative process. Outcome variables need to be identified (e.g., patient satisfaction, employee satisfaction, retention) and measured after each change in SOC to determine if the changes were effective from a holistic standpoint. Additional refinement may be necessary after measuring outcomes to achieve optimal SOC. We also recommend that determining the optimal SOC be done on a unit-by-unit basis. Because of the number of factors that are relevant when determining SOC, there is not a single optimal number for all units or departments within an organization.

THE CASE STUDY

The organization in this case study is a 22-hospital system in the western U.S. with more than 30,000 employees in small, medium, and large hospitals that range in bed count from less than 20 to more than 600. The case study follows a systematic approach for exploring, analyzing, and optimizing an organization's SOC. The steps we outlined for achieving the optimal SOC start with an understanding of the data sources used for monitoring and analyzing an organization's leadership structure and SOC. The next step includes a full analysis of the data to identify outliers and exceptions. Step three includes a gap analysis and recommendations for improvement. The final step is designing and implementing a plan that will help the organiza-tion achieve its vision. The OD practitioner plays a vital role throughout the process by challenging the organization's thinking around structure, pro-viding a strategic view of the analysis and gaps, and finally by helping the organization with acceptance of change.

Understanding the Data Source

The first area of focus is the data source used for understanding the organization's SOC and layers of leadership (LOL). Most organizations use human resource information systems (HRIS) that can store and track the appropriate data to identify an organization's SOC and LOL , but the use of HRIS does not guarantee the integrity of the data. In order for the data to be valuable, there are a few assumptions that must be tested to validate the integrity of an organization's HRIS data:

- The process for entering data into the HRIS is reliable.
- The data fields with the HRIS are used effectively.
- Key data fields are used consistently and with common purpose.
- Role of leader is consistently defined in the HRIS.

Our analysis of the data source identified that data entry may need some improvement, the data fields are being used effectively, some of the fields used need clarity with different users, and leadership definitions are close in consistency. While this analysis identified opportunities for improvement, the data was reliable enough to proceed with the next step in the process. The OD practitioner's role in this step is to partner with HRIS staff and gain acceptance of the reliability and effectiveness of the data source.

Analyzing the Data

Once the data source is assessed for reliability, effectiveness, and understanding, the next step is to analyze the current data. The data analysis includes looking at the distribution of SOC, the outliers, and the exceptions at the different levels in the organization. Data distribution will help uncover the range of the organization's SOC. Distribution will also help identify the outliers. Some of these outliers will be uncovered when assessing the data source, while others will need to be researched and analyzed. The key to reviewing the organization's data is to fully understand the outliers and remove the exceptions from the data review. Without removing the exceptions, the data may be skewed, presenting a false picture of the data results. The research into the case study data uncovered a few exceptions that could skew the data.

Understanding Exceptions in SOC

The first of these exceptions relates to contracted services an organization uses. A common scenario in health care is that occasionally the leadership function of a service is contracted out, but the workforce supporting the service is employed by the organization. An example of this could be a food services function where a contracted company provides the management of the service; however, the food preparation, delivery, and sterilization are performed by employees of the hospital. Within the HRIS, the employees may be assigned to a single manager, but this may not be the individual to whom they report. This manager may have up to 100 direct reports, but is not performing supervisory duties. Supervisory duties may be performed by a contracted leader who is not linked to a supervisor code within the HRIS. This type of outlier can be managed, but unfortunately, the SOC for this group will need to be calculated manually. This exception can be found in other industries that use contracted functions.

Another exception comes from a function somewhat unique to health care. Within a hospital setting, some functions and structures use a registry for part-time or contracted nurse support. This is largely due in part to registered nurse shortages across the country. The staff that are used from a registry are assigned to different sections of a hospital based on demand and skill; however, assignments are not always permanent or long-term. A registry nurse could work for several leaders over a short period of time. Because of the constant movement of these employees, they are assigned to a single manager within a staffing function. This manager can have more than 100 employees showing as direct reports within the HRIS. This exception is easy to identify and should be filtered out when analyzing the data.

The next exception to be aware of is leaders with only one direct report. If an organization has a large number of leaders with only one direct report, the data can be skewed or misleading if one is looking at the averages. There are some legitimate reasons for leaders to have only one direct report; however, the organization needs to assess this group thoroughly to understand the reasons for such a small SOC. The known exceptions should be minimal and may not need to be isolated from the data analysis.

Filtering Data

Data used during the review is a moving target and will only provide a snap-shot in time. Understanding that the source data is active and continuously changing is critical when presenting the results of the review. A useful technique in looking at the data is to filter it by the key factors that make up a leader's SOC. Filtering the data allows you to focus on a core set of data and usually involves aggregation of data (e.g., totals broken down by position title, leadership level, or even organization structure). There are several slices of the data that we found useful in our analysis. These include filtering by number of direct reports, leadership levels, and chain of command. Further filters to consider are by regions, facility, and role in the organization. Our initial analysis only explored the data at a system level (all 22 facilities).

Filtering by Number of Direct Reports

The first slice of data to review relates to the number of direct reports each leader has assigned. This view shows grouping of leaders by the number of direct reports they have. The data provides a good picture of distribution when placed into a simple bar chart. The chart can reveal the ranges of SOC and to what magnitude they occur. The case study data set shows that the normal distribution ranges from 1 to about 40 direct reports, with the tail expanding out to over 130 (Figure 11.1). 80% of the leadership group falls within the 1 to 19 range. Leaders with 40+ direct reports only make up 4% of the leadership population and are outliers that need exploration. Another issue evident from this view is the number of leaders (114,

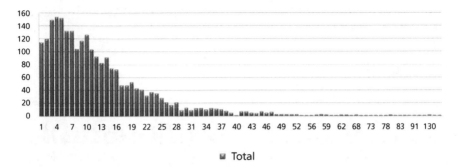

Figure 11.1 Number of leaders by number of direct reports.

or 5%) with only one direct report. This is an area that will require some exploration, as well.

This method of looking at the data will show frequency and distribution of the organization's SOC. From here, the depth and span of some of the outliers can be seen.

Filtering by Leadership Levels

When the HRIS uses leadership levels, another pivot table can be created showing the number of direct reports by leadership level. This slice into the data is a good way to look at an outlier group to see where the issues are. A bar graph (Figure 11.2) that compares leadership levels will reveal some interesting points about the outliers. The case study organization identifies leaders into 4 categories. Level 1 (not shown) is emergent leaders. These are individual contributors aspiring to become formal leaders and who currently have no direct reports. Level 2 leaders supervise individual contributors. Level 3 leaders supervise formal leaders, and level 4 leaders lead the enterprise. This view of the data can identify a specific level of leadership that has large SOCs. The case study data shows that the Level 2 leader (supervises individual contributors) has a larger number (69%) of leaders with large SOCs. In this data sample, this is most frequently a clinical manager (front-line nurse manager). The definition for a large SOC needs to be defined by the organization and usually is dependent on the function of the organization and other variables mentioned previously. It can also identify some key outliers, such as four level 4 leaders with greater than 50 direct reports. This same slice of data can be run against the leaders with less than 3 direct reports. This can help identify whether there is a specific group of leaders that fall into this group. Results showed that level 2

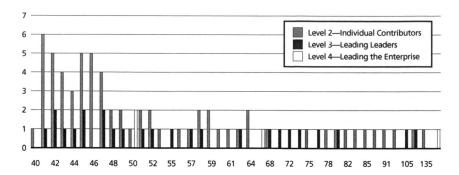

Figure 11.2 Number of leaders by leader level.

and 3 leaders made up 88% of the leaders with less than 3 direct reports (data not displayed).

Understanding the Chain of Command

Looking at the numbers is a good starting point for assessing the organization's SOCs and can be very telling. It is also a place to start the analysis; however, the SOC does not reveal the organization's structure. This will require a review of the data through a different lens. When the HRIS is used effectively, a report can be generated that shows the layers of leadership an organization has within its structure. The top of the pyramid is considered the 1st layer. The number of layers below the 1st layer can tell you a lot about the structure of the organization. Figure 11.3 is a representation of these layers related to healthcare systems. This shows seven layers of leaders between the company's CEO and the individual contributor.

This is a rather simple view of the organization's leadership structure. Comprehensive organization charts that show reporting structures are the best source for understanding the organization's structure. This is a critical element in assessing layers of leadership and associated SOC. This view of leadership can help with determining the proper SOCs needed for the organization. It can also identify possible areas for improving structure. One area to note is the names of the roles associated with each level of leadership. If the role descriptions are not consistent within the HRIS, this could prove to be a painful process; however, the insight gained through this slice of the data will help uncover true exceptions of the data that may be perfectly acceptable. Some of the leaders with only one direct report may be indirect leaders of larger groups of leaders that are aligned with their functional responsibilities. Their only direct reports in the HRIS may be their administrative supports. The analysis of the case study data showed

Figure 11.3 The organization's leadership structure.

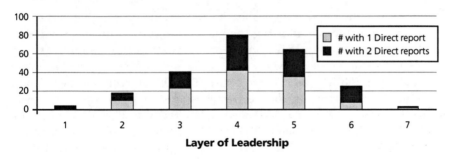

Figure 11.4 Number of leaders with one direct report by leadership layer.

that directors made up 24% and managers/supervisors made up 33% of the leaders with fewer than 3 direct reports (See Figure 11.4).

Figure 11.4 is a look at the number of leaders with fewer than 3 direct reports and what layers of leadership they report to. This slice of the data can help clarify some of the outliers. The OD practitioner provides assistance in understanding the organization's structure and in exploring the outliers. They also provide guidance to the team conducting the analysis by challenging the thinking and understanding of the data.

IDENTIFYING THE GAPS AND OPPORTUNITIES FOR IMPROVEMENT

Understanding the structure of the organization and a thorough analysis of its current SOC should uncover some opportunities for improvement.

Exploring the outliers will also uncover some quick wins and possible restructuring opportunities. The case study uncovered a need to decrease the number of direct reports for a group of leaders and relook at the leaders with only one direct report. The exploration of the layers of leadership also uncovered a need to look at how the organization is structured to support the organization's mission and vision. This organization is still struggling with determining the optimal number of direct reports a leader should have, largely due to the significant number of variables that factor into determining optimal SOC. The data provides a picture that looks good on the surface, but after a deeper dive, it uncovered some trends and practices that were causing large SOCs across the organization. The OD practitioner can assist with identifying cultural issues that cause some of the gaps and help assess the acceptance of the overall analysis.

PLANNING AND IMPLEMENTING CHANGE

Regardless of the opportunities that the analysis identifies, a big part of the gap analysis includes identifying the magnitude of the changes needed in order to close the gap. This is all a part of the implementation planning process. This step is often overlooked, which will cause issues in closing the gaps identified during the analysis phase. The OD practitioner is extremely helpful to the team during this step by focusing the team on options to overcome resistance and to manage the change effectively. Part of the planning process is to figure out what actions need to be taken and then determine the feasibility for success. Some key factors to explore when doing the feasibility check are financial impact, human capital impact, and operational impact. The OD practitioner provides great insight in the planning process by keeping the team focused on the human aspect of change.

CONCLUSION

When determining the appropriate SOC for an organization, a multitude of factors impact the optimal SOC. Healthcare systems have some unique factors that make this decision even more complex. We conclude that determining appropriate SOC is an iterative process for an organization, one that should take into consideration all variables related to the employee, the manager, the work itself, and the organization. It is not appropriate to set a one-size-fits-all related to SOC, so we recommend that it be looked at on a unit-by-unit basis. Leadership of that organization should keep their ear to the ground, observe behaviors, and measure outcomes. This iterative method can be effective because the factors that can impact SOC are dynamic, human behavior is hard to predict, and the iterative process allows for continual checking and correcting of SOC (Hopej & Martan, 2006). The OD practitioner adds value by bringing forth knowledge of good organizational structure; thinking strategically; and, from a systems perspective, keeping the team focused on all the influencers related to SOC and by acting as a change agent to help the organization manage the human side of change. Although no quick fix is available and no exact SOC can be recommended, using the expertise of the OD practitioner to optimize SOC can dramatically improve organizational effectiveness and employee satisfaction.

REFERENCES

American Association of Critical-Care Nurses. (2005). *AACN standards for establishing and sustaining healthy work environments.* Aliso Viejo, CA: Author. Retreived from http://www.aacn.org/WD/HWE/Docs/HWEStandards.pdf

Altaffer, A. (1998). First-line managers: Measuring their SOC. *Nursing Management, 6,* 36–39.

Bell, R. R., & McLaughlin, F. (1977). SOC in organizations. *Industrial Management, 19*(5), 23–26.

Cathcart, D., Miller, S., Jeska, S., Pechacek, J., Karnas, J., & Rheault, L. (2004). SOC matters. *Journal of Nursing Administration, 34*(9), 395–399.

Davison, B. (2003). Management SOC: How wide is too wide? *Journal of Business Strategy, 24*(4), 22–29.

Dive, B. (2003). When is an organization too flat? *Across the Board, 40*(4), 20–23.

Dohm, A., & Shniper, L. (2007). Occupational employment projections. *Monthly Labor Review, 130*(11), 86–125.

Doran, D., Sanchez McCutcheon, A., Evans, M. G., MacMillan, K., McGillis Hall, L., Pringle, D., Smith, S., & Valente, A. (2004, September). *Impact of the Manager's SOC on Leadership and Performance.* Retrieved from http://www.nursingleadership.org.uk/publications/doran2_final.pdf

Hattrup, G. P., & Kleiner, B. H. (1993). How to establish the proper SOC for managers. *Industrial Management, 35*(6), 28–29.

Hechanova-Alampay, R., & Beehr, T. A. (2001). Empowerment, SOC, and safety performance in work teams after workforce reduction. *Journal of Occupational Health Psychology, 6*(4), 275–282.

Hopej, M., & Martan, J. (2006). The determination of SOC. *Badania Operacyjne i Decyzje, 2*(9), 55–62

McConnell, C. R. (2000). The changing face of health care managers. *Health Care Manager, 18*(3), 1–17.

McManus, K. (2007). Losing our span of control. *Industrial Engineer, 39*(9), 22.

Meier, K. J., & Bohte, J. (2003). SOC and public organizations: Implementing Luther Gulick's research design. *Public Administration Review, 63*(1), 61–70.

Morash, R., Brintnell, J., & Lemire-Rodger, G. (2005). A SOC tool for clinical managers. *Nursing Leadership, 18*(3), 83–93.

Pabst, M. K. (1993). SOC on nursing inpatient units. *Nursing Economics, 11*(2), 87–90.

Simet, D. P., & Dewar, R. D. (1981). A level specific prediction of SOCs examining the effects of size, technology, and specialization. *Academy of Management Journal, 24*(1), 5–24.

Siela, D., Twibell, K. R., Keller, V. (n.d.). The shortage of nurses and nursing faculty: What critical care nurses can do. *AACN.org*. Retrieved from http://www.aacn.org/WD/Careers/Content/TOC-3.pcms?pid=1&&menu=

Texas State Classification Office. (2003, September). *Assessing your organizational SOC*. Austin, TX: Author. Retrieved from http://jobfunctions.bnet.com/abstract.aspx?docid=83069

CHAPTER 12

INNOVATION AND ENGAGEMENT

What Works When Diligence and Good Intentions Are Not Enough

Lisa Kimball and Carlos R. Arce

ABSTRACT

Although some quality problems in healthcare settings can be solved with new technology or breakthroughs in medical practice, many problems turn out to be simple in the sense that changes in how caregivers do basic things—like hand washing—turn out to make the critical difference. *Positive deviance* (PD) is based on the belief that in every community there are certain individuals or groups whose special practices or strategies enable them to find more successful approaches to these behavior change problems than their colleagues who have access to exactly the same resources. The PD process is a great example of an engagement process-driven OD intervention, quite different from some of the analytic quality problem solving approaches more familiar in hospitals. Based on the experience of implementing the PD process at Billings Clinic in Montana as well as other hospitals involved in a PD initiative focused on reducing the transmission of "superbug" infections, the authors identify special challenges and opportunities when introducing and facilitating a process-driven intervention like PD in a hospital setting.

Organization Development in Health Care, pages 231–241
Copyright © 2011 by Information Age Publishing
All rights of reproduction in any form reserved.

231

POSITIVE DEVIANCE

When Billings Clinic faced the serious issue of rising rates of Methicillin-resistant *Staphylococcus aureus* infections, also known as MRSA, a diverse team of lay leaders and clinical staff embarked on an innovative strategy to engage everyone in figuring out how to solve the problem. In 2006, Billings joined a group of hospitals working with Plexus Institute to pilot the application of a change approach called *positive deviance* (PD) to the reduction of MRSA infections. The PD process is a great example of an engagement process-driven OD intervention, quite different from some of the analytic quality problem solving approaches more familiar in hospitals. The authors have been deeply involved in introducing this process in healthcare settings—Carlos as Director of OD at Billings Clinic and Lisa as a member of the Plexus Institute team of PD coaches currently working with dozens of hospitals in the U.S., Canada, and Latin America. Reflecting on the facilitation of the PD process in hospitals provided us with an opportunity to identify some particular challenges as well as opportunities for OD practice in health care.

In contrast to most "best practice" approaches, PD is a change methodology based on the insight that knowledge alone does not change behavior. Although some problems can be solved with new technology or breakthroughs in medical practice, many problems turn out to be simple in the sense that changes in how caregivers do basic things—like hand washing—turn out to make the critical difference. Because MRSA bacteria survive on people's hands and on other surfaces such as clothing, furniture, and medical instruments, the primary means of MRSA transmission is via healthcare workers themselves. Everyone "knows" which practices keep that from happening but few hospitals have figured out how to get everyone to comply with these practices consistently. The primary hypothesis of PD is that within any organization, there are people who find unique ways to get around obstacles to finding solutions to problems that most in the organization have been unable to solve. They have the same resources as everyone else and they work within the same culture under the same constraints as everyone else, and yet they have found a better way. The PD approach engages everyone at all levels and from all parts of the organization to determine who those members are, discover their "positively deviant" practices, and design collaborative approaches that enable everyone to adopt or create practices that work in their unique situations.

For example, during one of the "discovery and action" dialogues that are part of the PD process in another hospital, staff discovered a problem that technicians were not wearing gloves consistently in isolation rooms where patients were identified as colonized with MRSA. They did not have a knowledge problem—they knew that they should be wearing the gloves—but further exploration uncovered the fact that isolation carts were frequently missing gloves in all sizes and glove supplies were not readily available to staff on the floor. However, there was at least one unit where all the sizes of gloves seemed to be available all the time. How did they manage that, given that they did not have a bigger budget for gloves, did not have more staff to work on glove supply, did not have a more "caring" culture? A few exploratory field trips to that unit later, many creative ideas to deal with the issue emerged from conversations that included not only those who needed to wear the gloves but also those who supplied the carts, ordered the gloves, and took responsibility for infection control. By replicating the process by which one unit solved the problem—not the specific solution itself—other units in the hospital found ways that worked locally for them to ensure that gloves were available. And when the gloves were available consistently, staff wore them consistently.

BILLINGS CLINIC

Billings Clinic is a not-for-profit, multi-specialty group practice with a 272-bed hospital in Billings, Montana. It is the largest employer in Billings, with 3,500 employees, including more than 250 physicians and 65 non-physician providers. Patterned after the famous Mayo Clinic in Rochester, MN, Billings Clinic is a not-for-profit organization, governed by the community, with physicians in leadership positions. While infection rates for the deadly MRSA pathogen have been rising in most U.S. hospitals, Billings reduced house-wide healthcare-associated MRSA infections by 84% in the past two and a half years, a spectacular achievement, especially as infection rates had increased relentlessly in previous years. CDC analysts determined that Billings Clinic has achieved a highly statistically significant decline—meaning that it is highly likely that the drop is associated with the MRSA-fighting initiative and did not happen by chance.

An analysis of the data by John Jernigan, MD, MS (the CDC's MRSA expert) and colleagues at the CDC and Billings was presented at the March 2009 meeting of the Society for Healthcare Epidemiology of America. "This hospital has apparently dramatically reduced the risk of acquiring MRSA for its patients, and that's a goal we hope every hospital would try for," Dr. Jernigan said of Billings Clinic (Singhal & Buscell, 2009). Referring to the recent analysis, he said,

> These extremely encouraging findings add to a growing body of evidence that hospitals can make a difference in their endemic MRSA rates, and further might be able to improve the chances that patients have the best possible treatment options available. It shows that hospitals can make an important difference in antimicrobial resistance even at a time when the availability of new antibiotics has stagnated. (Singhal & Buscell, 2009)

How did Billings Clinic achieve such positive results? At the core of the PD process is the notion that it is easier to act your way into a new way of thinking rather than think your way into a new way of acting (Sternin, 2003). This idea took on real life at Billings when one of the Plexus coaches, Keith McCandless, suggested improvisational theater as a way for staff members to practice infection control procedures like setting up an isolation room, donning gowns and gloves without contaminating them and then removing them safely, and handling difficult conversations in a safe place. "Improvisational play takes the edge away from difficult conversations, creating a safe space to discover possibilities that may not be initially obvious" noted McCandless.

In one of the MRSA improvisation sessions, employees acted out various solutions for taking food trays out of rooms for patients in isolation. Some suggested the use of disposable food trays; however, one employee spoke up and shared her experience that if you want patients to feel unwanted, like pariahs, give them a cardboard tray with cold food. The group brainstormed other ways to address the problem until a simple solution emerged in which the nurse wipes the bottom and edges of the tray with anti-bacterial wipe and hands it to someone outside the room (Singhal, Buscell, & Lindberg, 2010).

More than 50 improv sessions were conducted by the end of 2007, involving over 500 Billings Clinic frontline staff. The dozens of improv scenarios explored practical matters such as preparing a room for an MRSA patient, transporting an infected patient within the hospital, dealing with rehab patients who are not exclusively room-bound, and wearing and disposing of protective gear safely. The improv scenes were proposed by different units, including several from the PD MRSA Prevention Partnership at Billings Clinic, a multi-disciplinary in-house team to curb the spread of deadly pathogens.

FIVE CHALLENGES AND AN OPPORTUNITY

Based on the experience at Billings and the other hospitals involved in the PD MRSA initiative, we have identified some challenges to introducing and facilitating a process-driven intervention like PD in hospital settings.

1. The Challenge of Time and Space

We know that the primary drivers of the hospital engine, clinicians, are scheduled tightly around patient care when they are on campus. The challenge with space and time is creating spaces where the process-driven conversations and interactions we need to facilitate with and for them can occur. When we make time for lay leaders, it does not include clinical leaders, and vice versa. "The very nature and pace of what we're doing in health care and the way we've structured it isn't necessarily conducive to the types of interactions that allow you to harness the energy of the collective," explains Carlos. The interdisciplinary team and offsite meetings OD practitioners tend to rely on for process work are just not part of the culture in most hospitals.

One strategy that worked at Billings Clinic was to find spaces when there was an existing gathering—even one with a clinical purpose—and to try to create moments within those that lent themselves to discovery of the value of either learning or collaboration in a way that maybe it had not had in the past. For instance, Billings has a standing monthly lay leadership meeting of about an hour and a half. Traditionally, it was very didactic—it was "Here are the financials, here is what we are doing, and here is what you need to do." The challenge was that participants were used to just coming to that meeting to be told something and then leaving. One of the little changes that worked was to create something called *15 minutes of learning.* Carlos got a little bit of space on the agenda on the front end where he would start with a provocative question and invite the group to have a 2–3 minute tabletop conversation to just talk about issues in their departments related to the question. "Folks seem to appreciate the opportunity to share or just listen to the issues others were dealing with," says Carlos, "and then I'd interrupt the group and give this little mini session, this little mini learning moment around a concept like 'trust' or 'fear' and then suggest they go back and see if it resonated with their staff." Over time, that has created a new sense of appreciation for more interactive encounters. Creating a "brand" associated with learning helped create openings for OD work, including the PD process.

Another strategy that has worked at Billings is to bring OD topics into the Grand Rounds setting, which has historically been set aside for clinical work. Now, this already existing time/space is occasionally used for presentations about performance and creating high-performance teams. For this group, basic topics such as how to give constructive feedback, how to manage change, and what is emotional intelligence have provoked curiosity and powerful dialogue. For some physicians, these topics were new, but the Grand Rounds setting is a familiar and comfortable setting for learning.

2. The Challenge of a Hierarchical and Individualistic Culture

In healthcare institutions, we depend on the fantastic expertise and experience of key individuals in a wide variety of roles. These are definitely expert-driven cultures with sharply defined hierarchies and divisions. We often want to acknowledge that someone is, for example, a fantastic nurse and really has discovered through her or his rich experience important and successful ways to do something. But we may also need to convey that there might be something that nurse can add to or change about her or his practice without implying that the person has been doing anything wrong or that she or he is not as expert as she or he and others believe.

What can we do to make talking about behavior change a positive thing rather than something that is perceived to threaten someone's status in the system? A key element of the PD process is engaging the very people whose behavior needs to change in identifying and choosing new ways of working to experiment within their own practice. This is very different from a training model in which you are trying to sell people on an idea that is being presented by someone else as "better" than what they currently do.

Most of our medical schools train our physicians to be self-reliant individuals, capable of doing things on their own—being great solo artists or solo performers. Now we are starting to see some different expectations of the community and of society. "We require a new level of performance," suggests Carlos,

> and that level of performance is going to require taking individual athletes, if I may use that term loosely, and make them into team athletes. And that's not easy. It's not easy to be able to take that great performer who really is used to carrying it all on his or her back, of doing everything themselves, and put them in a mode where they're going to be on a team where those relational dynamics and interactions are much more complicated. Yet we know there are all kinds of great results that come out of healthy collaboration that can't be pulled off by an individual alone.

The PD process includes an important component: going to staff in every role and figuring out ways to include them in the process, even if it is not immediately apparent how their job impacts an issue such as infection control. The experience of working with some of the "unusual suspects" (transporters, cleaners, chaplains, and even patients and their families) who are central to the PD process is new for many clinicians. However, most have been surprised and appreciative of the insights generated when those with very different roles and perspectives are added to the mix. "We feel like we've all been deputized," explained a transporter. "Now we're all on the lookout for little things that may be creating problems." For example, a janitor at one facility using the PD process made the observation that the trash cans in one of the units were not filling up as quickly as those in other units. He suggested, "They may not be using their gowns as much as they should because if they were, they'd be generating more trash faster. Maybe we need to go there and talk about when you're supposed to wear gowns." When the Infection control doctor tells the story, he shakes his head in amazement: "When you have janitors making clinically relevant observations, you've got a lot more power on the team."

3. The Challenge of Gaining Credibility for OD

How does OD develop credibility in a culture that values science and clinical experience a lot more than what may be perceived as "soft" process wisdom? One approach that seems to work is to demonstrate true curiosity, appreciation, and humility in the face of being surrounded by an incredible level of technical expertise. "The collective intelligence of our physician team and nursing leaders, of our executive team, is awesome," says Carlos. By taking on the role of student and being curious about the great work that happens on a daily basis with patients in the clinic, he has created an openness where colleagues believe that he can provide resources, concepts, ideas, and tools that will allow them to do what they do even better. For example, a room of experts was working on a clinical process. While, as an OD practitioner, Carlos had a very limited understanding of the process itself, he noticed that they were growing frustrated with their efforts to prioritize, so he suggested a tool that could help them with that specific part of what they were doing. The strategy was to try to contribute to the existing objectives, the aim of the department or organization, and the leader rather than introduce "leadership development" skills as a stand-alone initiative.

There may also be ways that lacking technical and clinical expertise is an advantage for OD practitioners, as long as they believe in their own heart that they can contribute something that has its own source of credibility. Even in systems outside health care, it is common for OD practitioners to walk into a place of business where they do not necessarily understand the nature of the work and must become a student of something completely new. OD brings a new and perhaps unique perspective to the table. What has worked for Carlos at Billings was

> to demonstrate value with whatever expertise I did bring, not as something in competition with anyone else's technical expertise, but rather something that was actually enhancing the collective expertise of the group. We don't need to prove that we know or don't know as much as others, but that we can actually help.

4. The Challenge of Introducing a New Knowledge Domain

Unlike leaders in some other fields, most leaders in health care have not been introduced to core ideas and thinkers from the domain of OD or even leadership as part of their training. The pace and the rigor associated with 24/7 operations in health care means that there is a certain depth of expertise that cannot be acquired unless someone carves out the space and time to acquire it in addition to the five- or ten-year apprenticeship needed to develop an expertise in a medical specialty. Most have not been afforded opportunities to understand the basics of how to build a high-functioning team or how to improve the performance of a teammate through some basic coaching conversations. Health care does not necessarily afford experts in that field the chance to develop the kind of cross-functional expertise that one might see in some other industries. While there are always individuals who read and pay attention to that literature, one cannot assume that the majority have facility or actual experience with the language we in OD have come to depend on about teams, change, and group dynamics. While there is greater awareness of some quality management tools, this tends to be centered on use of data and analysis, and there is much less experience applying even basic tools such as brainstorming, nominal group technique, or dialogue.

One of the reasons PD has been more successful than some other change processes in these settings is that it brings in concepts like dialogue, self-organized teams, and appreciative coaching in the context of working on critical issues that have been identified and selected by the community as priorities for them. Although these practices are totally transferrable to any other problem the community wants to tackle in the future, they are never presented as important in isolation from the work. Skills are always learned in the process of doing, most often from a colleague (as opposed to a trainer) in an apprenticeship model.

5. The Challenge of Finding Collaborators

Related to the challenge of introducing a new domain is the challenge of finding or developing a group of people to collaborate with you in bringing an OD perspective to the organization. Most hospitals have very few people identified with the OD role (some have none!) According to Carlos, "It's about finding those folks who are already doing work that connects with something related to what you want to introduce and promote, even if they are calling it something different." In the PD projects in hospitals, this has often been people involved in quality and safety projects. Although much of the quality literature and methodology tends to be quite linear and focused on engineering processes, the goals are the same. Most quality processes include "employee engagement" as an important component. However, most do not spell out how to engage people and they typically promote a traditional "rollout" methodology designed to get "buy-in" but lacking in ways to achieve real ownership on the part of the community. By reaching out and asking, "Hey, how can we help you further some of these ideas around the quality agenda?" we have recruited some valuable teammates. One approach that has served us well is to differentiate between defining the *what* of change (practice "bundles" from credible sources like the Center for Disease Control or the hospital's own Infection Control department) and approaches like PD designed to work on the *how* part of the change equation.

Many of those who have stepped up as the most valuable collaborators in PD projects are from places one would not necessarily expect. Carlos spent a lot of time

> looking for those pioneers, those folks in the front end who are interested in moving forward and doing the work. And in the long run, over time, what's been very exciting has been the ability to simply be a scout for the types of talent and resources that might contribute to the work that we're going to do.

Many of the leaders of the PD initiatives have not come from Human Resources or OD or even Quality departments, but have been individuals from both clinical and non-clinical roles who chose to step up because they were attracted to the opportunity to participate in making a difference. Many of the heroes in hospitals across the MRSA initiative have been housekeepers and those in other support roles. For example, Jasper Palmer from Albert Einstein Medical Center in Philadelphia invented a method for removing gowns and gloves that was both effective and efficient, and the video of his demonstration has gone viral.

THE OPPORTUNITY TO LEVERAGE THE CALL TO SERVICE

> An advantage when working in healthcare settings is that, even when people are complaining or in a negative mood about various organizational challenges, you do not have to press very far before you find their core passion about helping people, taking away pain. There is a very deep core purpose that is beyond the other organization purposes, like economic viability, that is a terrific lever to have in doing this work because most of the people in health care are very motivated to serve.

Carlos remembers a physician early on in a meeting looking at his peers and making this extraordinarily impassioned reference to the calling of health care and how we can never lose sight of what it is we do and how we are the providers of an extraordinary service beyond imagination and that we are connected with humans at their most basic level. "His ability to capture the essence of this noble calling as he addressed his colleagues was really a crucial piece of my journey of understanding and appreciating the opportunity afforded to me in my role," says Carlos.

The PD process provides many opportunities to leverage those purely affect-related experiences where people say, "I am in the right place and I am contributing to something that is bigger than just me." That is an important part of what we try to do in OD—to get beyond the individual and connect to the collective. A central concept in the PD process is that there is something that every person in the system—no matter his or her role—can offer, and that contribution with others will take the organization to a whole new level. What is particularly satisfying about how this notion plays out in the PD initiatives is that it goes beyond talk and produces hundreds of specific, small, yet important examples that make a difference and that individuals and teams can point to as a result of their work together. Finding ways to make sure that these small changes are noticed and communicated across the system is an important part of the process. One group in a VA hospital points proudly to the new hand gel dispensers in public areas that the group identified as needed and carefully placed and says, "Those are *our* dispensers." Families of long-term care patients have written a pamphlet in "real language" to help explain MRSA precautions to other families so that they are enlisted in the effort. Assistants in one unit have redesigned the signs on isolation rooms to make them more noticeable and share in the pride when data shows significantly increased use of proper precautions on that unit. We cannot know which of the hundreds of specific PD-generated actions contributed what to the overall reduction in MRSA transmissions. However, we have learned that results come not from promulgating the handful of "best practices" associated with infection control but rather from the hundreds of locally generated strategies for implementing those practices consistently and with rigor.

It is not uncommon for participants to say something along the lines of, "We never get a chance to talk like this. I didn't know how many others were thinking and feeling the same things I've been thinking and feeling." One day last year, as the PD team at Albert Einstein looked at the data on MRSA transmissions, they talked about how the changes they had made resulted in a lot more than a better looking graph: "This means that these patients are going home earlier to their families, they are going back to their jobs. It's not just that they are not here in the hospital; they are back in the lives they want to be in." One of the participants in the group burst into tears, saying, "It seems that what we're doing really makes a difference." Making and supporting that connection between what healthcare workers do every day and the service they care so much about providing is a great mission statement for OD in health care.

REFERENCES

Singhal, A., & Buscell, P. (2009). From invisible to visible: Learning to see and stop MRSA at Billings Clinic. 3–5. Retrieved from http://www.plexusinstitute.org

Singhal, A., Buscell, P., & Lindberg, C. (2010). *Inviting everyone: Healing healthcare though positive deviance.* Bordentown, NJ: PlexusPress.

Sternin, J. (2003). Practice positive deviance for extraordinary social and organizational change. In D. Ulrich, M. Goldsmith, L. Carter, J. Bolt & N. Smallwood (Eds.), *The change champion's fieldguide* (pp. 20–37). New York: Best Practice.

CHAPTER 13

ORGANIZATION DEVELOPMENT IN THE NEW AGE OF HEALTHCARE REFORM

Diane L. Dixon

ABSTRACT

The purpose of this chapter is to share three case examples of successful healthcare reform efforts and to describe how OD processes played a valuable role in facilitating transformational change. Case examples include the state of Vermont, Geisinger Health System, and Kaiser Permanente. They reveal that to achieve any aspect of healthcare reform requires collective transformational leadership that makes effective use of OD processes to facilitate complex system change. Leadership collaboration and teamwork across multiple stakeholder boundaries were enhanced by strategic change facilitation, strategy development, team development, and organizational learning. These processes helped make reform possible in the cases.

CONTEXT

This is a defining time for health care in the United States, as unparalleled challenges present tremendous opportunities for a better health sys-

Organization Development in Health Care, pages 243–260

tem. Throughout 2009, there was contentious debate in Congress, town hall meetings, and communities across the country about how best to provide quality affordable health care. Sharp differences fractured ideological and political divisions threatening to deepen the fault lines in a fragmented and dysfunctional system. The old issues of increasing costs on all fronts with insurance at the epicenter, inconsistent quality of care, and unequal access are new again after decades of on and off debate. And the old politics cast in the traditional Western paradigm grounded in seeing parts rather than wholes and systems continue to present roadblocks to whole-system change. Competing interests and values blur a shared vision for the common good. Shifting paradigms is a messy process because of emotional tensions associated with the push and pull of letting go of the old and transitioning to a new paradigm not yet clearly defined. However, in the midst of these layers of complexity, changes are underway to improve healthcare delivery.

Key reform components were funded through passage of the American Recovery and Reinvestment Act, H.R. 1 in February, 2009 (111th Congress, 2009–2010). These components included funding for a nationwide interoperable health information technology system that incorporates the electronic medical record, increased use of comparative effectiveness data to enhance medical decision making and evidence-based clinical and community-based prevention strategies. On March 23, 2010, the Patient Protection and Affordable Care Act, H.R. 3590, was signed into law (111th Congress, 2009–2010). This bill focuses on improvement of healthcare coverage for all Americans and health insurance market reforms. Other features of the bill are quality and efficiency of health, prevention of chronic diseases, improving public health, and healthcare workforce improvement. Passage of both bills has not lessened the contentious reform debate across the country. As these bills are being implemented, deep divisions still exist.

The good news is that hard work continues on the development of integrated delivery systems, improving the management of chronic diseases, continuous quality improvement, and collaborative team-based care supported by health information technology infrastructures. These efforts have been the focus of hospitals, health systems, physician practices, nurses, other healthcare professionals, stakeholder organizations, and several states even before the recent legislation. In many cases, there have been significant large and small achievements in improving health care in areas targeted in this new age of reform.

The purpose of this chapter is to share three case examples of successful healthcare reform efforts and to describe how organization development processes played a valuable role in facilitating transformational change in each case.

INTRODUCTION TO CASE EXAMPLES

The three case examples described in this chapter include the state of Vermont, Kaiser Permanente, and Geisinger Health System. These cases reveal that in order to achieve any aspect of healthcare reform requires collective transformational leadership that understands and uses OD processes to facilitate complex system change. In each case, leadership collaboration and teamwork across multiple stakeholder boundaries were enhanced by effective change management facilitation, strategy development, team development, and organizational learning. The Vermont example describes healthcare reform at the state level and teaches us lessons about the importance of stakeholder coalitions and collaboration that benefit from skillful development and facilitation in a large-scale change process. In another case, Geisinger Health System is a physician-led integrated delivery system that has been a frontrunner in implementing many of the healthcare reform components such as prevention and wellness, collaborative care delivery teams, and management of chronic diseases supported by electronic health information systems. Transformational leadership that creates value through innovation and effective facilitation of system change has been a hallmark of their success. And Kaiser Permanente gives us an example of how an integrated delivery system that has had a longstanding commitment to delivering affordable quality care is continuously improving its comprehensive health information system with the help of OD processes. These cases demonstrate that healthcare reform is possible and that OD enhances the transformational change process.

Case Example: Vermont's Healthcare Reform

Sources: Telephone interviews were conducted with Hunt Blair, Director for Health Care Reform in the Department of Vermont Health Access; Helen Riehle, Former Executive Director for Vermont Program for Quality in Health Care (VPQ); and W. Cyrus Jordan, MD, MPH, Former Medical Director for VPQ.

Background

In Vermont, the healthcare reform journey began at least two decades ago. The Vermont Program for Quality in Health Care (VPQ) was a leader, as it is today, in building an infrastructure for quality improvement across the continuum of care delivery. These statewide quality improvement efforts established the trust with providers needed to build the collaboration required for safe, patient-centered, effective, efficient, timely, and equitable care to all Vermonters. This work set the stage for the renewed focus on reform in 2004.

State legislators and healthcare stakeholders had made attempts to transform the entire healthcare system in previous years. Building upon lessons learned from VPQ and other initiatives, it was recognized that a renewed collaborative effort was needed. Coalition 21 was formed in July, 2004 with the help of the Snelling Center for Government at the University of Vermont (McCrae, 2007). The coalition was comprised of public and private stakeholders, including legislators and leaders from government and business, health insurers, health providers, and healthcare associations (including VPQ). This approach was a new way of working together that is uncommon in health care because of traditional boundaries that create silos between stakeholders. The coalition's mission was to gain consensus on how to transform Vermont's healthcare system. It had to develop the path to an integrated and coordinated system that provides coverage to all Vermonters. .

The Snelling Center acted as facilitator and process consultant to help the coalition achieve its goals. It provided organizational support, conducted research, coordinated communications between the stakeholders, and documented outcomes. Snelling consultants used the "getting the whole system in the room" approach so that participants from multiple organizations could gain consensus on common goals and remain focused on them (Weisbord, 2000; Bunker & Alban, 2006). They engaged the coalition by using a combination of OD processes such as group facilitation, team development, and strategy development to enable them to define common purpose, clarify beliefs, and determine the outcomes they wanted to achieve. These OD processes were designed to minimize the barriers to transformational change and leverage opportunities to develop a new way to approach healthcare reform. Snelling created a space in which productive working relationships could be developed. Snelling engaged the group in meaningful dialogue and decision-making processes that enabled the coalition to gain consensus on several core beliefs about the future of healthcare reform in Vermont (McCrae, 2007):

- The healthcare "system" does not function as an integrated system, and to address the challenges that this creates requires all stakeholders to work together.
- Successful change depends upon a healthcare system that works as a cohesive and unified whole. A real transformational change process must embrace the whole system in a coordinated process focused on what will be best for all Vermonters.
- Changes to the healthcare must be system-wide, initiated in a coordinated manner across the entire system.
- Implementation of system change must transcend the two-year political cycle so that change is sustainable.

These shared beliefs served as the foundation for their work. By January, 2005, Coalition 21 gained consensus on "Six Principles of Health Care System Change for Vermont in the 21st Century" (McRae, 2007, p.2). These principles were:

- Ensure universal access to and coverage for essential healthcare services for all Vermonters.
- Health care coverage needs to be comprehensive and continuous.
- Vermont's health delivery system will model continuous improvement of healthcare quality and safety.
- Financing of health care must be sufficient, equitable, fair, and sustainable.
- Built-in accountability for quality, cost, access, and participation will be hallmarks of the system.
- Vermonters will be engaged to pursue healthy lifestyles, to focus on preventive care and wellness efforts, and to make informed use of all healthcare services throughout their lives.

The Coalition 21 principles served as a framework for legislators as they worked to develop reform legislation.

Healthcare Reform Legislation

State legislators wanted to broaden the circle of inclusion in the change process. So, in the Fall of 2005, the Snelling Center on behalf of the state legislature organized a public engagement process and hosted a series of six day-long meetings statewide (Klein, McRae, & Eastman, 2005). These meetings gave legislators and the public an opportunity to work together to understand the complex Vermont healthcare landscape. Snelling used the basic change management premise that people who participate in the development of proposed changes are more likely to support the changes. Snelling facilitated focused conversations and dialogue as a means to share information, listen, reflect, stay informed, and set the stage for continuing dialogue. The findings were summarized and used to develop healthcare reform legislation in 2006.

The comprehensive healthcare reform legislation was signed in May, 2006. There are three key goals (Besio, 2008, p. 3):

- Increase access to affordable health insurance for all Vermonters.
- Improve quality of care across the lifespan.
- Contain healthcare costs.

Subsequent legislation was passed in 2007 and 2008. Since passing the wide-ranging legislation, implementation of over 60 initiatives has been a priority.

Implementation Examples

The Secretary of Administration is responsible for coordination of healthcare reform among the executive branch agencies, departments, and offices. Specifically, the Director of Health Care Reform leads and manages the implementation strategy statewide. This office is coordinating the large-scale transformational change process. Two examples of how reform policy is being translated into specific action follow.

VPQ continues to play a major role in improving quality of care across the lifespan. They have been using the "Quality through Collaboration: The Future of Rural Health Care" framework developed by the Institute of Medicine as the guidepost for transformational change (IOM, 2005). The key goals of this framework are to develop an integrated approach to addressing personal and population health needs and to build a stronger healthcare system through a quality improvement infrastructure. To accomplish these goals requires that the human resource capacity of healthcare professionals be enhanced through education programs that develop the core competencies of patient-centered care, work in interdisciplinary teams, implementation of evidence-based practice, application of quality improvement, and use of informatics to support these efforts. Inherent in this process is the development of health communities that engage all stakeholders in a collaborative process for comprehensive change.

An example of VPQ in action is the Quality Improvement Collaborative that targets practice and system improvements (VPQ, 2008). This is an eight-month process designed to bring clinical outpatient and inpatient teams and managers together to work on real quality issues so that measurable results will be achieved for patients and the workplace. This is a comprehensive approach that incorporates methodologies from the Institute for Healthcare Improvement's Breakthrough Program and the Chronic Care Model developed by Edward Wagner, MD, MPH, Director of MacColl Institute for Healthcare Innovation, Group Health Cooperative of Puget Sound. VPQ established learning communities statewide using the collaborative model to focus on chronic diseases such as diabetes. Learning communities received coaching on the Plan-Do-Study-Act framework for small, rapid cycle change.

After VPQ recognized that small practices were unable to close down to participate in learning sessions, the VPQ Learning Community was revised to include centralized/statewide single-day learning forums, multiple community-based mini-learning sessions ("The Collaborative on Wheels"), and a virtual learning community dimension. However, VPQ learned that optimal learning, sharing, and networking occurred in face-to-face sessions.

Learning sessions include plenary segments, educational sessions specific to four curricular tracks, team working time, and team sharing. Later, the "Clinical Microsystems" model was incorporated into the curriculum (http://dms.dartmouth.edu/cms/). This model views the practice team, which includes both clinical and administrative members, as a microsystem of patient care within the larger healthcare system. The belief is that small changes in this complex adaptive system can have large effects on the entire healthcare system. Based on rigorous evaluation, there is evidence that many teams have achieved quality improvements, and those who did not gained tremendous learning that is putting them on the path to positive outcomes. The Vermont Quality Improvement Collaborative continues with a focus on helping to create an empowered, engaged, and educated patient. This example demonstrates how VPQ is using education, coaching, group facilitation, team development, and collaboration processes as approaches to build a continuous quality improvement infrastructure.

Another example of efforts to transfer state reform initiatives into concrete and actionable steps is the Vermont Rural Health Alliance (VRHA). This alliance is a vehicle for the state's rural health centers, clinics, and small hospitals to collaborate in the effort to translate health policy into practice (VRHA, 2009). In addition to providing educational resources, the alliance provides a forum for members to share their experiences and learn from each other. The alliance creates a bridge between policy makers and rural providers that helps them better understand the successes and challenges of implementing the reform initiatives. Facilitating communication, dialogue, and feedback are valuable for supporting the change process.

Moving Forward

The examples are just two among many programs, services, alliances, partnerships, associations, and individuals that are working to implement healthcare reform in the state. As Hunt Blair indicated, reform involves multiple organizations, multi-layered hierarchies, programs, services, and overlapping systems that need to coordinate their efforts. One of the major lessons learned is that collaboration and teamwork focused on common purpose are essential for achieving the shared goals. The challenge and opportunity is making this happen in an effective manner. While many challenges lie ahead, a great deal of progress has been accomplished.

OD Implications for Healthcare Reform

Vermont health care is a complex adaptive system that encompasses multiple complex adaptive stakeholder systems forming a network of networked organizations that need to be aligned so that they can collaborate to achieve reform goals in a coordinated timeframe (Zimmerman, Plsek, & Lindberg, 2008). While OD processes have played a valuable role in various aspects of the state's healthcare reform change process, the complexity of networked systems that must work together in ways that they have not been accustomed to may indicate a different type of OD, such as *transorganizational*. Several thought leaders suggest that transorganizational development is planned change focused on the collective relationships of a variety of stakeholders to accomplish something beyond the capability of any single organization (Boje, 1999; Cummings, Blumenthal, & Greiner, 1983). It is a distinct level of practice that focuses on improving collaboration in higher-order complex social networks (Clarke, 2005). The Vermont healthcare system transformational change process suggests the need for transorganizational approaches to leading and managing change of this magnitude and complexity. The implication for OD practitioners is that they should be aware of the new realities and challenges associated with large emergent complex networked systems, which will likely lead to innovative OD processes that will be particularly useful in healthcare reform.

Case Example: Geisinger Health System

Sources: Telephone interviews were conducted with Ronald A. Paulus, Former Executive Vice President, Clinical Operations and Chief Innovation Officer for Geisinger Health System; Currently- President and CEO of Mission Health System. Meg Horgan, R.N., M.S.N., Vice President of Clinical Innovation and Consulting at Geisinger Health System.

Background

Geisinger is a physician-led, not-for-profit integrated delivery system based in central and northeastern Pennsylvania founded by Abigail Geisinger in 1915. This system is recognized for its innovative approaches to quality patient-centered care delivery and creating value through innovation. It has been a frontrunner for many of the components in healthcare reform, such as a focus on prevention and wellness, collaborative care delivery teams, management of chronic diseases, and utilization of the electronic health information systems. The system is dedicated to health care, education, research, and service to approximately 2.6 million people across 43 counties. There is a multispecialty group comprised of more than 740 physicians practicing at 40 community-based clinical practice sites that provide adult and pediatric primary and specialty care. In addition, the system has two acute care hospitals; specialty hospitals and ambulatory surgery centers; a 220,000-member Geisinger Health Plan; and many other clinical services, ranging from prenatal to community-based care for frail elders (Paulus, Davis, & Steele, 2008). It is an "open yet integrated system" that serves both its own Geisinger Health Plan (GHP) members and non-GHP consumers in its service area.

The system is organized in 22 clinical service lines that are each co-led by a physician-administrator pair. Operating units encompass all service lines, each hospital, GHP, and central support functions that are responsible for achieving their own annual quality and financial budget targets. Performance goals and incentives are aligned across the operating units and coordinated within the system. The only centralized services are innovation and quality, with robust linkages to operational leaders that often share common performance-incentive goals.

In 1995, an electronic health record (EHR) platform was adopted and is used across the ambulatory services system, and the Geisinger Medical Center has fully implemented EHR for all inpatient care. The other hospitals are in various stages of a phased implementation. "My Geisinger" enables consumers to access their medical records, communicate with physicians, view lab results, and schedule appointments.

Geisinger's enduring mission to enhance quality of life through an integrated health service organization based on a balanced program of patient care, education, research, and community service serves as a foundation for transformational leadership and change (Geisinger Health System, 2008).

Transformational Leadership and Vision

With the leadership of Glenn Steele, Jr., MD, PhD, President and CEO, Geisinger has made significant measurable progress using a continuous innovation approach to transformational change. Dr. Steele understood that transforming the system after a failed merger would require a clear and compelling vision for the future. As a transformational leader, he recognized the value of widening the circle of engagement and developing leadership throughout the system. One of the ways Dr. Steele did this was to develop a highly participative visioning process that he facilitated. He met with thousands of stakeholders in the system on all levels. These visioning meetings were designed to engage participants in reflective dialogue about the system from the short view within their sphere of influence to the long view of seeing how their work connected to the whole. Dr. Steele listened to honest feedback about what was working well and what needed to change. With that valuable information, the vision for the first five years (2000–2005) was created and built on the legacy of Geisinger's founder who said, "Make my hospital right; make it the best," and the enduring values to "heal, teach, discover, and serve." Strategic priorities and associated goals for integration and growth were aligned with the shared vision. Road maps for a coordinated approach to achieving the goals and measurable outcomes were developed along with financial models, budgets, and master facility planning to ensure viability. Yearly updates on the vision helped to chart progress and lessons learned.

Equally important was building a culture of quality, accountability, and organizational learning. Everybody was asked to learn from both success and failure. Four guiding themes focused the effort (Geisinger Health System, 2006, p. 4).

- Quality: Provide superb care uniformly across the organization.
- Value: Provide care at the right time and right place—efficiently and effectively.
- Partnerships: Develop strong partnerships with providers, businesses, and educational institutions; jointly disseminate new knowledge and provide training in healthcare delivery and administration for future generations of caregivers.
- Advocacy: Serve as a proponent for the needs of a rural population and identify resources for our patients and community.

These guiding themes continue to help leaders to develop a sustainable culture.

Building upon a strong foundation of success in the first five years, Geisinger began the second five-year (2006–2010) change process. The hallmark of this phase of the visioning process was innovation, which came as a challenge from the board of directors in late 2005 (Paulus et al., 2008). Dr. Steele personally led and facilitated visioning meetings with thousands of stakeholders on all levels, including consumers, to listen and learn from their ideas and feedback. He was assisted by Dr. Paulus who was at that time Executive Vice President Clinical Operations and Chief Innovation Officer. The result was a renewed vision: *Geisinger Quality—Striving for Perfection.* Speaking of this vision, Dr. Steele said, "It is our 'window into the future,' setting high goals for ourselves and aligning our strategic plan with the Geisinger mission" (Geisinger Health System, 2006, p. 5). He also renewed the commitment to the founder's charge to "be the best." Quality was identified as the highest strategic priority: "We will provide the highest quality continuum of care with complete focus on each patient" (Geisinger Health System, 2006, p. 5), he stated. With this as the guiding direction, building a culture of quality and innovation continues.

GAPP Innovations Transformational Change Process

As an organizing framework for this phase of change and OD, the Geisinger Accelerated Performance Program (GAPP) was developed. This leadership engagement process began with two full-day retreats with the top 140 leaders across the system. These sessions were co-led and facilitated by Dr. Steele and Dr. Paulus. Dr. Steele kicked off the retreats with a focus on the vision and accomplishments achieved thus far. Then Dr. Paulus facilitated further discussion, giving more detail about baseline performance data and setting the expectation that as a team they needed to determine the direction for quality and innovation. From there, participants moved into small breakout groups to engage in dialogue about where they wanted to be—in essence, their aspirations for the future. These groups were facilitated by clinical and operational staff that had received facilitation skills coaching from the Innovations Group. The small groups reported back to the full group which led to further discussion and distillation of ideas. As a result, redesign recommendations were identified.

On day two of the retreat, leaders reviewed the redesign recommendations from day one. Initially they broadly discussed the challenges and opportunities that these recommendations presented. Then they broke into small dialogue groups and engaged in a force-field analysis process to clarify the organizational barriers and enablers that would help them to implement the recommendations. Each group shared their results with the full group, considering what could be expected in the next 12–18 months in terms of the market and efficiencies. The closing phase focused on what it means to be a "Geisinger leader." Together they identified leadership attributes that would enable them to implement the redesign initiatives that they had agreed upon. This same process was used with middle management leadership in a series of three retreats.

As a result of the leadership engagement process, a network of 11 multidisciplinary redesign teams have been established. Each team has an executive sponsor and an accountable leader. Overall leadership and support to teams comes from the GAPP Steering Committee, comprised of Dr. Steele and his executive team. Team leaders participated in education and training sessions provided by the Innovations Group in collaboration with the Geisinger Quality Institute. These sessions focused on developing skills in team facilitation and quality improvement tools. Teams are taught to use multiple improvement methods such as continuous quality improvement, Six Sigma, and lean reengineering along with evaluating the impact of new care models and gaining insights for subsequent innovation. Other internal training and education efforts are being aligned with this effort.

GAPP teams focus on the business case for redesign and identify performance gaps, engage in fact finding and conduct analyses, identify goals compatible with organizational goals, and develop process and outcome metrics using a 120-day improvement cycle. In addition, teams work through clinical evidence definition, existing and future workflows, analysis of financial incentives, regulatory and safety reviews, and business-case modeling. These initiatives are aligned and coordinated with system goals and other redesign projects creating an "innovation infrastructure" that is adapting to emerging evidence and rapidly translating it into practice.

Lessons Learned

Quality and innovation have been embedded into the culture through a transformational change process that engaged stakeholders in highly collaborative visioning process and team approach to redesign focused on achieving the vision. An unending focus on the vision, mission, and values is the simple rule that manages the complexity of the process. A culture of quality mindset has been developed over time across the organizational, group, and individual landscape. As Meg Horgan said, "Never underestimate the value of involvement and engagement." It is critical that top leaders develop leadership throughout the organization so that they become owners of the process.

OD Implications for Healthcare Reform

Geisinger does not have a dedicated OD department or function, but rather the CEO assisted by the Department of Innovation are the leaders of OD. They are working toward a shared responsibility for OD leadership by developing operational leaders and other staff to become change agents that lead and manage the transformational process. This situation is ideal and illustrates how effective OD can be when top executives are authentically leading change. Ultimately, the responsibility for OD is that of top leaders who in turn develop that capability throughout the organization. Since Geisinger is not the typical healthcare system in the U.S., there is a compelling need for OD professionals to help leaders develop the capability and capacity to design and facilitate the complex change strategies required to achieve healthcare reform goals.

Case Example: Kaiser Permanente

Sources: Telephone interviews were conducted with Karen L. Kaufman, Principal Consultant, Organizational Effectiveness, Kaiser Permanente in Oakland, California and Susan Kuca, RN, MA, Cardiac Care Coordinator at Kaiser Permanente Colorado.

Background

Kaiser Permanente is the largest not-for-profit health plan, serving more than 8.6 million members, located in Oakland, California and with sites across eight regions in the U.S. (Kaiser Permanente, 2009). The system comprises Kaiser Foundation Health Plan, Inc.; Kaiser Foundation Hospitals and their subsidiaries; and the Permanente Medical Groups.

The plan was founded in 1945 in response to the challenge of providing medical care to many people who were not able to afford a physician visit during the Great Depression and World War II. Since then, Kaiser Permanente has continued to be an innovative leader in integrated delivery systems supported by technology. Its prepaid health plans are intended to spread the cost to make them more affordable. With targeted attention on achieving excellence, the plan focuses on managing chronic diseases that can have a negative impact on patients and drive up costs if not managed appropriately. To attain excellence requires that Kaiser Permanente analyze population data with goal-oriented tools, identify patients that need medical attention early, focus on prevention and wellness, support systematic process improvements, and encourage collaboration between patients and professionals to improve overall health (McCarthy, Mueller, & Wrenn, 2009). A comprehensive health information system, Kaiser Permanente HealthConnect™ integrates an electronic health record with tools that physicians need in order to deliver evidence-based medicine. This electronic system also includes an online patient portal that enhances member access and involvement in their care. According to the Commonwealth Fund Commission on a High Performance Health System's report on healthcare delivery systems, which includes six attributes of ideal systems, Kaiser has demonstrated significant progress in information continuity, care coordination and transitions, system accountability, peer review and teamwork for high-value care, continuous innovation, and easy access to appropriate care (McCarthy, et al., 2009).

Kaiser Permanente HealthConnect™ and the Role of Organizational Effectiveness

Organizational Effectiveness (OE) played a valuable role on the Kaiser Permanente (KP) HealthConnect™ cross-functional design and program-wide implementation strategy teams. Prior to KP HealthConnect™, the OE team provided typical services over many years, including assistance with strategic planning, collaborative team development, process consultation, group facilitation, leadership development, and large-scale system change management. KP HealthConnect™ provided the opportunity to expand clinical and non-clinical representation across KP to partner in developing a large-scale system change process to implement this technology. OE guided the change teams to understand that the impact on people and culture were key considerations for success. According to Ms. Kaufman, OE consultant, critical questions were discussed, including *What would it take for stakeholders to adopt the new technology and change behavior?*; *What cultural and environmental drivers and restraining forces would affect change?*; and *How do we embed sustainability, growth, and continuous improvement into the process?* These questions became essential guideposts for the change strategy and implementation activities in the regions.

Prior to each regional implementation, the OE team would study the organizational structure, cultural attributes, and leadership engagement. They knew that leadership commitment would be essential for implementation and sustainability. Change champions were then engaged to become key sponsors, training "super users" and peer support experts. Supervisors closest to service delivery were essential partners in change since employees respond more favorably to what their managers tell them rather than messages from leaders with whom they have no daily interaction. OE listened deeply and actively to people on all levels to learn from their ideas, challenges, and fears. Taking these factors into consideration, they were able to assess user readiness for "go live" and determine the best implementation option. The "big bang" approach meant implementing KP HealthConnect™ across all facilities and departments simultaneously, with a top-to-bottom organizational focus promoting rapid learning and problem resolution. It was found that this approach worked best when a region was already using an electronic medical record and just transitioning to another one. A phased approach was more effective in regions that were moving from paper-based charting to using an electronic medical record.

Preparation to "go live" required more than training and education, but rather a whole-systems approach to change aligning all variables to the vision. Teams needed to be developed and dialogue facilitated. Multiple forms of holistic communication had to be developed and disseminated. Staff engagement processes that leveraged involvement in action planning were executed. This systems and highly participative approach to change resulted in effective implementations of KP HealthConnect™ across the organization. Use and sustainability are still high, and continuous improvement is a key focus moving forward.

Reflective Learning

The KP HealthConnect™ Program-wide Team that was the hub for the implementation process has adjourned. While there is ongoing governance of technology, now the regions own the commitment to sustainability, continuous improvement, and growth. However, the OE team thought that it was important to reflect on key lessons learned. Early implementations in practice management and ambulatory clinicals were used to study these lessons (Kaiser Permanente, 2005). An action research project team interviewed project leads and conducted focus groups with end-user participants across seven regions.

Here are several of the key learnings about what facilitated the most effective implementations:

- Horizontal organization structures with employee empowered cultures and visible leadership.
- Demonstrated leadership commitment evidenced by active participation in technology training, presence at "go-live" dress rehearsals and demonstrations, and removal of obstacles to focusing on implementation. It is important to note that the CEO is passionate about the transformational power of technology.

- Supervisor engagement and motivation to share department-specific data such as workflows, give input into targeted training design and delivery, and provide empathetic support.
- Planned and organized approach to user readiness before the "go-live" date.
- Selection of the appropriate implementation approach depends on the situation and readiness of users.
- Minimize other major change initiatives during the implementation timeframe.
- Use a broad range of communication vehicles that are realistic and embrace both user and system perspectives.
- Training and support needs to be user-centric so that participants understand how the technology affects their jobs.

The national organizational effectiveness team is applying these lessons to other OE processes, particularly in unit-based teams providing coordinated and integrated care across the system. A key lesson learned is that the success of KP HealthConnect™ is not the result of any one group; it is the result of collaborative efforts of multi-functional groups across the system. OE was the facilitative process for getting the work done.

Case in Point
The Collaborative Cardiac Care Service (CCCS) team at Kaiser Permanente Colorado has received national recognition for results achieved with coronary artery disease (CAD). They have demonstrated that collaborative teams improve cardiac care with the KP HealthConnect™ system (Sandhoff, Kuca, Rasmussen, & Merenich, 2008). The CCCS team consists of the Cardiac Rehabilitation Program and the Clinical Pharmacy Cardiac Risk Service. Working with patients, primary care physicians, cardiologists, pharmacists, and other health professionals, they coordinate proven cardiac risk reduction strategies for CAD patients. The care teams created a new electronic registry and support program to enroll every CAD patient so that early treatment and intervention could be implemented. This program is built upon a platform of consistent clinical care guidelines and protocols that are integrated into the KP HealthConnect™ system which gives the care teams the decision-support tools they need to guide care delivery. The system gives immediate access to reliable evidenced-based information at each point of the care continuum. This enables the care team member to support the patient's care plan and encourage treatment plan compliance, and it helps different care teams to coordinate quality care. Several results include a 73% reduction in cardiac mortality, an 88% reduced risk of death due to a cardiac-related cause when the patient enrolls in the program with-

in 90 days of heart attack, and 73% of patients achieved their cholesterol goal—a dramatic shift from 26%.

As Ms. Kuca, CCCS coordinator, noted, the key reason for these results is an enduring focus on patient-centered care: "That is why we are here." It is also evident that CCCS has benefited from the use of technology that makes integrated seamless care possible. The OE team played a key role in laying the foundation for the appropriate use of KP HealthConnect™. The CCCS team's success is within an overall organizational culture that sets the performance bar high to attain the highest quality of care through leadership, collaboration, teamwork, innovation, and the integration of technological tools to achieve that goal.

Continuing Role of OE

OE continues to contribute to the development of a culture of quality, teamwork, collaboration, and accountability. The OE structure today includes a Vice President and Directors of Organizational Effectiveness and a staff of internal consultants at the program level, along with regional OE practice leaders. While they keep busy supporting leadership with many initiatives that help the organization to achieve optimal results, one of their largest OE processes has been keeping Kaiser Permanente on the cutting edge of information technology.

OD Implications for Healthcare Reform

The renewed focus on implementing and integrating electronic information systems into the care delivery continuum is a major challenge and a tremendous opportunity, as the Kaiser Permanente case example illustrates. Internal OE consultants demonstrated the critical importance of OD partnering with executive and operational leaders to facilitate a coordinated and integrated systems approach to complex change. OE modeled how to help leaders to embrace the essential roles of people and organizational culture as they work to achieve business results through transformational change. With $19 billion allocated for health information technology in the American Recovery and Reinvestment Act of 2009, the lessons learned here demonstrate the vital role that organization development can play as hospitals, health systems, physician practices, and other medical providers implement technology creating record-sharing networks designed to improve quality of care delivery across the country.

WHAT THE CASES TEACH US

The case examples confirm that leadership and OD play a critical role in facilitating the complex change processes needed to transform health systems. In each case, the dynamic interplay of basic OD elements—leadership, shared vision, engagement, teamwork and collaboration, group process facilitation, planning and execution, education, and learning—was evident. This affirms the processes that we know to be effective in leading change. However, in the new age of healthcare reform there are additional layers of complexity and uncertainty because of a much more complex national and global environmental context. This increased complexity is further impacted by political and ideological divisions. Also, there is the emergence of new organization forms such as a network of complex adaptive systems that need to collaborate and align their actions to achieve the shared purpose of reforming health care, as the Vermont case suggests. This has implications for more collective and networked leadership that requires leaders to balance responsibilities in their respective organizations with shared leadership of networks. Healthcare reform depends on a new level of leadership collaboration and partnership across stakeholder organizations, functions, and disciplines that need to become more loosely bounded to co-create solutions to what seemingly have been intractable problems. OD, as each case demonstrates, is a valuable asset that helps leaders to develop these capabilities that enable the transformation of complex health systems. Building on a rich foundation of theory and practice, specifically focused on all aspects of leading and managing change, the OD field is continuing to discover innovative approaches to transformational change in growing complexity. As the healthcare reform journey continues, it is evident that OD can help make a significant difference.

REFERENCES

American Recovery and Reinvestment Act, H.R. 1: 61–67 (2009). Retrieved April 26, 2010 from http://www.recovery.gov/About/Pages/The_Act.aspx

Besio, S. (2008). *Overview of Vermont's health care reform.* Montpelier, VT: State of Vermont Agency of Administration. Retrieved from http://www.hcr.vermont.gov

Boje, D. M. (1999). *Transorganizational development: An introduction and overview.* Retrieved August 6, 2009, from http://web.nmsu.edu/~dboje/TDtransorgtext.html

Bunker, B. B., & Alban, B. T. (2006). *The handbook of large group methods: Creating systemic change in organizations and communities.* San Francisco, CA: John Wiley & Sons, Inc.

Clarke, N. (2005). Transorganizational development for network building. *The Journal of Applied Behavioral Science, 41,* 30–46.

Cummings, T. G., Blumenthal, J. F., & Greiner, L. E. (1983). Managing organizational decline: The case for transorganizational systems. *Human Resource Management, 22,* 377–390.

Geisinger Health System. (2006). *Geisinger quality striving for perfection: A vision for the second century.* Danville, PA: Author. Retrieved August 5, 2009, from http://www.geisinger.org/about/index.html

Institute of Medicine (IOM) (2005). *Quality through collaboration: The future of rural health care.* Washington, D.C.: Author. Retrieved from http://www.iom.edu/

Kaiser Permanente. (2009). *Fast facts.* Oakland, CA: Author. Retrieved August 11, 2009, from http://xnet.KaiserPermanente.org/newscenter/aboutKaiser Permanente/fastfacts.html

Kaiser Permanente. (2005). *Kaiser Permanente HealthConnect early implementations practice management and ambulatory clinicals: Overall key learnings, June 2004–February 2005.* Oakland, CA: Author.

Klein, H., McRae, G. & Eastman, J. (2005). *Vermonters working together and speaking out on health care reform.* Shelburne, VT: Snelling Center for Government. Retrieved July 29, 2009, from http://www.snellingcenterorg./ppol.html

McCarthy, D., Mueller, K., & Wrenn, J. (2009, June). Kaiser Permanente: Bridging the quality divide with integrated practice, group accountability, and health information technology. *Case study: Organized health care delivery systems.* New York: The Commonwealth Fund. Retrieved from http://www.commonwealthfund.org/Content/Publications/Case-Studies/2009/Jun/Kaiser-Permanente.aspx

McCrae, G. (2007, March). *Health care reform in Vermont hard choices for transformative change: Coalition 21—An overview of its work and perspectives of members on what lies ahead 2007 and beyond.* Shelburne, VT: Snelling Center for Government. Retrieved from www.snellingcenter.org

Patient Protection and Affordable Care Act, H.R. 3590 (2010). Retrieved April 26, 2010 from http://www.govtrack.us/congress/bill.xpd?bill=h111-3590

Paulus, R. A., Davis, K., & Steele, G. D. (2008). Continuous innovation in health care: Implications of the Geisinger experience. *Health Affairs, 27,* 1235–1245.

Sandhoof, B. G., Kuca, S., Rasmussen, J., & Merenich, J. A. (2008). Collaborative cardiac care service: A multidisciplinary approach to caring for patients with coronary artery disease. *The Permanente Journal, 12,* 4–11.

Vermont Rural Health Alliance. (2009, January). *Putting health policy into practice.* Montpelier, VT: Bi-State Primary Care Association. Retrieved from www.bistatepca.org

Vermont Program for Quality in Health Care (VPQ) (2008). *The VPQ learning community: Improving care for people with chronic disease.* Montpelier, VT: Author. Retrieved from http://www.vpqhc.org/

Weisbord, M., & Janoff, S. (Eds.). (2000). *Future search: An action guide to finding common ground in organizations and communities.* San Francisco, CA: Berrett-Koehler Publishers, Inc.

Zimmerman, B., Plsek, P., & Lindberg, C. (2008). *Edgeware: Lessons from complexity science for healthcare leaders.* New Jersey: Plexus Institute.

CHAPTER 14

LEARNING TO RESIST "RESISTANCE TO CHANGE" IN ACADEMIC MEDICINE

Marvin Weisbord

"Historically, health professionals have tended to learn management skills in their own group, physicians with physicians, nurses with nurses, and so on, thus replicating the model in which professional training was provided. However, effective management practices require integrative behavior and nowhere is this more obvious than in the relatively new and rapidly-expanding area of primary care."

—Rachel Z. Booth, Associate Dean
University of Maryland School of Nursing
December 4, 1979

ABSTRACT

Diagnosis means specifying gaps between how things are and how they should be. Both "are" and "should" are loaded words, for the first law of diagnosis can be summarized as follows: "Seek and ye shall find." In workplaces, if you look for resistance, you will find it everywhere. When I went into organizational consulting in 1969, the systems reputed to be most resistant to change

Organization Development in Health Care, pages 261–271
Copyright © 2011 by Information Age Publishing
All rights of reproduction in any form reserved.

were those where expert professionals worked—medical schools, hospitals, laboratories, law firms, and universities. Professional experts demanded answers and advice from consultants. Answers they treated skeptically. Advice they were reluctant to take. Few systems were less receptive to OD than those of physicians in the 1970s.

During a decade of consulting and research in 10 medical schools and 25 teaching hospitals, I learned a great deal about OD and its discontents. I reported on this work (much of it with Paul Lawrence and Martin Charns) in a series of articles, notably one on why OD had not worked (so far) in medical centers (Weisbord, 1976). While writing the update of *Productive Workplaces* in the early 2000s, I had occasion to revisit this phase of my career. My last academic medical project was with the University of Maryland's primary care program from 1978 to 1980. In helping to develop an interdisciplinary training seminar, I had a rare opportunity to integrate all I had learned about medical systems. How I came to revise some of my ideas about what you can and cannot do with OD is the subject of this memoir. Like any good mystery story, there are a few twists. These I will save for the end.

THE DIAGNOSIS: GREAT DIFFERENTIATION, LITTLE INTEGRATION

To appreciate my story, it helps to know a bit about OD's hybrid origins. Some were odd indeed, resulting from action research projects undertaken between 1939 and 1946 to apply social science knowledge to critical societal problems.

For example, you can trace the first formal studies of the consequences of authoritarian, democratic, and laissez-faire leadership behavior to arts and crafts projects with preadolescent boys' clubs.[1] The power of self-managing groups emerged from an experiment with leaderless teams by British Army Officer Selection Boards in World War II.[2] Participative management grew out of experiments with Iowa housewives during that war to change family eating habits, reserving scarce meats for the armed forces.[3] T-groups evolved from Connecticut Interracial Commission workshops to improve leadership skills in tense communities just after WWII.[4] (You can find details in my 2004 book.)

Output- Versus Input-Focused Organizations

Despite these diverse origins—boys' clubs, officer candidates, housewives, and community organizers—OD blossomed not in higher education where the experiments originated, but in business and industry where the promise of economic success wedded to collaborative values seemed too good a prospect to ignore. Indeed, business organizations demanded collaboration as a condition for success. In academia (as in medicine, law, architecture, and OD consulting—any profession built on individual autonomy), OD for several decades following its debut proved a hard sell.

If you studied academic medical centers in the 1970s, the reasons for resistance to planned change were not far to seek. Exactly those systemic factors that made businesses amenable to OD were missing. On four critical organizational features business firms and academic medical centers were diametric opposites.

Business leaders managed *output-focused* organizations, emphasizing quantity and quality of goods and services produced. Output-focused systems typically had (1) clear-cut formal authority, (2) concrete goals, (3) high interdependence, and (4) agreed-upon performance measures. Customers evaluated businesses on the "output" end, based on satisfaction with goods and services.

Academic medical centers, by contrast, were *input-focused*, evaluated on the staff members' professional credentials and the acquisition of state-of-the-art technology. Such systems tended to have (1) diffuse authority, (2) abstract and often conflicting goals, (3) low interdependence, and (4) few or no widely accepted performance measures.

Autonomous medical professionals, of course, had personal standards for quality care, based in part on individual patient needs. So variable were (and are) these standards that it was (and is) hard for third parties to impose standard diagnoses and treatments to control costs. Indeed, until hospitals began competing aggressively in the late 1980s, there was little organized effort to satisfy patients. Today, in an age of free market medical care, you see TV testimonials from patients for medical centers and an emphasis on outcomes that was not evident in the 1970s.

Differentiation/Integration in Business and Academic Medicine

There was another key difference, peculiar to academia and greatly amplified in academic medicine. In industry, people tended to wear only one hat at a time: production, or sales, or R&D, or engineering, and so on. Coordination meant getting diverse functions to collaborate for shared economic results that none could achieve alone. Industry, then, honored general managers who could integrate specialized functions. In medical schools, each faculty member wore as many as four hats at once: administration, patient care, teaching, and research. Each professional had two, three, or four individual bottom lines.

Administrators could hardly keep track of who wore which hats on what days. Faculty could pick research, patient care, or educational goals, depending on the month, the day, or the hour. They could switch in an eye blink, a phenomenon I came to call "the hat dance." Indeed, *individuals* had no trouble sorting out their own work. Often one program's budget was used to subsidize another's. Those charged with managing the *whole*, however, could hardly keep track of, let alone prioritize, so much differentiated activity. This was made more mind-numbing by nearly two dozen board-certified specialties (e.g., medicine, pediatrics, obstetrics, surgery, etc.) and numerous subspecialties. No wonder medical faculty shunned administrators. Managerial attempts to integrate threatened everybody's freedom.

During many years of action research in academic medical centers I and my colleagues interviewed scores of faculty (Weisbord, Lawrence, & Charns, 1978). When we asked about leadership, we often heard stereotypical personal characteristics named as problems, particularly for associate and assistant deans. This one was too young, only recently out of residency. ("Prejudice toward youth?" I wrote in my notebook.) That one was a woman, and women had a hard time gaining acceptance from male faculty. ("Women too?") Another was Black, at a time of few Black faculty. "No prejudice, an interviewee assured me, but...you know." (What I knew was that I could find racism anywhere. "Prejudice toward nonwhites, too!" I mused.)

Then there was the veteran faculty member, nearing retirement, now an assistant dean. People scratched their heads, "He must be over-the-hill." ("They don't like seniors, either," I noted). But the interviewee who confounded me was the one who said of a distinguished, prize-winning clinician, "I don't know what happened to him. He used to be a pretty good doc, but ever since he got on the Dean's staff, he seems out of touch with everybody." ("They don't even like each other!" I observed.)

Back at my desk, I got out my notebook and began contemplating this grim litany of isms. Except for a thunderstorm of negative projections, what could these diverse medical professionals—young, old, male, female, Black, White—have in common? And then a bolt of lightning struck me too. They were all administrators! Their goal was to inject order, predictability, and modest controls into systems where personal preference and free choice defined the work. Each was seeking to integrate a system whose members thrived on differentiation. Standard procedures and paperwork were unwanted bureaucratic intrusions.

People in diffuse structures with few organizational constraints tended to personalize everything. Anyone who sought to integrate the many hats of medical faculty on behalf of the whole was seen as acting in ways inimical to good research, teaching, and patient care. No wonder I found so few takers in professional systems during those years for methods advancing self-awareness, teamwork, and commitment to shared goals. (This was not true then of nursing, for nurses were trained to deliver coordinated care.)

In business firms, rewards and prestige went to generalists who could manage on behalf of the whole. In medical care, rewards went to awe-inspiring specialists. Consulting to companies and medical schools, I lived in contradictory worlds. I became aware that most management technologies were adopted first by industry. All were designed to affect what I called the "task system," the core process of delivering products or services. Task systems thrived on clear authority, goals, interdependence, and measures. Business was relentlessly bottom-line: higher profits, lower costs, increased shareholder value. Self-awareness, personal growth, and collaboration—core OD values—were touted as paths to more productive workplaces, not just better human beings.

Medical centers in the 1970s, by contrast, represented a force field of three interlocking systems. There was a task system, to be sure, producing education, research, and patient care. And administrators ran the task system—with its diffuse goals, dispersed authority, unrecognized interdependence, and few measures—as best they could, seeking to impose structure, policy, and procedure amid piles of paperwork. Indeed, as Just Stoelwinder, an Australian physician and medical administrator, pointed out, physicians controlled up to 90 percent of hospital costs in the 1970s (Weisbord & Stoelwinder, 1979). Doctors decided who got hospitalized, what treatment and medicines patients received, and how long they stayed in. Administrators were left with supporting these decisions as efficiently as possible.

The professional medical staffs, however, danced to more subtle melodies than the relentless drumbeat of bureaucracy. The two most powerful of these I dubbed the "identity system" and the "governance system." Professional identity in medicine was based on academic training and certified by outside agencies and licensing boards. Credentials were the name of that tune. If you asked the general physician with the little black bag who visited your grandparents' house in the 1930s what he did for a living he would say, "I'm a doctor." If you asked your personal physician 40 years later, she replied, "I'm an internist" or "I'm a family practitioner." They were board certified, their identities validated, updated, and policed by diverse civil and professional agencies—the governance system—where the rules for professional conduct and competence were made.

It is no wonder so many medical professionals, socialized by training and licensure to autonomy in thought and deed, resisted methods intended to make them collaborative. Why should psychiatrists care whether surgeons showed up for work in the morning? Few specialists saw the value of behavioral science-based training for managing work. Many considered administration a necessary evil, inimical to good patient care, research, and teaching.

A PRESCRIPTION: TRAINING AS ACTION RESEARCH

It was from this perspective that I began working with William S. Spicer, Jr., a feisty physician heading up the Office of Coordination of Primary Care Programs (OCPCP) at the University of Maryland in Baltimore in the late 1970s. Spicer's goal was a joint training program in medical management for primary care professionals. He wanted all to become competent service coordinators, and he hoped to train a generation of health professionals capable of integrating multiple disciplines. The vehicle would be an annual three-day workshop for interns, residents, and practitioners of medicine, nursing, and pharmacy.

Spicer, who had attended the Management Advancement Program of the Association of American Medical Colleges, recruited a physician and hospital administrator with a master's degree in management from MIT and a noted nurse-educator to plan the program. I was invited to join the staff by virtue of my consulting and research in medical systems. The plan was to develop content similar to what the physicians had learned at MIT, then pilot the course with primary care faculty. We would start with a five-day workshop for faculty members in the three disciplines. They would be expected to support and in some cases staff three-day training events with graduate students. Modules included large systems change theory, management practices, group dynamics, interpersonal skills, and personal leadership.

I would coordinate the workshop design and "stage manage" the faculty workshop. Something troubled me about the plan. My years of research and consulting in medical schools had taught me that the managerial bag of tricks was much more highly valued by administrators than by medical professionals. The theory and practice of OD taught in business schools derived largely from industry. I was reluctant to prescribe this medicine for doctors, nurses, and pharmacists without more systematic clinical trials.

Kurt Lewin, the pioneer social scientist behind field theory and the primary ancestor of "change managers" today, held that reducing forces resisting change was easier than increasing driving forces (Weisbord, 1987). Pushing content that some considered antithetical to good medical practice might increase negative forces in this system. For years I had heard colleagues in medical systems tell me that doctors insisted that you be an expert too, a projection I resisted, though with much anxiety and self doubt. How could I force collaboration on people and unilaterally insist on more democratic practices? I considered my medical school consulting a form of Lewinian action research. None of us could say for sure what would work in upside-down organizational settings. We needed to enter into joint inquiry with the professionals.

In this sense, I consciously emulated Lewin's model of shared agreement between clients and consultants on goals, procedures, and outcomes. That medical systems might require an exception to this core practice always troubled me. Still, I was not ready to advocate techniques that medical professionals might not appreciate the same way I did. In fact, as our research had shown, much integration in medical schools actually took place inside individuals—who did some mix of patient care, education, and research—rather than by administrators. Even Spicer's title reflected this: He was the "coordinator" of primary care programs. In formal organizational terms, he could not order anybody to do anything.

Building on Individual Autonomy

With these thoughts rattling in my head, I proposed another format for the faculty workshop. Instead of treating the OD repertoire as essential knowledge for medical professionals, why not invite the faculty to do action research with us? We would present the proposed training modules for their evaluation. These would include personal style instruments, interpersonal, group and meeting skills, role analysis and problem solving, and large systems change strategies. The faculty's/participants' task would be to (1) try each activity as potential content for graduate training and (2) decide what should be dropped, modified, or presented to graduate students. We would work out with them the relevant connections to medical management. Nobody was expected to change their personal behavior, work systems, or organizational norms. Participants need not like everything. We need not defend anything. The deal was accepted and we conducted this experiment with 20 faculty members in January, 1978.

Despite much anxiety, the event was successful. We refined the program's content, emphasizing aspects of the training repertoire that faculty considered most useful for medical professionals in building program manager skills.

No Right Answers

A key feature of the Maryland program centered on cases written by faculty members based on their actual experiences. Students, as part of their training, would use the cases to "diagnose" organizational problems and work out new solutions. One typical case had a person coming into the primary care clinic with severe dizziness. She says she is taking "pressure pills" four times a day. Except for unusually low blood pressure, the nurse practitioner finds nothing wrong. A medical resident confirms her findings. "Just get her to take her pills right," says the resident. "You've got to educate these people if you give them this sort of medicine." The nurse points out that the patient took her medicine for months and was fine until now. The nurse also notices, though, that the records show a different dosage than the patient's bottle. "The pharmacy messed up again!" she says. "I'm calling them."

"Don't bother," says the resident. "They don't listen anyway. Give her a new prescription." The nurse practitioner writes and the resident signs a new Rx. A few days later, the woman is back in the emergency room after a fainting spell. This time she brings two bottles of the same medicine, one generic, one brand name. She is taking both, thinking she has two medicines. A resident on duty calls the pharmacist who finds two prescriptions written two weeks apart.

"You should have caught this!" says the resident to the pharmacist. "Don't you talk to your clients?" To which the pharmacist replies, "This is what happens when doctors just countersign Rx's and don't really evaluate the case!" Whereupon the screening resident calls the clinic resident and both agree it was the nurse's fault for not taking the first bottle away from the patient. The nurse practitioner says, "This is what happens when you have physicians sitting around in offices reading journals instead of helping us out!"

Finding an Organizational Solution

To work on the case, we formed groups by specialty: nurse practitioners, clinical pharmacists, and physicians. We asked each group to "diagnose" the situation. How did the patient get into trouble? Each group presented a diagnosis emphasizing its blameless behavior. Participants then were reorganized into cross-disciplinary groups. We introduced these groups to the technique of "responsibility charting." This method, devised in the 1960s, requires making a matrix. In the left column are listed all the decisions to be made relevant to the situation (e.g., prescribing, filling, and monitoring patient medications). Across the top are listed all the professionals involved in the case (e.g., physicians, nurse practitioner, pharmacist, clerks, etc.). For each person and each decision, a letter symbol is assigned. One person, and only one, gets the "A" for *authority*, meaning the buck stops here. Only the "A" can reverse a decision. Others get the "R" or *responsibility* for making and implementing the decision. Still others get an "S," meaning their *support* is required; and still others get an "I," meaning they must be *informed* before the decision is implemented so that they can tell the "R" what they know, the better to avoid mistakes.

The diverse professionals were asked to make a responsibility chart insuring that this troubling case would not occur again. Each of several groups came up with creative solutions. However, there was a big surprise. No two solutions were exactly alike. What happened next raised the hairs on my neck. One of the physicians jumped up from his chair, clapped a hand to his head, and said, "Omigod, there's no right answer to this!" When people put the system at the center of the action, they realized that the right answer could only be collaboration. The best answer had to be the one everybody agreed upon.

The workshop, with similar cases, was repeated for several years thereafter. It had considerable faculty support and a big impact on the primary care program. Which brings me, at last, to what I learned from all this.

LEARNING FROM EXPERIENCE

Two noteworthy things happened in Maryland, challenging ideas that I had considered OD gospel. First, we expected the primary care faculty to put systems theory and matrix management high on the relevance list for graduate training. After all, these were the key to understanding the system's many ins and outs at the theoretical level. We expected personal, group, and interpersonal skills training to rate relatively low. This was the "soft" stuff that people needing to be in control found so threatening. In fact, the faculty rated all the content as relevant, hard and soft alike. However, for graduate students, the faculty proposed, much to our surprise, that the large system concepts and theories be sacrificed in favor of personal, interpersonal, and group methods of interaction. Personal skills, they said, would be instantly useable on the job!

Huh? This was the very content that for years medical professionals in other contexts had dismissed as "touchy-feely." Given first-hand experience, no pressure, and no expectations, the faculty wrote their own prescriptions. Despite the temptation to play the medical game and prescribe desirable techniques, our training staff got more openness to new ideas by treating the techniques as hypotheses for action research. Had we taken the other approach, the faculty would surely have confirmed our built-in prejudice about their built-in resistance.

Whence Cometh New Behavior?

My second "aha" had to do with *transfer-of-training*, the conditions under which people apply at work what they have learned in seminars. Earlier research had shown that newly-learned skills and attitudes faded quickly once a workshop ended. To overcome this, people in training seminars were invited to make action plans. We reserved up to 20 percent of our workshops in those days for "back-home" applications. People would write and even rehearse action plans. Despite this, they often had a hard time affecting their systems. This was especially so when people came alone and went back to find that existing organizational norms, policies, practices, and/or leaders did not support new behavior.

In the faculty workshop, participants were not expected to use what they had learned. There were no "back-home" exercises. All we asked of faculty was help in refining the curriculum. What we did not anticipate is that the faculty—researchers, clinicians, teachers all—began applying what they had learned anyway! In follow-up interviews, many reported using responsibility charting, conflict management techniques, and meeting skills back on the job. OD wisdom had it that "just training" was an inferior way of inducing organizational change. Here we saw the stirrings of significant changes in the way primary care professionals worked with each other. Our faculty were not constrained by the corporate sanctions reported by business people.

How could this be happening? I concluded that the same features that led Cohen and March (1974) to call universities "organized anarchies" also made possible effective action by individual faculty. In systems with diffuse authority, abstract goals, low interdependence, and few performance measures, all were queens and kings of their own domains.

"If the fans won't come," baseball's legendary phrase-maker Yogi Berra once said, "nobody can stop them!" In academic medicine, if faculty wished to act in constructive ways, then nobody could stop them! Professional autonomy could work for, as well as against, better organizational practices. After Maryland, I stopped stereotyping experts and dropped "resistance to change" from my vocabulary.

ACKNOWLEDGMENT

This memoir is adapted from "Management Training in Academic Medicine," Chapter 13 in *Productive Workplaces Revisited: Dignity, Meaning and Community in the 21st Century* (Jossey-Bass/Wiley, 2004). Copyright 2009 by Marvin R. Weisbord.

NOTES

1. By Ronald Lippitt and Rakph White, under Kurt Lewin's supervision in 1938.
2. By Wilfrid Bion and Eric Trist.

3. By Kurt Lewin and Margaret Mead.
4. By Kurt Lewin, Ronald Lippitt, Kenneth Benne and Leland Bradford.

REFERENCES

Cohen, M. D., & March, J. G. (1974). *Leadership and ambiguity: The American college president.* Hightstown, NJ: McGraw-Hill.

Weisbord, M. R. (1976, Spring). Why organization development hasn't worked (so far) in medical centers. *Health Care Management Review,* 17–28.

Weisbord, M. R. (1987). *Productive workplaces: Organizing and managing for dignity, meaning and community.* San Francisco: Jossey-Bass. Revised in 2004 as *Productive workplaces revisited.*

Weisbord, M. R., Lawrence, P. R., & Charns, M. P. (1978). Three dilemmas of academic medical centers. *Journal of Applied Behavioral Science, 14*(3), 284–304.

Weisbord, M. R., & Stoelwinder, J. U. (1979, Spring). Linking physicians, hospital management, cost containment, and better medical care. *Health Care Management Review,* 7–13.

CHAPTER 15

ORGANIZATION DEVELOPMENT IN HEALTH CARE

The Dialogue Continues

Heather Hanson, Mark J. Moir, and Jason A. Wolf

ABSTRACT

The concluding chapter of this volume provides a set of provocative considerations raised by the contributing authors in this book as well as the day-today
challenges faced in applying OD in the healthcare setting. In examining the
challenge of transforming an already moving system, why this conversation is
critical, where we go from here, and then offering suggestions for beginning
to journey, the authors push us to dig deeper than the simple application of
OD to consider the implications of our actions and the impact we can have
in this dynamic sector. The chapter leaves us with a powerful thought: that
the practice of OD within health care is a proud and exciting endeavor. It is a
journey of both meaning and purpose.

Organization Development in Health Care, pages 273–279
Copyright © 2011 by Information Age Publishing
273

THE CHALLENGE OF TRANSFORMING AN ALREADY MOVING SYSTEM

Health care is a unique endeavor with an unwavering purpose to improve the human condition. It is one of the most important social, economic, and political issues of our time. With a growing list of significant challenges including access to care, increasing costs, the volume of both under-insured and uninsured individuals, and a decline in general health, health care is characterized by many as being in a state of crisis. These challenges and others have given rise to calls for fundamental changes in the system.

While the industry and system as a whole is experiencing pressure for desired transformation, it is also constrained by numerous interests and forces that seek to maintain the status quo. Issues embedded within this complex and sensitive narrative range from financial factors (such as repayment and reimbursement) and inherent cultural conflicts to care-related concerns and the specialties and technologies focused on effective treatment. Throughout this discourse there are interdependent pressure points involving concepts such as competition, margin, equality, choice, history, social wellbeing, diversity, hierarchy, disintegration, and suffering. At the same time, themes emerge related to innovation, creativity, mission, collaboration, care, passion, compassion, paradox, privacy, life, and death.

As this work suggests, the role of OD professionals within this broad and complex context is both necessary and complicated. OD has evolved over the years from its early uses as a management tool around planned change. It has now perhaps reached one of its greatest challenges with its expanding application in the healthcare industry. Health care today is vast sea of people, processes, and policies, churning at the speed of change. Applied to health care, the need to address the issue of change has become more apparent as we engage in reform and needed transformation. OD will need to move beyond its traditional forms to now address an environment of constant and often chaotic change, an age of "permanent whitewater" (Vaill, 1989; Weisbord, 2004) in which information, technology, markets, and people are emerging and advancing at breakneck speed (Beer, 2001; Marshak, 2002) and pushing the very scope and boundaries of healthcare systems across the globe.

The healthcare system, in the broadest sense—the global network of care services and solutions—is growing ever more interconnected and interdependent. While each nation still examines its healthcare delivery models in the general confines of national borders, patients are less restricted in terms of care choices. This changes the nature of care delivery, the way in which patients interact with the system, and the even more critical nature of understanding the human interfaces and systems implications for delivery of care. This challenge helps us (or perhaps challenges us) to look at health care on multiple levels. While this book focused on change, leadership , engagement, and new views, there are also issues of culture, teams, information technology, and others that need to be explored as well as the reality that health care is now a global issue. This leaves us more questions than answers and only suggests that as we think about transformation we need to remain open to the perspective that we are already dealing with a consistently moving system.

WHY THIS CONVERSATION IS CRITICAL

With continuous conversations of healthcare successes and woes around the world, and with the clear grip the healthcare debates have in the U.S. in particular, we continue to see a rising level of energy and interest in how we manage the stresses placed on organizations that touch on the delivery of care and health care overall. The web is widening daily and requires that we find new and innovative ways to engage more and more people in the dialogue.

Research indicates that the ability to engage in meaningful conversation within ourselves and among colleagues begins the process of change. Wheatley's (2009) experience within organizations and communities all across the world leads her to believe that "there is no more powerful way to initiate significant change than to convene a conversation. When a community of people discovers that they share a concern, change begins" (p. 26). Our intention with this work was to create a space and invitation for dialogue and offer a challenge for our readers to think about how you lead the issues of OD and change in your organizations.

This handbook provided valuable and applicable insight into successful practices in healthcare organizations, from how change is lead and individuals engaged to how new ideas can be applied across healthcare settings. We offered a collection of new tools and processes, as well as expanded perspectives and knowledge for OD scholar-practitioners engaging in the work of OD and leaders driving organization transformation in health care. We catalyzed new thought around how OD practitioners can improve their practice and share their learning within the healthcare community. We encouraged leadership at all levels to recognize that good OD practice is not owned by one's internal or external consultants, but by every individual committed to high-performance, vibrant healthcare organizations.

If we are truly committed to making a difference in the healthcare setting, providers, support staff, and others must recognize that the conversation must extend beyond clinical delivery of care. The way in which a healthcare organization lives, breathes, and operates is at the core of any effective healthcare encounter. While historically the healthcare setting has focused on clinical successes as indicative of effective outcomes, there is now a much broader recognition of the critical pieces of the puzzle. In the U.S., for example, the Joint Commission now focuses on leadership performance and the Center for Medicare & Medicaid Services (CMS) looks beyond core measures to service and the patient experience through the Hospital Consumer Assessment of Healthcare Providers & Systems (HCAHPS). These shifting priorities raise the need for the very work that OD is focused on: creating healthy and effective organizations and systems and "creating adaptive organizations capable of repeatedly transforming and reinventing themselves" (Woodman, 1993, p. 73). Today's healthcare environment may need nothing more urgently than organizations and systems capable of doing just that.

SO WHERE DO WE GO FROM HERE?

Meaningful challenges deserve meaningful consideration. Health care, and the inherent complexity and spirit that it possesses, is one of the most meaningful and complex challenges facing us all. Complexity, however, does not contradict a pragmatic and thoughtful approach toward working with this unique and somewhat sacred environment. OD professionals are delivering meaningful and pragmatic solutions to the complex affairs of health care while improving the outcomes of those touched by this enterprise.

As demonstrated, OD practitioners are working within these challenging arenas with evidence-based protocols that engender engaging work environments. Through authentic interaction within systems and processes, OD practitioners and their colleagues are leading change, often in very sustainable ways, within their respective enterprises. OD practitioners, who have embraced life-affirming dialogue, have turned the ethereal and inescapable adage of the inability to be a "prophet in one's own land" on its prodigious ear. Meaningful change as revolution for the healthy advancement of organizations and industry is a central deliverable of the OD profession.

OD as a strategic consideration is helping to shape people and organizations in very demonstrable ways. OD practitioners are working with professionals to build engaging environments that invite its members to belong to meaningful endeavors. These endeavors provide a continuing opportunity to find one's central purpose and meaning—to answer the broad existential questions that shape our time and reason. This environment encourages the connection to a deeper meaning of work, the "common caring" (Senge, 1990, p. 206) that binds us together rather than fragmentation that tears us apart.

Beyond the obscure, improved outcomes to the human condition within these organizations leads to improved organizational performance. More highly engaged workers are tending to the complexity in a more compassionate and respectful way while serving enterprise sustainability. While all of this generative activity denotes positive change, what does the future portend? What meaningful challenges await the OD practitioner and how will she confront these challenges with passion and integrity? As we consider these exciting challenges, we posit a few thoughts for the journey:

- Constancy of Change: Within this redundancy one can find significant opportunity for the development of stronger communities. Change invites renewal. OD practitioners need to harness the energy of evolution for the betterment of their respective communities. Leading change in organizations can be a rejuvenating exercise that allows for the pruning and shaping of systems for the purpose of sustainability.
- Centrality of Common Purpose: Beyond the isomorphic tendencies of competing organizations rests the internal binding mechanism of an organization's unique sustainability, its core purpose. OD practitioners will be charged with coalescing a plurality of internal interests around the prime directive, in a sense syncing the organization in a rhythmic cadence with mission. As externalities place pressure on organizations to move with the herd, OD practitioners will be challenged with ensuring that each organization delivers on its promises.
- Returning to Connectedness: "To bring health to a system, connect it to more of itself" (Wheatley, 1999, p. 145). The culture of health care has shifted away from the humanness inherent in the work and has neglected the authentic relationships, communication, and connections necessary for health and effectiveness. OD practitioners will need to return to the roots of health care, the caring values that birthed this industry. The need to recreate health care with internal conditions embodied by wholeness, connectedness, and relationships is paramount if we seek greater outcomes and opportunities to reignite the purpose and calling that brought us together.
- Retaining Our Humanity: As shifts in the overall landscape of health care continue to emerge, we as OD practitioners may need to balance the speed and pace of change with our own human limitations for adaptation and reformation. The way in which we usher in the constancy of change will be a leading indicator of our ability to retain the relative soul of our endeavors. A challenge for OD practitioners will be to ensure that the form of organization does not become the focus of the work, but rather the mechanism that sustains the individuals within the work.
- Seeing OD as a Focus of "The Work": Peter Vaill (1989) has challenged many a practitioner to consider the quality of their theories

and accompanying action by suggesting that "the theory's honesty about itself, its openness to change in the phenomena it refers to, and its advocates' own willingness to take the theory's medicine are the three key qualities that will produce a responsible stewardship in theories and theorists" (Vaill, 1989, p. 139). OD practitioners applying OD principles to their work can bring a generative authenticity to the process and ensure some level of stewardship within the profession. Forgoing the allure of dogmatic showmanship for the pragmatism of meaningful questioning can help engender integrity and sustain us in our endeavor to deliver and authenticate our calling.

- Being Available to Our Ignorance: As science advances the work of the OD field, recognizing and embracing our own lack of knowing leaves open a door for discovery. Retaining our curiosity within a growing field of knowledge will be crucial for a field built on white space activity. As we become more refined in our processes, we risk being unavailable to that which we do not know.

As OD practitioners continue to advance the cause of health care through the support of those who touch the lives of so many, we must remain humble to the calling to retain our integrity. As we seek to master our work, we must recognize the limitations of our own design. What will sustain us is our intention for meaningful dialogue directed toward the betterment of those we serve. OD practitioners efforting in the advancement of meaningful change are Sherpas of a better tomorrow.

BEGINNING TO JOURNEY:
SURROUNDED BY POETIC "FRINGES"

The philosopher and sociologist Alfred Schutz (1970) described the nature of the relationship between language, context, and knowledge as one that was "surrounded by fringes." Schutz stated that

> Every word and every sentence is, to borrow a term of William James, surrounded by "fringes" connecting them, on the one hand, with past and future elements of the universe of discourse to which they pertain, and surrounding them, on the other hand, with a halo of emotional values and irrational implications which themselves remain ineffable. The fringes are the stuff poetry is made of; they are capable of being set to music but they are not translatable. (Schutz, 1970, p. 97)

As noted previously, it is an immense challenge to transform an "already moving system." In seeking to affect change within healthcare systems, OD practitioners are faced with complex narratives that often possess the poetic and the emotional. In some ways, the narrative *transition*, where the past and future elements meet, is the potential rhythmic space where the OD practitioner plies her trade—shaping tone and tenor, setting change in motion. As unique and untranslatable as this reverberation may feel, this is a place where the potential for change moves from emergence to pattern, from chaos to order, from mere sound to melody and harmony.

This book has provided a glimpse at the intentional and inspirational work of OD professionals who are leading significant change for the betterment of the organizations they serve. Health care is a complex and interesting environment that holds the entirety of the human condition, all of which intensifies the space within which the OD practitioner moves. All of this makes the OD practice within health care a proud and exciting endeavor—a journey of meaning and purpose.

REFERENCES

Beer, M. (2001). How to develop an organization capable of sustained high performance: Embrace the drive for results-capability development paradox. *Organizational Dynamics, 29*(4), 233–247.

Marshak, R. J. (2002). Changing the language of change: How new contexts and concepts are challenging the ways we think and talk about organizational change. *Strategic Change, 1*(5), 279–286.

Schutz, A. (1970). *On phenomenology and social relations.* Chicago: The University of Chicago Press.

Senge, P. (1990). *The fifth discipline: The art and practice of a learning organization.* New York: Doubleday.

Vaill, P. (1989). *Managing as a performing art.* San Francisco: Jossey-Bass.

Weisbord, M. R. (2004). *Productive workplaces revisited: Dignity, meaning, community in the 21st century.* San Francisco: Jossey-Bass.

Wheatley, M. (1999). *Leadership and the new science: Discovering order in a chaotic world.* San Francisco: Berrett-Koehler Publishers.

Woodman, R. W. (1993). Observations on the field of organizational change and development from the lunatic fringe. *Organization Development Journal, 11*, 2.

ABOUT THE CONTRIBUTORS

EDITORS

Jason A. Wolf
Jason is the Executive Director of The Beryl Institute, an organization committed to improving the patient experience in healthcare. An explorer of organizations and radical catalyst for organizational effectiveness and cultures of service, he has over 16 years of leadership and consulting experience. Jason has led major initiatives both as an OD Leader at HCA and Owens Corning and in external consulting roles working with numerous organizations in the public, private and not-for-profit sectors. He has his Ph.D. in OD from Benedictine University.

Heather Hanson
Heather works as an OD Manager for Kaiser Permanente based out of Denver, CO. In this role she is responsible for developing physician leaders and teams that support and drive the integrated healthcare model. She is pursuing her Ph.D. from Saybrook University in Organizational Systems. Through her career and educational journey, Heather has the opportunity to tap into her passions for improving the health of healthcare organizations by engaging with others to develop environments and conditions that allow individuals and teams to thrive.

Mark J. Moir
Mark is the VP of Organization Development for Sanford Health, the largest, rural, not-for-profit integrated healthcare system in the nation serving 110 communities in six states, including 30 hospitals and 111 clinic loca-

Organization Development in Health Care, pages 281–285
Copyright © 2011 by Information Age Publishing
All rights of reproduction in any form reserved.

tions. He received his MBA from the University of South Dakota and his Doctorate in Leadership Development and Organizational Change from Antioch University. A student of organizational life, Mark is a member of the American Psychological Association and the Organization Development Network.

CONTRIBUTORS

Carlos R. Arce is currently the Director of Organizational and Leadership Development at Billings Clinic. In this role, he continues to create and implement innovative leadership and staff experiences that improve organizational performance and achieve enterprise wide cultural change. He is driven by the intention of inspiring others to be better.

Dawn E. Bowden, PhD, is Assistant Professor, School of Business and Economics at the University of Wisconsin–Stevens Point and Visiting Professor, International School of Management, Paris. Her recent research focused on the innovation and integration capacity of U.S. health care organizations.

Susan Burns-Tisdale, MPH, RN, has been a healthcare leader for thirty years. She began her career as a clinical nurse, transitioned to clinical leadership and is now currently a senior vice president for a health care system. Ms. Burns-Tisdale has co-authored several chapters on the role of the nurse practitioner in the home care setting.

Rosa M. Colon-Kolacko, Ph.D., MBA, is VP of System Learning for Christiana Care Health System, one of the largest non-profit, teaching health systems in the US, with approximately 10,000 employees. Before joining Christiana Care, Rosa was the Director, Change Management & Learning for Global Supply Chain Operations for Bristol Myers-Squibb.

Stacy B. Cupisz, BS, MOD, SSBB extensive educational background in Psychology and Organizational Development has prepared her to lead and facilitate significant quality, process and performance improvement activities using Lean Six Sigma, Change Acceleration Process (CAP)™, and Work-Out™ methodologies within the healthcare industry. Stacy is committed to building positive relationships, transforming organizational culture and sustaining change.

Dan Dangler is founder of Authenticity, a consulting firm dedicated to maximizing human performance and collaboration within organization. With over 25 years of strategic business experience, Dan works with organizations to establish effective leadership and management practices, and innovative collaborative work approaches.

Jon H. Desjardins has over 20 years of experience in organizational development. His OD journey started in the US Air Force as a Wing Quality Advisor and transitioned to Arizona state government as a Quality Consultant which led to his current role as an Organizational Development Director for Banner Health.

Diane L. Dixon, EdD, is Managing Principal of D. Dixon & Associates LLC, an independent consulting practice specializing in leadership and organization development primarily in the healthcare and human services sectors. She has taught leadership and organizational behavior for the Business of Medicine Program at Johns Hopkins University.

Diane Doumas has 25+ years of experience in senior living, a B.S. in Gerontology Services Administration from UTHSCD and M.Sc. in Organization Development/Knowledge Management from GMU. She is currently Managing Partner, Vantage Advisory Group, a professional services firm dedicated to advancing quality senior living worldwide through unparalleled consulting and training.

Kathryn Kaplan, PhD, began her career as an Occupational Therapist and has been an OD practitioner in major medical centers since receiving her doctorate in Management and Organization Behavior from the George Washington University in 1994. She is currently the Chief Learning Officer at Maimonides Medical Center in Brooklyn, NY.

Josephine M. Kershaw, PhD, is an Associate Professor of Healthcare Management in The University of Findlay's College of Business. Dr. Kershaw has several peer-reviewed publications and a research focus on minority health disparities. She is a consultant on national grant review panels and served as principal investigator on numerous grants.

Lisa Kimball, PhD, is President, Plexus Institute, a nonprofit social enterprise that applies ideas from complexity science to solve social and organizational problems. With Plexus she has worked with health care facilities on action research projects applying Positive Deviance methodology to eliminate transmission of hospital acquired "superbug" infections and other quality initiatives.

Charlotte Lofton worked for 14+ years in healthcare and service-related industries. She's a consultant with Red Phoenix Consulting Group, an adjunct faculty with Northeastern University's College of Professional Studies in Boston and Kent State University's Corporate and Community Services. She's an executive leadership doctoral candidate at The George Washington University.

Tabitha Moore is Manager of Organizational Effectiveness for ARAMARK Healthcare at a major hospital system in Denver, Colorado. She received a BA in Psychology from the University of Texas and a MA in Organizational Psychology from Columbia University. She specializes in the fields of leadership development, teambuilding, and employee engagement.

William E. Ruse is President Emeritus of the Blanchard Valley Health System, an integrated rural health care system located in Findlay, Ohio. He served as President and CEO of the organization for 36 years. Mr. Ruse currently teaches health care administration at in the MBA program at the University of Findlay.

Joanne Schlosser, MBA, ACC, SPHR, has a vibrant business career spanning over 25 years has included leadership positions in healthcare, economic development and non profit work. Joanne has provided leadership development, change management, executive coaching and organizational development services to thousands of leaders.

Stanley J. Smits, PhD, is Professor and Chair Emeritus, Department of Managerial Sciences, Robinson College of Business, Georgia State University; Visiting Professor, International School of Management, Paris, and a Licensed Psychologist. His recent research focused on the effectiveness of physician-led interdisciplinary health care teams in VA hospitals.

Beth B. Stiner, MOD, is the Senior Director of Organizational Development at Banner Health, one of the largest non-profit healthcare systems in the nation. Beth has a Master's in Organizational Development from Bowling Green State University and a Bachelor's in Communication from Michigan State University.

Howard Straker, Director of Community Medicine for the George Washington University Physician Assistant Program, is an assistant professor of Health Sciences and Prevention and Community Health. He has been a physician assistant in various health care settings for over 20 years. He's an executive leadership doctoral candidate at GWU.

Kelly Topp, PhD, has more than 15 years of experience in OD working for organizations such as Banner Health, Tyson Foods, Anheuser-Busch, and Southwestern Bell. She has a Ph.D. in Organizational Psychology and broad experience with change management, performance management, group dynamics, and organizational design.

Rosalind Ward, Ph.D., MPH, has helped numerous organizations bridge the gap between engaging individuals and creating sustainable shifts in organizational culture through building intrinsic capacity. She holds a degrees in kinesiology, public health, and a Ph.D. in Organization in Management where she focused on organizational culture, intrinsic motivation and coaching.

Marvin Weisbord is co-director of Future Search Network, an international non-profit community service organization. During more than 20 years of organizational consulting he worked with many large corporations, medical schools, and hospitals. He received a lifetime achievement award in 2004 from the Organization Development Network, whose members named his book *Productive Workplaces* one of the most influential of the past 40 years. He is the author of *Organizational Diagnosis, Productive Workplaces, Discovering Common Ground, Productive Workplaces Revisited,* and co-author with Sandra Janoff of *Future Search,* 3rd edition and *Don't Just Do Something, Stand There!*

CPSIA information can be obtained at www.ICGtesting.com
Printed in the USA
237849LV00001B/25/P